Embedding Agricultural Commodities

Over the past 500 years, Westerners have turned into avid consumers of colonial products and various production systems in the Americas, Africa and Asia have adapted to serve the new markets that opened up in the wake of the 'European encounter'. The effects of these transformations on the long-term development of these societies are fiercely contested. How can we use historical source material to pinpoint this social change? This volume presents six different examples from countries in which commodities were embedded in existing production systems – tobacco, coffee, sugar and indigo in Indonesia, India and Cuba – to shed light on this key process in human history. To demonstrate the effectiveness of using different types of source material, each contributor presents a micro-study based on a different type of historical source: a diary, a petition, a 'mail report', a review, a scientific study and a survey. As a result, the volume offers insights into how historians use their source material to construct narratives about the past and offers introductions to trajectories of agricultural commodity production, as well as much new information about the social struggles surrounding them.

Willem van Schendel has served as Professor of Modern Asian History at the University of Amsterdam and as head of the South Asia Department, International Institute of Social History. Among his recent books are *The Camera as Witness: A Social History of Mizoram, Northeast India* (with Joy Pachuau); *A History of Bangladesh* and *Global Blue: Indigo and Espionage in Colonial Bengal*. Recent co-edited volumes are *Labour Migration and Human Trafficking in Southeast Asia: Critical Perspectives* and *The Bangladesh Reader: History, Culture, Politics*.

Embedding Agricultural Commodities

Using historical evidence, 1840s–1940s

**Edited by
Willem van Schendel**

LONDON AND NEW YORK

First published 2017
by Routledge
2 Park Square, Milton Park, Abingdon, Oxon OX14 4RN

and by Routledge
711 Third Avenue, New York, NY 10017

Routledge is an imprint of the Taylor & Francis Group, an informa business

© 2017 selection and editorial matter, Willem van Schendel; individual chapters, the contributors

The right of Willem van Schendel to be identified as the author of the editorial material, and of the authors for their individual chapters, has been asserted in accordance with sections 77 and 78 of the Copyright, Designs and Patents Act 1988.

All rights reserved. No part of this book may be reprinted or reproduced or utilised in any form or by any electronic, mechanical, or other means, now known or hereafter invented, including photocopying and recording, or in any information storage or retrieval system, without permission in writing from the publishers.

Trademark notice: Product or corporate names may be trademarks or registered trademarks, and are used only for identification and explanation without intent to infringe.

British Library Cataloguing in Publication Data
A catalogue record for this book is available from the British Library

Library of Congress Cataloging in Publication Data
Names: Schendel, Willem van, editor.
Title: Embedding agricultural commodities : using historical evidence, 1840s-1940s / edited by Willem van Schendel.
Description: Farnham, Surrey, UK ; Burlington, VT : Ashgate, [2016] | Includes index.
Identifiers: LCCN 2015045584 (print) | LCCN 2016000841 (ebook)
Subjects: LCSH: Agriculture – Economic aspects – Developing countries – History. | Agriculture – Social aspects – Developing countries – History. | Farm produce – Developing countries – History. | Colonies – Economic policy. |Developing countries – Colonial influence.
Classification: LCC HD1417 .E53 2016 (print) | LCC HD1417 (ebook) | DDC 338.109172/409034 – dc23
LC record available at http://lccn.loc.gov/2015045584

ISBN: 978-1-4724-6186-5 (hbk)
ISBN: 978-1-315-57912-2 (ebk)

Typeset in Bembo
by HWA Text and Data Management, London

Contents

List of figures vii
List of tables viii
Notes on contributors ix

1 Embedding agricultural commodities: an introduction 1
  WILLEM VAN SCHENDEL

2 Staying embedded: the rocky existence of an indigo maker
  in Bengal 11
  WILLEM VAN SCHENDEL

3 Multatuli, the liberal colonialists and their attacks on the
  patrimonial embedding of commodity production in Java 30
  ULBE BOSMA

4 Smallholdings versus European plantations: the beginnings
  of coffee in nineteenth-century Mysore (India) 55
  BHASWATI BHATTACHARYA

5 'Keeping land and labour under control?': reporting on
  tobacco-shed burnings in Besoeki (Java) 78
  RATNA SAPTARI

6 Embedding cigarette tobacco in colonial Bihar (India):
  a multi-dimensional task 99
  KATHINKA SINHA-KERKHOFF

7 Cuba, sugarcane and the reluctant embedding of
   scientific method: Agete's *La Caña de Azúcar en Cuba*   119
   JONATHAN CURRY-MACHADO

8 Globalization's agricultural roots: some final considerations   146
   MARCEL VAN DER LINDEN

   Index   190

Figures

2.1	Delivering fresh indigo to the factory	15
2.2	The indigo harvest	16
2.3	Stick fighters and javelin fighters, rural Bengal, 1850	18
3.1	Portrait of P. J. Veth	30
3.2	Portrait of Eduard Douwes Dekker ('Multatuli'), the author of *Max Havelaar*	32
3.3	Regent and Resident in colonial Java	38
4.1	Excerpt from the 15-page 'Complaint of Mr. Lonsdale' (1864)	57
4.2	Map of nineteenth-century southern India	60
5.1	A tobacco-drying shed of the Soekowono company	79
5.2	Producers, foremen and a supervisor posing in a tobacco field	83
6.1	Title page of *Studies in Indian Tobaccos*	101
6.2	Map showing the location of Pusa in early-twentieth-century India	103
6.3	Furrow irrigation for tobacco as propagated by scientist Gabrielle Howard at the Imperial Institute of Agricultural Research	110
6.4	Cross-bred tobacco plants at Pusa	111
7.1	Concentration of cane cultivation in Cuba, 1943	123
7.2	Main sugarcane varieties used, 1943	127
7.3	Sugar factories, and concentration of POJ 2878 cane in the sugar crop, 1943	129
7.4	Origin of cane varieties grown in Cuba, 1943	130
7.5	Sugar centrales with Cuban cane varieties, and total land with cane in district (1943)	134
7.6	Relationship between amount of Cuban cane varieties grown for a sugar factory, and proximity to other Cuban cane-variety crops	134
8.1	The 'triangulation' of agrarian production	149
8.2	Picking coffee in Brazil in the early twentieth century	156
8.3	Wardian cases	166

Tables

4.1	Annual revenue from coffee in Mysore, 1822–61	62
4.2	Land under coffee cultivation in Mysore in the early 1860s	64
4.3	Share of European and Indian planters in the excise duty on coffee in Mysore, 1863–64	65
4.4	Loss of forests in some districts of the Western Ghats, Karnataka, 1920	66
5.1	Frequency of tobacco-shed burnings in Bondowoso and Djember, 1898–1902	81
7.1	Numbers of sugar factories in Cuba, with Cuban cane varieties grown in related farms, 1943	133
8.1	The Columbian and Magellan exchanges of crop species	148
8.2	World coffee production: geographical distribution, c. 1852–2010	157
8.3	Sugarcane production, 1456–2010	161
8.4	Tobacco production	163
8.5	Some botanical gardens that played a role in long-distance plant transfer, sixteenth–nineteenth centuries	165
8.6	Development of productivity on a world scale	173

Contributors

Bhaswati Bhattacharya is a Research Fellow at the Centre for Modern Indian Studies (CeMIS) at the Georg-August-Universität Göttingen (Germany). Her recent publications have focused on networks of Asian merchants in the Indian Ocean. Her current research project traces the history of coffee consumption in India.

Ulbe Bosma is a Senior Research Fellow at the International Institute of Social History in Amsterdam (The Netherlands) and Professor of International and Comparative Social History at the Free University, Amsterdam. His most recent book is *The Sugar Plantation in India and Indonesia: Industrial Production, 1770–2010* (Cambridge University Press, 2013).

Jonathan Curry-Machado is Coordinator of the 'Commodities of Empire' Project (Open University, UK) and a Research Fellow at University College, London. Among his recent publications is *Cuban Sugar Industry: Transnational Networks and Engineering Migrants in Mid-Nineteenth Century Cuba* (Palgrave, 2011).

Ratna Saptari is Assistant Professor of Anthropology and Development Sociology at Leiden University (The Netherlands). She has co-edited *Labour in Southeast Asia: Local Processes in a Globalized World* (Routledge, 2004) and *Pemikiran Kembali Penulisan Sejarah Indonesia (Rethinking Indonesian History-Writing)*. Her current project is on 'The Making and Remaking of the Cigarette Labour Communities in East Java.'

Kathinka Sinha-Kerkhoff has served as Director of Research at the Asian Development Research Institute (ADRI) and as Regional Representative for South Asia of the International Institute of Social History, based at Ranchi (Jharkhand, India). She is the author of *Colonising Plants in Bihar (1760–1950): Tobacco Betwixt Indigo and Sugarcane* (Partridge, 2014); *Tyranny of Partition: Hindus in Bangladesh and Muslims in India* (Gyan, 2006) and has co-edited *Autobiography of An Indian Indentured Labourer: Munshi Rahman Khan (1847–1972)* (Shipra, 2005).

Marcel van der Linden is Senior Research Fellow and former Research Director of the International Institute of Social History. He also teaches Social History at the University of Amsterdam. His recent publications include *Transnational Labour History: Explorations* (Ashgate, 2003) and *Workers of the World: Essays toward a Global Labor History* (Brill, 2008).

Willem van Schendel served as Professor of Modern Asian History at the University of Amsterdam and as head of the South Asia Department, International Institute of Social History. Among his recent books are *The Camera as Witness: A Social History of Mizoram, Northeast India* (Cambridge University Press, 2015; with Joy Pachuau); *A History of Bangladesh* (Cambridge University Press, 2009) and *Global Blue: Indigo and Espionage in Colonial Bengal* (The University Press Limited, 2006). Recent co-edited volumes are *Labour Migration and Human Trafficking in Southeast Asia: Critical Perspectives* (Routledge, 2012) and *The Bangladesh Reader: History, Culture, Politics* (Duke University Press, 2013).

1 Embedding agricultural commodities
An introduction

Willem van Schendel

How can we use historical source material to pinpoint social change? *Embedding Agricultural Commodities* shows six different ways, based on different types of historical source. Each chapter is concerned with the same process: the embedding of commodities in existing agrarian systems. Embedding is the term we use for the process of forging an agricultural commodity chain: introducing a new cash crop and making sure it endures.

Approaching this process from six different vantage points, we demonstrate how important it is to pay close attention to the sources of knowledge on which we base our analyses of social change. They shape our understandings of the past but what do they tell us, and what not? The more we understand how they came about – who wrote them, for whom they were intended, and how they impacted on subsequent social change – the more we are able to assess their usefulness and their limitations.

This volume presents an introduction to the use of sources and it does so by looking at a key process in human history: the way we seek to manipulate the world around us to our own advantage. The focus of this book is on how different historical sources help us understand the insertion of new agricultural commodities into pre-existing social and economic arrangements. To this end, we consider different locations and periods. Our case studies deal with Indonesia, India, Bangladesh and Cuba and they run from the mid-nineteenth to the mid-twentieth century. The main commodities that we look at are tobacco, coffee, sugar and indigo. The book concludes with a chapter that considers these four commodities together to explore the global dimensions of embedding and to argue for the agricultural roots of globalization.

The sources

We have selected six types of historical source on the embedding of commodities. We explore the usefulness of a diary, a petition, a 'mail report', a book review, a scientific study and a survey. Each chapter features one of these sources and, as we shall see, each source has its own strengths and limitations. Historians would label these documents 'primary sources' because they were created by participants in (or observers of) the historical events that they describe.[1] They are also similar in that they are texts – rather than images, material objects, or other relics of the past.[2]

But they differ from each other in many other ways. First, they began life in diverse places: three of them were crafted in various locations in British India, and one each in Cuba, the Netherlands East Indies and the Netherlands. Second, they were written in the languages of three different colonial regimes – English, Spanish and Dutch – over the course of a century of rapid change, from the 1840s to the 1940s.[3] Third, half of them remained unpublished (and can now be found in archives in India, the Netherlands and Britain), two were published in limited editions by government presses (a few copies are now in specialized libraries) and one was published as an article in a Dutch literary journal. Only this last one can currently be found online in full-text version. Finally, these sources vary in size from a couple of pages (the petition) to a five-volume manuscript running into hundreds of pages (the diary).

Variation is even more striking if we consider the authors and their intentions. The creators of four of the texts were Europeans writing in colonial settings, one was in post-independence Cuba, and one in the Netherlands. Three texts had a single author, one was co-authored by a married couple, and the other two were a group effort. All authors except one were male.

The position of the authors with regard to agricultural commodity production differed for each source. At the time of writing they were, respectively, the manager of an indigo factory in rural eastern India (the diary), 21 coffee-planters in South India (the petition), a bureaucrat (the mail report), an essayist (the review), two botanists (the scientific report) and an agronomist (the survey).

Who were they writing for and with what intentions? The audiences they targeted ranged from a single private individual (the diary writer's father) to the general educated public. Three texts were meant for the eyes of government officials only, and one sought to reach fellow researchers. It is hard to reconstruct exactly which combination of factors motivated the authors but their main concerns were clear enough. The diary was written as an act of self-expression and to sustain personal communication with a faraway relative. The main purpose of the petition and the book review was political lobbying – an attempt to change government policy. The mail report was a cog in the bureaucratic machine, intended to facilitate administrative processes. The scientific report and the survey were all about knowledge production and economic development.

These six sources provide contrasting entry points into the realities of how new commodities get – and stay – embedded in agrarian societies. They give an indication of the types of information that different remnants of the past can provide. But how do researchers use such disparate information to create a convincing narrative? This is what we turn to next.

The historian's craft in action: how do researchers interact with their sources?

The contributors to this volume have been working in the same field for several years and they have met as participants in a comparative research programme, workshops and conferences.[4] Their individual projects have resulted in scholarly monographs and articles. One of the issues that kept coming up in discussions among them was the extent to which diverse sources of information constrain comparisons between cases. Another issue was how each researcher used and interpreted the historical sources at his or her disposal. Obviously, they all based their insights on many sources but the idea of this joint volume is to highlight just one. Each chapter concentrates on a single revealing source to explore its peculiarities and to demonstrate how the researcher used it in constructing a historical narrative, thereby shaping memory.[5] The chapters demonstrate the historian's craft in action. They are not proffered as models to be emulated, but rather as an introduction to the quandaries and possibilities of the everyday work of historians.

In the following chapters, the contributors explain why they consider their selected sources to be especially significant and relevant. They explore the uses and limitations of each source: the perspective it offers, its biases and its silences. They also share parts of the source with us, both to give us a sense of the 'raw data' and to help us assess the veracity of their interpretations.

Interpretation of historical sources can take different forms, depending on what the researcher wants to accomplish. The shared interest of the contributors to this volume is to explore what the embedding of new agricultural commodities meant, how it was done and how successful it was. The selected texts act as empirical building blocks in the construction of narratives about this process in concrete cases. The case studies themselves are intended as building blocks for the construction of comparative understandings of how commodity production begins and continues.

The dynamics of embedding

The concept of 'embeddedness' first emerged as a significant scholarly concept when Karl Polanyi published his *The Great Transformation* in 1944.[6] In this book, Polanyi analysed economic activities as being 'socially embedded.' Since then, the term has been used in many different ways.[7] Of special interest to this volume is how the concept has been used in the study of commodities. In 1985, economic sociologist Mark Granovetter published an article in which he argued that standard economic accounts are 'under-socialized': they do not take sufficient note of the socio-structural contexts that shape economic behaviour.[8] This idea – that 'economic activity is embedded in social relationships, not the other way round'[9] – has had a considerable impact on researchers in the field of commodity chains. These researchers focus on the meso-level and assume that economic activity is embedded either in network structures or in social, economic or political institutions.[10] But they 'typically do not analyse the long-term or underlying causes of the networks themselves'.[11]

This is precisely what we aim to do in this book. First, we look at longer-term processes of embedding during the nineteenth and twentieth centuries. Second, unlike much commodity chain research, which puts emphasis on the behaviour of firms, we concentrate on how economic activity was embedded in agrarian networks and arrangements. And third, we treat embedding as a continuous process rather than as a single action; embeddedness is not a state but a balancing act.

In the following chapters, we explore several dimensions of the concept. All chapters deal with embedding in the sense of introducing a new commercial crop into a pre-existing agrarian order and the ensuing struggles between those who benefit from it and those who wish to dislodge, or disembed it. As all of our examples are from what is now the Global South – the ex-colonized world – the peculiarities of colonial rule play an important role. Chapters 2 and 3, especially, investigate how the exploitative relationship between Europeans and local populations was predicated upon entrenching the colonial administration in pre-colonial, patrimonial structures. We also examine moral issues beyond the mere profitability of colonial commodity production, notably discourses about property rights, labour relations, social justice, human mobility, coercion and environmental impact (for example, Chapters 2, 3 and 5).

In several chapters, embedding takes on additional meanings. For example, it is also employed to examine the application of technical knowledge (notably Chapters 6 and 7), the competition between different forms of embedding (for example, smallholder versus plantation production, as in Chapters 4 and 5), and the embedding of production-enhancing commodities such as fertilizers, pesticides and improved varieties (Chapters 6 and 7). Embedding was also predicated upon ecological conditions and the biological requirements of individual crops, which put restrictions on their cultivation (Chapter 2). The interplay of various factors became apparent only by trial and error; the essentially experimental dimension of embedding is especially evident in Chapters 6 and 7. Finally, the embedding of new cash crops implied – or at least raised fears of – disembedding other crops, notably food crops and agricultural commodities produced for local markets rather than for Northern ones. The new cash crops also endangered trade in agricultural commodities within the Global South. Much of the resistance against new agricultural commodities stemmed from this perceived threat to local subsistence and South–South trade. This dimension – disembedding resulting from embedding – is examined primarily in Chapters 2, 3 and 7.

Giving a face to the agents of embedding

Each of the six chapters following this introduction uses a particular historical source as its starting point to explore the emergence of a new commodity production system. Rather than presenting this process as the outcome of faceless economic forces and high-level abstractions (world market, state, empire), each chapter calls attention to the agents of embedding. Who were the driving forces behind this process and how did they achieve their goals? The answers show a remarkably varied picture. When we look at the everyday experience of the agents of embedding, it is important to keep in mind that successful embedding was far from assured: the history of agricultural commodity production is strewn with examples of failure.[12] Even in the best of circumstances inserting a new crop required careful social engineering. In none of our case studies did the process go smoothly; it always entailed a tussle between opposing social forces and its long-term outcome was determined by the relative power that the agents of embedding could exert over their opponents.

It is no surprise that each of the selected historical sources bears witness to this power struggle. The contributions to this book show that processes of embedding are complex and nuanced. Many players are involved in the initial phase, the start of a new production system. Once this is in place, however, the relationship between the players continues to develop and embedding becomes a process of continual readjustment and renegotiation to keep the forces of disembedding in check. Thus, embedding is not merely the insertion of an agricultural commodity and the formation of a commodity chain. It is the recurrent tending of that insertion lest the commodity chain snap. The social tensions involved can be enormous and they can play havoc with the wider agrarian system.[13] The embedding of commodities is not an act; it is an iterative process.

Between forced cultivation and disembedding

The following chapters all deal with these dynamics. Ulbe Bosma (Chapter 3) describes the production of coffee, sugar and indigo in colonial Java as 'forced cultivations' and he also shows that it is essential to identify the primary power relations that allow forcible embedding. In the case of Java, it was an alliance between a colonial government seeking a stepped-up *mise en valeur* of their possessions and rural elites controlling a pre-existing system of labour services that forced unpaid cultivators to produce export crops. Once in place, the system required relatively little attention because cultivator resistance was weak and mostly took the form of avoidance rather than confrontation.[14]

Embedding was a far less steady process in colonial Bengal (in British India), as shown in Willem van Schendel's contribution (Chapter 2). Here the protagonists were factory managers, landlords and peasants who formed an unstable and contested triangle of power. Unlike in Java, embedding the cash crop (in this case indigo) was a permanent headache because power alliances shifted incessantly. The managers – the main proponents of the indigo commodity chain – could never establish lasting partnerships. For over a century they lived precariously because they had to live in the countryside, close to the indigo fields, and they had to face seasonal confrontations with landlords and smallholding indigo cultivators.

Such patterns were not 'colonial' in the sense that they could be said to typify commodity production in a specific colony. As the contributions of Bhaswati

Bhattacharya (Chapter 4) and Kathinka Sinha-Kerkhoff (Chapter 6) show, the process of embedding cash crops was far from uniform in British India. Local social and environmental conditions, the attributes of individual crops, and variations in policy produced distinct local patterns. Bhattacharya describes competition between two strategies to introduce coffee in South India: here local smallholders found themselves pitted against European plantation owners. The situation differed from that in Bengal (Chapter 2), where local enterprise was negligible. European coffee entrepreneurs in South India sought the active intervention of the state to outflank their local competitors and thus the state became a more prominent player in the process of embedding coffee plantations. In the case of cigarette tobacco in Bihar (northern India; Chapter 6) the state was even more directly engaged in promoting the crop and in uprooting a competing variety, tobacco for water-pipe consumption. As Sinha-Kerkhoff reveals, the colonial state invested in improving the quality of cigarette tobacco by means of botanical research and outreach. This chapter provides pointers to the intended and unintended effects of state-initiated 'research and development' on processes of crop embedding.

The contributions to this volume show that agents of embedding could be entrepreneurs, managers of plantations or factories, smallholders, landlords or state officials. They could be outsiders or locals. They could form alliances to enhance their impact but they were never able to get their way without opposition. None of our cases support the idea of all-powerful cash crops effortlessly imposed on supine colonized societies. Resistance took many forms. We have seen how some Javanese cultivators used avoidance protest: they moved away from areas of forced cultivation. In his essay on sugarcane growers in Cuba, Jonathan Curry-Machado (Chapter 7) explores another form of defiance when he speaks of 'reluctant embedding.' Cultivators showed aversion to new varieties, were deliberately sluggish in developing Cuban cane hybrids and postponed the introduction of scientific approaches at all stages of cane farming. Such foot-dragging has been described as a practice of everyday resistance.[15]

A more confrontational strategy is highlighted in Ratna Saptari's analysis of the burning of tobacco-drying sheds in Java (Chapter 5). Taking her cue from an official's report, she explores how this official, and other bureaucrats in Java, interpreted these incidents. They were worried about the breakdown of law and order, which the burnings seemed to indicate, and they were confused about their meaning. Was arson a weapon in the hands of disgruntled tobacco cultivators? Or were the arsonists actually employees of tobacco companies? Could the fires be seen as attempts to disembed tobacco cultivation, or were they better understood as tactics to improve work conditions, or eliminate the competition?

Linking colonial empires

Chapters 2 to 7 in this volume are arranged chronologically, according to the date of the historical source from which they take off. This means that we take the reader on something of a rollercoaster ride through three colonial empires

– British, Dutch and Spanish – and their aftermaths. Chapters 2, 4 and 6 provide examples from the huge colony of British India. Our cases deal with three distinct regions. Bengal (now divided between India and Bangladesh) is in the east, Mysore (an indirectly-ruled kingdom; today part of the Indian state of Karnataka) is in the south, and Bihar (today a state of India) is in the north. Unfortunately, sketching the broader contours of this colony is beyond the scope of this volume – but for a first introduction to its agrarian history, we can refer the reader to David Ludden's *An Agrarian History of South Asia*.[16] Chapters 3 and 5 take their cases from Java, the central island of the Netherlands East Indies (today: Indonesia), which became a testing ground for one of the world's most ambitious and massive colonial attempts at embedding agricultural commodities for the European market, the 'Cultivation System.' For overviews of Indonesia's agrarian history, see Elson's *Village Java under the Cultivation System* and Pelzer's *Pioneer Settlement in the Asiatic Tropics*.[17] Chapter 7 examines Cuba, which was part of the Spanish empire until 1898. For a classic introduction to its agrarian history, see Fernando Ortiz's *Cuban Counterpoint*.[18]

Even though each case study in this volume focuses on local networks and agricultural arrangements, the sources reveal that embedding commodities involved long-distance connections that went well beyond the boundaries of empire. In addition to tracing the obvious links to metropolitan markets, the following chapters also document connections across imperial boundaries, for example, between the Caribbean, India and Java (Chapters 2 and 7); and between India and Arabia (Chapter 4). The historical trajectories that agricultural commodities followed across the world should be studied from the perspective of multiple colonies and empires, just as we must study them across pre-colonial, colonial and post-colonial periods.

This is exactly what Marcel van der Linden does in the final chapter (Chapter 8), which can be read as an extensive epilogue and contextualization to the six case studies. A wide-ranging excursus on the *longue durée* of agricultural embedding, it does not focus on a particular source but provides a global framework to the four agricultural commodities – indigo, sugar, coffee and tobacco – with which this volume is concerned. Drawing from a wealth of evidence, this chapter traces myriad commodity connections across the world, resulting from mobile agricultural commodities being sequentially embedded in – and disembedded from – local production systems. It demonstrates the importance of looking at agricultural commodities as plural rather than single, both in terms of succession – how, over the centuries, commodities succeeded each other in local agricultural production systems – and in terms of coexistence – how several commodities were often embedded simultaneously in such systems.

But it also tells an even larger story. It argues that the very notion of 'mobile production' – the idea that production systems that generate commodities for global or regional markets may be transferred from one part of the world to another – *originated* in agriculture, and only later gained ground in the processing industries. Hence the chapter's title, 'Globalization's Agricultural Roots'. It throws new light on the importance of agriculture in the making of today's world.

Plants, sources and historians

The iterative nature of embedding – the forging *and* tending of an agricultural commodity chain – is reflected in each of the historical sources and the six different entry points they provide to six historical examples of embedding. Together with the comprehensive overview of the final chapter they present an unusually broad vista of the vicissitudes of embedding cash crops in existing agrarian orders. They help us to understand the forces that 'agents of embedding' employ as well as the opposition they unleash as a result of their actions.

Each of these historical sources has its limitations and biases. Assessing these, as we do in the following chapters, requires knowledge of how they came about, who wrote them, for whom they were intended, and how they impacted on subsequent social change. Such an assessment establishes the usefulness of a source for historians in constructing convincing narratives of the past – in this case, promoting insights into the dynamics of embedding. Thus, the contributions to this volume explore histories of agrarian embedding but, beyond that, they allow us to observe how historians embed historical sources into their renderings of social change in the past.

Notes

1. Primary sources are the raw materials of history. The term 'secondary historical sources' refers to works, such as this volume, that offer interpretations of primary material to support an argument. For introductions, see John Tosh. *The Pursuit of History: Aims, Methods and New Directions in the Study of History* (New York, NY: Routledge, 6th ed., 2015), 74–88; and Miriam Dobson and Benjamin Ziemann (eds.). *Reading Primary Sources: The Interpretation of Texts from Nineteenth- and Twentieth-Century History* (London and New York: Routledge, 2009).
2. These sources are not entirely textual; some contain illustrations.
3. The diary is the earliest (1840–56), followed by the book review (1860), the petition (1864), the mail report (1902), the scientific report (1910) and the survey (1946).
4. The contributors participated in the research programme 'Plants, People and Work: The Social History of Cash Crops in Asia, 18th to 20th Centuries' (International Institute of Social History, funded by the Netherlands Organisation for Scientific Research (NWO)) and participated in conferences of the 'Commodities of Empire Project' (funded by the British Academy), the German Centre of Excellence 'Cultural Foundations of Integration' (University of Konstanz, Germany), the Department of History, Gadjah Mada University (Yogyakarta, Indonesia) and the International Convention of Asia Scholars, Daejeon (South Korea). We wish to express our sincere gratitude for the financial support our research programme has received from the Netherlands Foundation for Scientific Research (NWO) and the International Institute of Social History.
5. Georg G. Iggers. 'The Role of Professional Historical Scholarship in the Creation and Distortion of Memory', *Chinese Studies in History*, 43:3 (2010), 32–44.
6. Karl Polanyi, *The Great Transformation* (Boston: Beacon Press, 1944).
7. For overviews, see Greta R. Krippner and Anthony S. Alvarez. 'Embeddedness and the Intellectual Projects of Economic Sociology', *Annual Review of Sociology*, 33 (2007), 219–40; Jens Beckert. *The Great Transformation of Embeddedness: Karl Polanyi and the New Economic Sociology* (Cologne: Max-Planck-Institute for the Study of Societies, 2007; www.econstor.eu/).

8 Mark Granovetter. 'Economic Action and Social Structure: The Problems of Embeddedness', *American Journal of Sociology*, 91:3 (1985), 481–510.
9 Timothy J. Sturgeon. 'From Commodity Chains to Value Chains: Interdisciplinary Theory Building in an Age of Globalization'. In Jennifer Bair (ed.) *Frontiers of Commodity Chain Research* (Stanford, CA: Stanford University Press, 2009), 120.
10 Bob Jessop distinguishes three levels on which the study of social embeddedness can focus. In addition to interpersonal relations and networks it can concentrate on inter-organizational relations ('institutional embeddedness'), or on relations between different institutional orders ('societal embeddedness'). Polanyi's work dealt with this third level; most economic sociologists' with the first two. Bob Jessop. 'The Social Embeddedness of the Economy and its Implications for Economic Governance'. In Fikret Adaman and Pat Devine (eds.) *Economy and Society: Money, Capitalism and Transition* (Montreal: Black Rose Books), 199–222.
11 Gary G. Hamilton and Gary Gereffi. 'Global Commodity Chains, Market Makers, and the Rise of Demand-Responsive Economies'. In Bair (ed.) *Frontiers of Commodity Chain Research*, 140.
12 See Alfred Crosby. *Ecological Imperialism: The Biological Expansion of Europe, 900–1900* (Cambridge: Cambridge University Press (rev. ed.), 2004); Brett M. Bennett. 'A Global History of Australian Trees', *Journal of the History of Biology*, 44 (2011), 125–45; and Sandip Hazareesingh. 'Cotton, Climate and Colonialism in Dharwar, Western India, 1840–1880', *Journal of Historical Geography*, 38 (2012), 1–17.
13 For a consideration of the term 'agrarian system', see Willem van Schendel. 'What Is Agrarian Labour? Contrasting Indigo Production in Colonial India and Indonesia'. *International Review of Social History*, 60:1 (2015), 1–23.
14 Michael Adas. 'From Avoidance to Confrontation: Peasant Protest in Precolonial and Colonial Southeast Asia', *Comparative Studies in Society and History*, 23:2 (1981), 217–47.
15 James C. Scott, *Weapons of the Weak: Everyday Forms of Peasant Resistance* (New Haven: Yale University Press, 1987).
16 David Ludden. *An Agrarian History of South Asia* (Cambridge: Cambridge University Press, 1999).
17 R. E. Elson. *Village Java under the Cultivation System, 1830–1870* (Sydney: Allen and Unwin, 1994); Karl J. Pelzer. *Pioneer Settlement in the Asiatic Tropics: Studies in Land Utilization and Agricultural Colonization in Southeastern Asia* (New York, NY: American Geographical Society, 1945).
18 Fernando Ortiz. *Cuban Counterpoint: Tobacco and Sugar* (New York: Random House, 1970).

References

Adas, Michael. 'From Avoidance to Confrontation: Peasant Protest in Precolonial and Colonial Southeast Asia,' *Comparative Studies in Society and History*, 23:2 (1981), 217–47.

Bair, Jennifer (ed.) *Frontiers of Commodity Chain Research* (Stanford, CA: Stanford University Press, 2009).

Beckert, Jens. *The Great Transformation of Embeddedness: Karl Polanyi and the New Economic Sociology* (Cologne: Max-Planck-Institute for the Study of Societies, 2007; www.econstor.eu/).

Bennett, Brett M. 'A Global History of Australian Trees,' *Journal of the History of Biology*, 44 (2011), 125–45.

Crosby, Alfred. *Ecological Imperialism: The Biological Expansion of Europe, 900–1900* (Cambridge: Cambridge University Press (rev. ed.), 2004).

Dobson, Miriam, and Benjamin Ziemann (eds.). *Reading Primary Sources: The Interpretation of Texts from Nineteenth- and Twentieth-Century History* (London and New York: Routledge, 2009).

Elson, R. E. *Village Java under the Cultivation System, 1830–1870* (Sydney: Allen and Unwin, 1994).

Granovetter, Mark. 'Economic Action and Social Structure: The Problems of Embeddedness,' *American Journal of Sociology*, 91:3 (1985), 481–510.

Hamilton, Gary G., and Gary Gereffi. 'Global Commodity Chains, Market Makers, and the Rise of Demand-Responsive Economies'. In Jennifer Bair (ed.) *Frontiers of Commodity Chain Research*, 136–61.

Hazareesingh, Sandip. 'Cotton, Climate and Colonialism in Dharwar, Western India, 1840–1880,' *Journal of Historical Geography*, 38 (2012), 1–17.

Iggers, Georg G. 'The Role of Professional Historical Scholarship in the Creation and Distortion of Memory,' *Chinese Studies in History*, 43:3 (2010), 32–44.

Jessop, Bob. 'The Social Embeddedness of the Economy and its Implications for Economic Governance'. In Fikret Adaman and Pat Devine (eds.) *Economy and Society: Money, Capitalism and Transition (Montreal: Black Rose Books)*, 199–222.

Krippner, Greta R., and Anthony S. Alvarez. 'Embeddedness and the Intellectual Projects of Economic Sociology,' *Annual Review of Sociology*, 33 (2007), 219–40.

Ludden, David. *An Agrarian History of South Asia* (Cambridge: Cambridge University Press, 1999).

Ortiz, Fernando. *Cuban Counterpoint: Tobacco and Sugar* (New York: Random House, 1970).

Pelzer, Karl J. *Pioneer Settlement in the Asiatic Tropics: Studies in Land Utilization and Agricultural Colonization in Southeastern Asia* (New York, NY: American Geographical Society, 1945).

Polanyi, Karl. *The Great Transformation* (Boston: Beacon Press, 1944).

Scott, James C. *Weapons of the Weak: Everyday Forms of Peasant Resistance* (New Haven: Yale University Press, 1987).

Sturgeon, Timothy J. 'From Commodity Chains to Value Chains: Interdisciplinary Theory Building in an Age of Globalization'. In Jennifer Bair (ed.) *Frontiers of Commodity Chain Research*, 110–35.

Tosh, John. *The Pursuit of History: Aims, Methods and New Directions in the Study of History* (New York, NY: Routledge, 6th ed., 2015).

Van Schendel, Willem. 'What Is Agrarian Labour? Contrasting Indigo Production in Colonial India and Indonesia'. *International Review of Social History*, 60:1 (2015), 1–23.

2 Staying embedded

The rocky existence of an indigo maker in Bengal

Willem van Schendel

Thomas Machell was a remarkable character. Born in 1824, he was the son of a Yorkshire parson who wanted him to become a clerk in a mercantile house. But Thomas showed an adventurous streak. Not enamoured with 'the idea of quill driving in an office', he decided, at the age of 15, to run away from home to seek his fortune. His ten-year-old brother demanded to be taken along. 'We walked three hundred miles [to London, Portsmouth and Brighton] and endured considerable hardships before we discovered that we had left our good fortune behind us and that we had better go back and look for it'. After this adventure, Thomas begged his father to send him to Australia 'where I secretly determined to amass an immense fortune and bring it all home to him'.[1] Instead, his father sent him to sea.

This was the beginning of a roving life that took him to Hong Kong during the first Opium War, to the Marquesas Islands in the South Pacific, to Chile, to Arabia and several times to India before he died at the age of 37. In India he spent two periods as a manager of indigo factories in Bengal and a third period managing a coffee plantation in South India.

There were many seafarers, travellers and planters like him, crisscrossing the mid-nineteenth century world in search of adventure and wealth. What makes Thomas Machell special, however, is his deep attachment to his father back in Yorkshire. Not only did he return to England as often as he could, but when he was away he also kept an extensive and detailed journal for his father.

This journal survives as a memorial of his life and times. It provides information about an enormous range of topics but here we are concerned with his two stints as a manager of indigo factories in Bengal, first in 1845–7 and then in 1850–2. His journal entries are not the only surviving personal writings on the indigo industry but they are the most perceptive and informative that we have.[2] They provide an insight into the workings of indigo production that is quite unique.

Thomas Machell's 'Journals' provide a primary source that is intensely personal. Historians have long used such sources and evaluated their significance for constructing narratives about the past. They have proposed the term 'ego-documents' to refer to a category of intimate documents that includes diaries, journals, autobiographies, family chronicles, travelogues, letters and memoirs.[3] Such diverse private writings can be treated as historical sources that impart singular human vitality to our understanding of the past – but they can also be approached as literary texts or as cultural artefacts.[4] Their historical value varies enormously and questions of reliability, veracity and perspective must always be considered.

Machell's writings are not only voluminous and original but also of high relevance. He meticulously enters his thoughts, and he does so daily or shortly after the events he records. He writes about his own experiences, observations, thoughts and doubts. The value of this diary lies in its being an unpublished, little known and highly detailed witness account of events and people that do not feature in other historical sources, or appear only marginally. His observations form a rich – but as yet largely unexplored – resource for the study of mid-nineteenth-century Bengal. Here I will use the 'Journals' merely to look at one aspect of indigo production: its techniques to survive in a largely hostile society. But first I will give a brief introduction to indigo.

Indigo and its production

Indigo is an intense blue dyestuff made from plants. People in different parts of the world mastered the art of making indigo and using it to dye textiles well before recorded history.[5] For millennia, it was the preferred blue dye – brilliant and colourfast. It can be derived from different species of plants, so there is no single source of indigo. Each world region relied on its own favourite variety and there were old routes by which the best qualities were traded. For example, ancient Greece imported the dye from India and called it *indikon* ('from India'), hence the modern term indigo.

When Europeans began to expand their power to other parts of the world, they soon discovered that indigo could be produced more profitably in their tropical colonies than at home (where a plant named woad had been used for centuries) or by importing it from the traditional export region, western India. There was a growing European demand for the blue dye, so indigo emerged as one of the major and most valuable commodities to be traded between the colonies and Europe. First, the Spaniards controlled much of the trade, with indigo made in San Salvador, Guatemala and Southern Mexico. Then, the French emerged as major competitors with indigo from Haiti. And, finally, the British became major producers in what is now the southern United States.

Not only was indigo an important trade item across the Atlantic, but it also turned into a crucial tool of imperial competition. This became very clear when, in the late eighteenth century, all three production hubs went into decline. The reasons were varied but wars and revolutions were important factors. The American war of independence (1775–1883) stopped the flow of indigo to Britain. In the Spanish possessions plant disease, war and problems of labour supply and quality control led to a gradual decline. Haiti's indigo industry, which had been based on slave labour on French-run plantations, collapsed rather suddenly as a result of slave uprisings and independence from France (1791–1804). This crisis in the supply of indigo from the Americas had European powers scurrying for new production areas, mainly in Asia.[6] The Spanish tried to develop indigo production in the Philippines, the French and British in their colonies in India – Pondicherry and Bengal – and the Dutch in Indonesia.[7] Remarkably, only one of these attempts was really successful. By 1810 British Bengal had cornered much of the world export market and Britain supplied indigo to the rest of Europe and most of the world.[8] This situation would not change until 1900 when the entire world production of indigo ran into a brick wall. By 1897 chemists in Germany had managed to synthesize indigo artificially from coal tar and, within a few years, cheaper artificial indigo wiped natural indigo off the market. Since then, natural indigo has not played any role in international trade and its former significance is largely forgotten. It is only in recent years that we see a very modest revival in the use of indigo, largely as a result of an increasing interest in natural dyes and sustainable development.

Embedding indigo in Bengal

After the loss of their American colonies, the British were eager to set up an indigo industry elsewhere. Not surprisingly, their eye fell on their newly acquired colony, British India. In 1757, the British East India Company had become masters of the large province of Bengal in the east and its main trade city, Calcutta (today: Kolkata), now became the capital of British India. Over the next 100 years the British would expand their control over the entire Indian subcontinent but, for the moment, the traditional indigo-producing areas in western India were beyond their reach. Therefore, they decided to start a new industry in the hinterland of Calcutta.

The point of colonial rule was to make the land yield economic and strategic benefits for the motherland. Early British rule rested on two economic supports, the collection of land tax and the export of opium to China, but experiments with other potentially profitable cash crops were going on all the time. One of these was an indigo-producing plant (*Indigofera tinctoria*). It grew naturally in the region but it had never been used for export.

Setting up indigo works required investments. These were difficult to come by during the first 20 years when British rule was still uncertain. But by the 1770s, it became more effective. Now European entrepreneurs came forward to set up indigo factories as well as silk filatures and sugar mills. The first indigo factory was built in 1777 by a Frenchman who had learned his indigo skills in the Caribbean and now tried his luck near Chandernagore, a tiny French holding in Bengal. Soon others followed: by 1785 there were 14 export-oriented factories and their numbers climbed steadily; by 1829 there were hundreds of factories, spread over more than 40 districts of north-eastern India and employing thousands of labourers. Indigo production had turned into by far the largest rural industry.

It was a commercial success story. Returns to investments were high, Bengal indigo conquered the world market and it secured Britain the position of kingpin in the international indigo trade. Thus, in 1783 Britain imported £1.2 million of indigo and only 7 per cent came from Bengal. Fifteen years later Britain imported £4.0 million, 96 per cent of which came from Bengal. In other words, indigo imports from Bengal had increased 40-fold. By this time Britain consumed 45 per cent of the indigo it imported (mainly to dye textiles) and re-exported the rest. Business merchants did a roaring business.[9]

What is surprising in all this is that export-oriented indigo could be produced so successfully in Bengal at all. Certainly, the natural conditions were auspicious: climate, rainfall, soil and water supply were all favourable. There was also a large supply of cheap labour. In addition, capital was forthcoming and technical knowledge could be applied to the process. And yet, there were huge obstacles to the free play of market forces and entrepreneurial zest. Embedding indigo production was hampered by two related factors: the colonial government's dependence on land tax and its bar on Europeans living in the countryside.

The British had inherited an intricate pre-colonial system of land taxation that turned out to be extremely effective and soon formed the bedrock of colonial rule in Bengal. Each plot of land yielded a specific amount of money that was collected from the cultivators by hereditary tax collectors/landlords known as *zamindars*. However, these zamindars and their staffs were more than tax collectors for the British. They also acted as the backbone of rural administration and control. Worrying that European capitalist enterprise might disrupt zamindari control of the countryside and the smooth flow of tax to the exchequer, the colonial authorities forbade Europeans to live beyond city limits, except with a permit, which was hard to get.

This was a serious problem for the indigo industry because its factories had to be located in the countryside. There were two reasons for this. First, indigo plants lose their capacity to yield dye soon after they are harvested, so factories had to be very close to the fields. Second, the complicated process of turning plants into dye requires large amounts of clear water, so factories had to be close to rivers and needed large reservoirs to store water. The result was a clash between the indigo industry, which wanted European managers in charge of its factories, and the authorities fearful of too many Europeans disturbing the system of rural control. The compromise was to allow entrepreneurs to run rural factories but not to allow them private possession of land for growing indigo. This resulted in a triangle of local power and animosity wherever indigo factories sprang up. The three parties in this struggle for control were the local zamindar (or his representatives; many zamindars were absentee landlords), the peasant in control of cultivable land, and the manager (and staff) of the indigo factory. The indigo industry was able to embed itself in rural society but always under conditions of duress. Staying embedded required constant vigilance and effort. This was the world in which Thomas Machell found himself when he decided to try his hand at managing indigo factories in Bengal.

Thomas Machell plays the embedding game

Managers of indigo factories were constantly aware of their precarious position. Living in obscure villages with poor connections to the city, they felt isolated and remote from other Europeans.[10] This is how Machell expressed the feeling in 1850:

My world here is half a dozen sugar boilers at Treemoney, 20 miles East, Mulnath [the headquarters of his indigo company], 20 miles north, and the Newcomers' at Hobna, 25 miles west. To the South a vast extent of jungle, swamp and wasteland extending to the sea, the residence of many a royal Bengal tiger, of Deer, Panthers, Buffaloes, Cheetahs &c &c.

They were surrounded by a rural population that was not particularly welcoming and could well do without their presence. They were under pressure from their superiors in Calcutta and Britain to get locals to grow indigo plants and deliver these to the factory at the right time. Then they had to make sure that they processed the plants properly so as to get as much dye of the best quality as possible. Finally, they had to take care that the dye reached the Calcutta warehouses safely. So why bother being an indigo manager? For most, it was the attractive pay. For Thomas Machell, it was also the adventure of running an establishment and learning about the society around him.

His journal describes how the factories he ran were forever in danger of losing their grip on the surrounding countryside. Staying embedded was a struggle. He was always aware of the possibility of being ousted by powerful zamindars or rebellious peasants and he strategized to prevent that from happening. The two chief concerns of any indigo manager were to protect the factory compound from physical attack and to ensure a steady supply of fresh indigo plants (Figure 2.1).

What makes Machell's journal especially interesting is that it describes two periods in which the strategies of control shifted. During his first stint as an indigo manager (1845–7), economic methods were more effective than during his second (1850–2) when armed violence was more prominent. Both times

Figure 2.1 Delivering fresh indigo to the factory[11]

Machell had a job with the Bengal Indigo Company, a shareholder company which owned many factories spread across rural Bengal.[12] It had its headquarters in Mulnath, a village in Nadia district. In introducing the company to his father, he describes both the complexity of the business and its violent nature.[13] He started as a trainee at Patkabaree factory (Murshidabad district) but soon was given charge of the Ballee division consisting of three factories.[14] His career would involve frequent shifts to other factories in what is now the borderland between West Bengal (India) and Bangladesh.

Economic embedding was based on providing advances to cultivators. Although a few factories were able to control some land directly (in effect becoming zamindars who ordered their tenants to grow indigo), this was not the usual setup in Bengal. Factories needed many more indigo plants than they could grow themselves and they persuaded independent cultivators to grow them by advancing money on the future crop (Figure 2.2).

The circumstances under which cultivators entered into this agreement varied widely. Some did so voluntarily, often finding out later that they could not escape as their debt became a rolling one, keeping them bound to indigo over the seasons (and sometimes generations). Others were pressured into accepting advances and yet others were simply told to grow indigo.[16] From the beginning of the indigo industry in Bengal, factory managers found it impossible to get sufficient raw material merely by using the economic compulsion of debt, even if backed up by the judicial system.[17] The industry was soon known for its violent treatment of cultivators who refused to do the managers' bidding and for fights between managers who were after each other's turf. In 1810,

Figure 2.2 The indigo harvest[15]

the government sent an urgent message to all its district magistrates about the 'abuses and oppressions committed by Europeans, who are established as Indigo Planters in different parts of the Country'.[18]

Thomas Machell was aware of the violent nature of the industry that he joined and clearly accepted it as the way things were. His early entries into the journal do not dwell on it – the dominating sentiment is his excitement of being, at the age of 21, in charge of factories employing hundreds of labourers. When he does mention violence, it is initially in a humorous fashion, accompanied by a stick-figure drawing (see Figure 2.3 and Box 'Enforcers of the Indigo Industry'[19])

It is only in his later entries that he indicates increasing unease about the treatment of the cultivators. His earlier reticence may have resulted from loyalty to the company or his desire to amuse rather than depress his father, the intended reader of the journal. In late 1850, however, there is a clear shift in the operations of the Bengal Indigo Company. Machell begins to describe the violent techniques by which it tries to squeeze the peasantry for more indigo more cheaply.[21] He begins by showing the resistance that factory managers put

Enforcers of the indigo industry

Ye Latteal [stick-fighter] and Soorkie Wallah [javelin-fighter] are two gentlemen of the Piada [footman] genus who are employed in times of riots to keep refractory Ryots [peasants] in order or to bully the Saheb for they will fight indifferently on either side and it is a common thing when one side has discharged them to go and tender their services to the opposite party in order to loot (i.e. plunder) the village of their former employers.

Living in gangs, they are a formidable set of men and their lawless life induces lawless habits. When they have our honest employment, as the[y] call fighting for or against a factory, they do a little in the Dacoity line (i.e. Highway robbery and Burglary). They do not however often try a European house for they well know the telling effect of a rifle ball. The Lattial is so called because his weapon is the Latty or Quarterstaff with which he is pretty expert.

The Soorkie Wallah or Spearman is a more dangerous enemy wielding an iron javelin some six feet long. He throws it with great force and precision insomuch that within fair range he will spit his man clean through the midriff. The pay of these men is 4 annas a day when not fighting 8 annas when at work – 4 annas is ¼ rupee or sixpence; 8 annas = ½ rupee or one shilling.

Of course, one never sees anything of this sort. It is the Planter's business to be out of the way on these occasions. Nevertheless, it does so happen that sometimes a set of fierce-looking wild men are seen hanging about and soon after one or two lame ducks are brought in. But quarrels will happen in the best-regulated families and it invariably is the case that these wounded men have been hurt in some extraordinary way not by fighting at all. One does hear of factories occasionally paying four or five hundred lattials but it always happened a long time ago: never nowadays although there are curious entries in the books of so many hundred rupees for law business when there happens not to have been any cases in court.

Figure 2.3 Stick fighters and javelin fighters, rural Bengal, 1850[20]

up against new superintendents who were eager to lower the price of indigo but were unfamiliar with the intricacies of the way its production was embedded in the Bengal land system. Pointing out that independent cultivators can be pushed only so far before they and their zamindar landlords will rebel, the factory managers try to warn against excessive greediness:

Well, [Captain Crawfurd, the newly appointed superintendent] determined to make a brilliant season or two before he went home, and he did so.

> 'Why, Mr Forlong [an experienced indigo manager], don't you make your indigo as cheap as Mr Campbell [manager of the Khalbolyah factories, where all indigo land is under direct lease from the government]?' says the Captain.
> 'I cannot', says Mr Forlong, 'consistently with the interests of the Company'.
> 'Why?'
> 'Because the Ryots [peasants] will not bear it'.
> 'But they do at Khalbolyah?'
> 'We shall see', is the reply.
> [Crawfurd] is gone and Battersby takes his place.
> 'Why don't you do as Mr Campbell did?'
> 'I cannot consistently with the interest of the concern'.
> 'But you must'.
> 'Very well, Captain, of course if I have your order I am not responsible for the consequences. I am not a shareholder'.
> 'Mr Forlong, you must do the same'.
> 'It will not answer'.
> 'It must'. ...[22]

The results were immediate. The cultivators recoiled from the new demands – which would mean a 20 per cent drop in their income from indigo – and refused to accept them.[23] Thomas Machell saw the existing rural balance of power shifting before his eyes. He understood that running a commercial enterprise by armed force might be possible but it would come at a high cost:

> with Ryot and Zemindar against me there is no alternative but a few battles royal. If they are determined to carry it out they had better send me five hundred lattials [fighters] at once. Of course there will be a few murder cases, which they will find rather more expensive than five bundles for the rupee.[24]

Their adversaries also knew how to use the courts to make life difficult for indigo managers, although their tactics sometimes backfired, as in a case of the 'dead body dodge'.[25]

Machell was in a quandary. He was vexed about the stark capitalist logic of his superiors and the coercion of the cultivators weighed heavily on his conscience.[26] He protested and seriously considered leaving his job but feared he would not be able to get another soon.[27] So he decided to carry out his orders, however repugnant and, in his opinion, ruinous for the industry:

> Now this is not right and yet whom to blame? I have my orders and must see them executed. If I don't choose to do so, there are plenty others who will. I by remaining may navigate but cannot avert the consequences of impolitic commands. "Obey orders though your break owners" is the sailor's creed … There is no doubt that the Planters generally [are] a great benefit to the country. The misfortune is when this great power for good and evil is vested in the hands of inscrupulous and inconsiderate men. Mr Hills who has been thirty years a planter, Mr White who has been twenty-five, Mr Maclogan & Mr Forlong all shake their heads at this cheap indigo work, another year or two and instead of a hundred per cent we shall have factories closed and the Company in difficulties again.[28]

He continued to waver, however, and suffered from depression:

> I am in excellent health but owing, I fancy, to the constant depression of spirits during the past year hot weather and loss of appetite, I am grievously reduced in strength and flesh but one does not require much of either in this country.[29]

Finally, he came around to the position that he could at least lessen the damage by staying in his post. This conviction led him to criticize a colleague who handed in his resignation:

> I have no great sympathy with men who, like Richard Sage, would throw up their employment as one in which they cannot conscientiously discharge their duties, as if that were not the very reason they should remain when so many unscrupulous men are ready to jump into their vacant places to increase that misery, which, if we cannot prevent we can at least alleviate.

But R. Sage is one of those hot-headed fellows who must have [it] only their own way or make it a point of conscience to ruin themselves.[30]

His frustration about the turn the indigo industry had taken made him think about his role in it. Earlier he had held the opinion that, 'there is no doubt that the Planters [are] generally a great benefit to the country' but now he reconsidered.[31] His diary entries become more disapproving. As the fighting escalated around him,[32] he wrote this on 6 January 1851:

> The object now is to make two or three bumper seasons and sell the factories, never mind the distress, the poverty, the utter ruin of the labourer, never mind how many are driven from their miserable homes to become beggars and robbers over the country. Great is the competition and consequent ratio, great is the pressure on the poor Ryot.
> I have heard the question argued at every Planter's table in the country and to hear the Planter eloquent, you would really think he was a most deeply injured individual, but let me ask what good he does in return. True, from the capital he brings into the country, from the energy he infuses into the district, waste lands are reclaimed, there is more traffic, more labour and more general activity in the country, but there comes the question: are the people better off? Is there less poverty? Less distress? More morality? More general prosperity? I shall say no.
> The poor remain poor, in the same low mental moral and physical distress as before, ignorance is just as gross amongst the mass as it was before we entered the country. The mud huts of the villages are just as clumsy and comfortless as ever for the uncertainty of their long tenure is as great as it was in the days of Surajood Dowlah [the last independent ruler, Nawab Siraj ud-Daulah (1733–57)] and as Ruskin says in his Lamps of Architecture, it is a bad sign when men build only for themselves frail temporary tenements and think not that they can hope for posterity to inherit the houses of their forefathers. That this is not the Bengali's fault is evident from the intense love of home that they all evince, and few are to be found who will leave their own neighbourhood to seek service abroad unless under pressure of extraordinary distress. The Bengali is bound to his family and home by the strongest ties of affection of custom and religion and yet that home is a miserable mud hut and why? Because of constant oppression and poverty.[33]

Machell's anxiety about what indigo managers 'do in return' spurs him into action. He makes a point of buying local: 'Contrary to the custom of most Sahebs, I use the common cloth made in the [district textile] factories for towels, sheets and trousers'.[34] He also buys his furniture locally. He begins to think of himself as a philanthropist and dreams of creating development projects that will benefit the local population: 'I am most anxious to carry out a course of usefulness, which will bring comforts and improvement to many who are now toiling from year to year without any hope of bettering their condition'.[35] The first plan is to set up a rural industry: 'if I continue here I meditate trying to introduce a little silk manufactory'[36]. He also builds better huts for his servants and improves the roads near his factory.[37]

Soon his thoughts turn to education. He hands out Bibles to his amazed servants and fancies his house becoming 'the most Literary Planter's Bungalow in Bengal'.[38] The next project is establishing a large school near the factory for instruction in English and Bengali, for which he contacts the secretary of the Bible Society of Calcutta who sends him 'books and tracts in the Bengali language' for distribution.[39] Upon reconsidering, he decides it is better to set up Bengali schools.[40] A few months later, Machell's journal includes a handwritten petition from nearby villagers who ask him to appoint their candidate, 35-year-old Gogun Chand Shurkar, as the new teacher.[41] By summer 1851 his school is completed and has 50 pupils. It looks:

> quite picturesque, especially if it is full of its little Bengali boys. It is very amusing to see them at work. They learn to write on the slips of palm leaf and what with the broad wooden pens and the ink which they rub off with their hands when they make a mistake and rub on their faces when they cry and on their little legs when they laugh. You never saw such figures, some of the children are very beautiful, especially those of higher castes. Their fair golden skins and large eyes and beautiful teeth, their small hands and feet and delicate shape and expression of features make them more interesting to my eyes than any of the hundred darling cherubs I have seen in England'.[42]

Meanwhile, further impositions on the cultivators, such as a more onerous system of weeding, lead to further open resistance. Four villages in Machell's area revolt. Machell protests but carries out orders. He thinks there is a good chance he will be blamed for it and lose his job but, by now, he does not care.[43] He is indignant: 'If we will tyrannize we must expect that even worms will turn'. Unlike most of his colleagues, he squarely blames the indigo establishment for the chaos.[44] Even his earlier conviction that he might do some good by staying on and lessening the impact of the extortionate system seems to be gone. He now feels that that would just prolong the suffering.[45] And yet, his indecisiveness continues: a little later, he returns to this view that it is best to stay in his job.[46]

By August 1851, he has lost all loyalty to the leaders of the Bengal Indigo Company. When renewed fighting breaks out, he writes: 'I am letting the cat out of the bag, must not tell tales out of school, but like the obstinate boy I don't care; I'll tell my father for all that and lick the unruly into the bargain'.[47] He dreams of a better Bengal in which he could be a benevolent and independent indigo entrepreneur in a prosperous land:

> I dream I see the view alive with boats plying to the city with country produce and returning with stores for labourers. Going with rich cargoes of silk, hemp, flax, cotton, tobacco, grain and the blue dye, and returning with iron, cloth, brazen vessels and such like goods. Dreaming still I fancy

myself surrounded with honest, well-educated and well-paid dependants with schools in every large village bringing up a generation of educated and intelligent and honest natives and that the Hindoo gong is not the only chime which marks the hours of the day. And let me ask: what is there improbable in all this? Change the accused old system to which the Planters and all our countrymen cling and the people will change themselves ... [T]he hope that some time I may set the neglected powers in action keeps me patiently grinding at the millstone and yet were I to open my lips on this matter to my practical neighbours I can imagine the look I should get.[48]

By now, Machell thinks of himself as an outsider, an eccentric in the colonial world.[49] But despite his denunciation of the way the indigo industry has developed, he does not plan to leave it just yet. It is only severe illness that forces him suddenly to give up his job at the age of 27; in April 1852, with mixed feelings, he sets sail from Calcutta.

Conclusion

In the historiography of colonial Bengal, the managers of indigo factories (or 'indigo planters') have been depicted as callous agents of a rapacious capitalist enterprise bringing ruin to peasant producers. The sources used to reconstruct the history of indigo provide ample evidence for the economic and physical coercion that was an essential part of its production. These sources are mostly the rich records of the colonial government dealing with court cases and reports of inquiry committees, notably the much-referenced Report of the Indigo Commission.[50] Additional sources are contemporary writings in Bengali and English exposing the cruelty of the system.[51]

Thomas Machell's five-volume journal provides a historical source of another order. It allows us to access the experience of being an indigo manager. So far, little is known about everyday life in the indigo industry and even less of the ideas and aspirations of those who worked in it. Machell's journal offers this perspective and does so in astonishing detail. For the first time, an indigo manager appears to us in more complexity than historians have been able to perceive so far. The journal forces us to reappraise the simple roles allotted to (or claimed by) indigo managers: fiendish exploiters, instruments of untrammelled capitalism, pioneers of free enterprise, adventurers, fortune-seekers, and so on. Machell allows us to look at the world through his eyes. What we see is certainly not always pretty but it is in full colour, three-dimensional and compelling.

In this chapter, we have explored only one aspect of indigo production as revealed in the journal. We have traced Machell's ideas about the techniques used to keep the industry anchored in a rural society that often rejected it. As these techniques turned more towards armed enforcement, Machell expresses his misgivings and the moral dilemmas he faces. As he struggles with his conscience, he attempts to counterbalance the violence that he is part of with acts of philanthropy. Starting out as a 20-year-old in high spirits, towards the end of his journal he has lost all loyalty to the company that employs him. We see him wavering between leaving the job and staying on in an attempt to alleviate the suffering of the cultivators.

We learn about the struggle between different sets of indigo managers. Some, like Machell, aim for production with a long-term view and less extreme oppression, whilst others are interested in quick returns, whatever the means applied. The latter view prevails. Within a decade, it leads to widespread rural rebellion and the almost complete collapse of the Bengal indigo industry.[52] Machell's voice gives us a rare inside view of this process of social rejection (or 'disembedding') as it gathers force.

Embedding an agricultural commodity, and making sure it stays embedded, always involves struggle and violence. This becomes clear when reading the other chapters in this volume. Ulbe Bosma (Chapter 3) deals with the tragic story of Saïdja and Adinda, a fictional account of the oppression of Javanese peasants under the 'Cultivation System'. Bhaswati Bhattacharya (Chapter 4) details how European coffee entrepreneurs in South India tried to use the force of the colonial state against local smallholding competitors. The burning of tobacco-drying sheds, analysed by Ratna Saptari (Chapter 5), typifies the tensions that developed around colonial cash-cropping in Indonesia. Kathinka Sinha-Kerkhoff (Chapter 6) and Jonathan Curry-Machado (Chapter 7) demonstrate how the embedding of agricultural commodities tends to be driven by commercial and industrial forces that pay too little heed to agricultural needs – resulting in stagnation and decline. Despite the best technical and scientific inputs, sugarcane production in Cuba lost its pre-eminent position and cigarette tobacco vanished from North India.

Thomas Machell's five-volume diary was a private account, only intended for his father's eyes. This allowed him to be as observant and frank as he wished. Although it is evident that he started out painting a rosy picture of the process of embedding indigo in Bengal, he finally decided to share the dark sides of this enterprise with his father. This makes his diary a uniquely valuable historical source.

Notes

1 'A Rough Sketch of My Life and My Brother Lancelot's, Written for the History of the Machell Family But Considered Too Long for the Purpose'. In Thomas Machell. 'Journals of Thomas Machell' (1840–1856) (British Library, India Office Private Papers, Mss Eur B369), Vol. III, 174–92.
2 The closest comparison is *Rural Life in Bengal: Illustrative of Anglo-Indian Suburban Life ... letters from an artist in India to his sisters in England* [by Colesworthey Grant] (London: W. Thacker & Co., 1860). For meetings between Grant and Machell in Bengal, see Machell, IV, 153/232 and Machell, IV, 205/34.
3 Kaspar von Greyerz provides an introduction to the literature as well as a critique of the term. Kaspar von Greyerz. 'Ego-Documents: The Last Word?' *German History*, 28:3 (2010), 273–82. On the sub-genre of diaries, see Christa Hammerle. 'Diaries'. In Miriam Dobson and Benjamin Ziemann (eds.). *Reading Primary Sources: The Interpretation of Texts from Nineteenth- and Twentieth-Century History* (London and New York: Routledge, 2009), 141–58.

24 *Willem van Schendel*

4 Jenny Balfour-Paul demonstrates this in her recent imaginative use of the 'Journals' to evoke Machell's life as mirrored in her own travels. Jenny Balfour-Paul. *Deeper Than Indigo: Tracing Thomas Machell, Forgotten Explorer* (Surbiton: Medina Publishing, 2015).
5 Jenny Balfour-Paul. *Indigo* (London: British Museum Press, 1998).
6 Willem van Schendel. 'The Asianization of Indigo: Rapid Change in a Global Trade Around 1800'. In Peter Boomgaard, Dick Kooiman and Henk Schulte Nordholt (eds.) *Linking Destinies: Trade, Towns and Kin in Asian History* (Leiden: KITLV Press, 2008), 29–49.
7 For a brief comparison of indigo in British India and the Netherlands East Indies, see Willem van Schendel. 'What Is Agrarian Labour? Contrasting Indigo Production in Colonial India and Indonesia'. *International Review of Social History*, 60:1 (2015), 1–23.
8 Prakash Kumar. *Indigo Plantations and Science in Colonial India* (Cambridge: Cambridge University Press, 2012).
9 John Phipps. *A Series of Treatises on the Principal Products of Bengal. No.1: Indigo* (Calcutta: Baptist Mission Press, 1832), 49.
10 Machell, 'Journals', III, 347–8.
11 *Rural Life in Bengal*, 113.
12 For a financial overview of this company in 1846, see Machell, 'Journals', I, 174-7; cf. III, 62–
13 '[T]he whole of the lands of the Bengal Indigo Company are divided into what they call concerns, over which there is one general manager (Mr Forlong), and each concern has its manager, as Patkabaree has Mr Verplough. Then each manager will have so many assistants according to the number of factories in the concern. Thus Patkabaree is divided into three subdivisions, one managed by Mr Verplough himself, the next or Ramnaghur division managed by Mr Bush, his head assistant, the third or Ballee division managed by Mr Snudden and the fourth or Santipore division managed by his younger brother. Each of these divisions again will have so many factories and over each Factory there is a native Ghomastah, or Factor, and even below this again there are subdivisions of Villages, with their respect in overseers and assistants.

It is a complete use of:
"Great fleas have little fleas
"And they have less to bite them
"Those fleas have less fleas
"and so ad infinitum.

Until when at last you come to the Ryot (i.e. peasant) you find him ground to the dust by his numerous overseers and, of course, the lower the overseer is, the more severely he rides on the necks of the people. It is [an] old story with them, "a poor man over a poor man, and no pity"' (Machell, 'Journals', I, 24–5).
14 Machell, 'Journals', I, 32.
15 *Rural Life in Bengal*, 116.
16 See the interviews that the Bengal Indigo Commission had with indigo cultivators, for example: 'Evidence given by Sri Bhobonath Joardar (inhabitant of Tarai, Hardi Police Office, Nuddea District (now: Chuadanga District)); examined on oath.

Q: Have you sown any indigo this year?
A: This year, in the month of Aswin and Kartik [September-November], the factory people made me sow indigo, i.e., they sent for my servants, five in number, and two pairs of bullocks, and made them sow seven beegahs and a half [1 hectare]. I had nobody to complain to. Mr Tripp [the indigo planter] is judge, magistrate, collector, and everything.

Q: Did you never receive any advances from the factory?
A: No, I never did. I can't say what they have written in the books, because the pen and ink and paper all belong to them. Last year I delivered 10 or 11 bundles of

plant to the factory. My grandfather sowed for the factory. My grandfather used to sow willingly. In those days they used to get cash, but since the factory has the ijaras [leases] and putnis [estate rights] we get nothing.

Q: Did your father sow indigo willingly?

A: I never saw my father sow at all. I have myself sown for 10 or 12 years.

Q: In the first year of those 10 did you get no advances?

A: I was laid hold of and taken to the factory, and told, as I was a well-to-do man, I must sow. The factory had then got the putni. It had the lease previously. It was in the Bengali year 1258 [1851 CE]. I did not get any cash advances. They simply told me to sow.

Q: Then the first year, when you took your plant to the factory, did you get nothing?

A: Not a thing'.

Source: *Report of the Indigo Commission*, 1860 (London: The House of Commons, 1861), 178.

17 'The lands of [the indigo division of] Khalbolyah are all alacka (i.e. rental from Government directly or indirectly); no firmer tenure than this exists in Bengal. The lands of Mulnath are partly alacka partly ba alacka (ba alacka is not leased but held by making advances to the small proprietors who rent or subrent it from Govt.). Now when you are Talookdar, Zemindar or even Izardar or Patnidar (i.e. renting directly or indirectly from Govt), you are Lord and master and, so long as you don't grind the Ryot [peasant] too hard, you can make him sow what you please, when you please, and how you please for you are his landlord. He pays rent to you, you to Government, but when you have no such hold you must advance loans that quietly pay your way and keep smooth or you must resort to the Lattial (Quarterstaff men) and Doorkee wallah (spear men). A few raids will teach the small neighbours that you have might. If you have not might on your side perhaps they will combine to resist and then you have a few number cases but the longest purse gains the day in an Indian lawsuit when the magistrate rarely knows more about the matter than his omlahs [staff] choose to tell him and very often not much of that. "Thank heaven," said an old judge on closing his Cutchery [court] for the last time. "Thank heaven I have been five & twenty years in the country and don't know a word of your blackguard language" (Machell, 'Journals', III, 48–49/336–9).

18 Factory managers were known as 'planters' in British India. The circular stated the following offenses:

'1. Acts of violence, which although they amount not in the legal sense of the word to murder, have occasioned the death of natives.

2. The illegal detention of natives in confinement, especially in stocks, with a view to the recovery of balances, alleged to be due from them, or for other causes.

3. Assembling, in a tumultuary manner, the people attached to their respective factories and others, and engaging in violent affrays with other Indigo Planters.

4. Illicit infliction of punishment, by means of a rattan or otherwise, on the cultivators or other natives'.

Copies of the Circular Letters Sent on the 13th and 20th of July 1810 by Orders of the Governor General in Council of Fort William to the Magistrates under that Presidency; Ordered, by the House of Commons, to be printed, 27th April 1813 (London: His Majesty's Stationery Office, 1813).

19 Machell, 'Journals', II, 179–80.

20 Machell, 'Journals', II, 180.

21 'December 22nd[1850]. I have been rather disgusted to day at the new orders. So long as Captain Crawfurd confined himself to cutting coolie hire, horse allowances and gun orders, when the said horses were to be fed and how their manes and tails were to be combed, all was well enough. But now he has just acquired enough insight into factory affairs to give mischievous orders.

I am one of the old school who have been taught that to hear is to obey, however, I shall take the sailor's liberty: growl you may go you must. I don't consider that in thus unburdening myself to you I am violating any secret. This is a private journal like a private letter for your sole amusement, so here goes for a little account of the affairs of the Bengal Indigo Company' (Machell, 'Journals', III, 48/336–7).

22 Machell, 'Journals', III, 49/338.

23 'In consequence of our merely being tenants on sufferance instead of Landlords, we have to make advances and pay higher for our Indigo. Here therefore we manufacture more expensively. It costs us a rupee for only four bundles and we never succeed in getting more than five and a half maunds [5½ x 36 kg] per thousand bundles. In Khalbolyah during the last year Campbell made his indigo at 70–80 Rs per maund whilst we make it at 100–120 per maund, both selling at the same price 170–200 Rs per maund. This in two concerns adjoining each other each making from 12 to 1300 maunds makes a great difference in the accounts and the Captain is now determined to work after Campbell's system, alacka or ba alacka [whether the land is held as landlords or not]. Consequently I have today received an order to make my arrangements with Ryots as in Khalbolyah and Mulnath at one rupee per five bundles. Now as it is we can hardly coax these men who are independent to take our advances and grow indigo for us at four bundles for the rupee. How will they like to be compelled to rear it for us at five? Already the Ryots of Khalbolyah have risen against their Landlords. What then am I to expect from the independent Ryots [here]? Why, already a rival Zemindar is urging the ryots to annoy us ... He made over the Izaarah [lease] on much lower terms than we offered to a native holding a much smaller factory near one of mine on condition that he should not allow us to sow a single Beegah [bigha = 1/3 acre] of indigo on his grounds and that he should incite the neighbouring Ryots and small talookdars to annoy us as much as possible and deny taking advances from or cultivating Indigo for us. This single man's influence extends over thirty villages in the factory of Peepulergatchi' (Machell, 'Journals', III, 49–50/338–41).

24 Machell, 'Journals', III, 50/341.

25 'I hear that Khalboyah is already up and the Captain has gone to the station to ascertain the progress of a few Mooker dunnehs (law cases) in the civil and criminal courts. I have not heard how many indictments there are for coons (murders) but of course there will be a few for Bengalis are not particular. They tried the dead body dodge the other day (i.e. slashing and mutilating a corpse for the purpose of getting up a case) but the Surgeon found them out, much to their surprise. The wounds having been given after death they'll have to look smart to get a corpse away from here for it is a two days' journey to the station all through our factories, so they could only travel by night and they'd have a nosegay by the time they got there, especially in the hot weather when I expect we shall have the worst tussling' (Machell, 'Journals', III, 51/342).

26 'Captain Crawfurd [is a] thorough man of the world, one who has subdued all impulse of a generous or benevolent nature, he thinks only of reducing the outlay to the lowest possible amount, regardless alike of the poor Ryot who is ground down beyond what he can bear and the result which his poverty and despair must eventually create. It is the old story of Manufacturer and his workmen. Competition lowers prices and consequently the labourer suffers but who cares, for the man who makes his Indigo at eighty rupees a maund is a fine fellow and a good planter' (Machell, 'Journals', IV, 11/11).

27 'All this I have represented but my representation remains unanswered. I can hardly reconcile it to my conscience to enforce such proceedings but I must do so or resign my berth and employment is not as easy to be obtained, as the last twelve months experience plainly teaches me, and yet what can I do. Enforced these measures will be either by might or my successor and so I console myself. Poor consolation for dirty work. The consequences will fall heaviest however on the destroyers of the goose that lays the golden eggs' (Machell, 'Journals', III, 54/350).

28 Machell, 'Journals', III, 52/345.
29 Machell, 'Journals', IV, 19/26.
30 Machell, 'Journals', IV, 13/14.
31 Machell, 'Journals', III, 52/345.
32 'Trip Saheb sent out three of our fellows at the head of a hundred men to Tonghy to settle matters with Bhamun Dos Baboo but when they got there they found five hundred soorki wallahs (men who fight with iron javelins), so the hundred lattials (quarterstaff men) bolted, but our three men stood firm, but what would they do with tulwars [sabres] against soorkies. Nevertheless they gave some wounds and one was speared through the thigh, the other fell with a soorki clean through his shoulder and the third with a severe cut on the side of his head' (Machell, 'Journals', IV, 8/4; cf. IV, 113/206–7).
33 Machell, 'Journals', IV, 11–12/11–12.
34 His clothes look so good that he also gets orders from other Europeans and he prides himself on always paying the manufacturers promptly. 'I can congratulate myself on being the cause of prosperity to one branch of trade in my district'. (Machell, 'Journals', IV, 22/32–3).
35 Machell, 'Journals', IV, 22/33.
36 Machell, IV, 22/33. See also Machell, 'Journals', IV, 174–5/323–4.
37 Machell, 'Journals', IV, 23–4/34–7.
38 Machell, 'Journals', IV, 26/41. For later plans to start a missionary station manned by 'native Christians', see Machell, 'Journals', IV, 194/14; Machell, 'Journals', IV, 200–1/25–6.
39 Machell, 'Journals', IV, 26/41, 29/46, 31/50.
40 'March 19th [1851]. Rode over to old Baragoria factory with Ramchunder Roy, my head Ghomastah, partly to see how the lands are and how the plant looks and partly to make arrangements for establishing a school at this place, having on consideration changed my original design of establishing an English school at Rooderpore for seeing the uncertainty of my stay at this place of what use would a slight smattering of English be to a set of village boys whilst what they learn in Bengali will be of real use, however little that may be, for instance if they only learn their letters they will be able to potter out a receipt and thus save themselves from imposition when their mahajans [money lenders] try to fudge them by giving false papers which when a second demand is made they produce as receipts and find to their horror that it is no receipt. If I remain they shall have Geography and History taught them in the vernacular and I intend to give prizes so that two Bengali schools, one at Baragoria and one at Rooderpore, will I think after all be better and more useful than the first idea of having a Bengali and English school at Rooderpore. Besides from what I have seen of English students I do not much like them. They get forward and disrespectful, saying "Good Morning" instead of the good Oriental salutation of "Peace be with you," and coming into the presence with their shoes on whilst their seniors and superiors are standing barefoot before you'. (Machell, 'Journals', IV, 50/88).
41 Machell, 'Journals', IV, 86(b)/156–7.
42 Machell, 'Journals', IV, 99/180–1. See also Machell, 'Journals', IV, 160/299 for his anger at the well-off Brahmins of Goga who try to persuade him to shift his school to their village because 'they are all Brahmins and respectable men. A set of Locusts, mean, overbearing, deceitful scoundrels. Why, my object is to educate the poor who cannot afford to pay, that by acquiring the rudiments of their own language they may not fall a prey to these vampyres who taking advantage of the dense ignorance of those beneath them avail themselves of their own low cunning to plunder and ruin them on all sides'.
43 'Well, I am not afraid; though berths are not plentiful, steady men are scarce and I can tell "how many blue beans make five"'. (Machell, 'Journals', IV, 102/186).
44 'It is my humble opinion that more disturbances are the result of unnecessary severity and ill management on the part of the masters and masters' servants than,

as is generally reported, the deceitfulness and turbulence of the Ryots. I am not one to be blinded with prejudice either for or against masters or servants; on one side you have an utterly uneducated poor, half-starved animal who will cheat if he can to get a few extra pice [cents] for his half-starved family, on the other side you have a master bent on having his full due, with a swarm of underlings to watch that he is not robbed, all of them bent on having all they can get for themselves firstly and for their master secondly'. (Machell, 'Journals', IV, 102/186).

45 'I am now only an instrument for a very different purpose and though by remaining I may mitigate in some measure, I believe the only really good I could do would be to leave the Ryots to their masters and the masters to the Ryots. The burden is very heavy, let them feel the full weight of it and they will fling it off. Helping them now is merely prolonging their sufferings' (Machell, 'Journals', IV, 102/187).

46 For my own part, though it may appear to be conceited my giving any opinion contrary to every experienced planter in the country, I do honestly believe that if there were no oppression there would be no cause for fighting, that there would be infinitely less law and a great deal more justice, prosperity and happiness, both for the Ryot and the Planter. But such opinions I think it best to keep to myself at present for I can do no good by declaring them but should make enemies, be deprived of employment and thus be unable even to alleviate in the smallest degree the condition of those for whom I express pity. By remaining I at least help to alleviate what I cannot remove, by going I only loose my own bread and make room perchance for someone with less philanthropical and more practical notions than myself. This is my notion and I consider it justifies me in remaining where I am, though the Planters are oppressors in spite of their violent denial of such accusation. I will add this in their favour: they are ten times more lenient than the Native Landlords. There indeed it is the tyranny of a poor man over a poor man, remorseless [...], unconscionable injustice and crimes of such a dark hue that when [one] only catches a glimpse behind the veil one draws back shuddering 'can such a thing be?' Aye, under our very noses and we in utter ignorance' (Machell, 'Journals', IV, 114/208–9).

47 Machell, 'Journals', IV, 119/219. At times he feels his current job is not the most repugnant in the company and he still feels indigo production itself is great endeavour. He dreams of running his own indigo factory on his own terms: 'The longer I remain here the more I feel convinced of the agreeableness of my present employment and though the drawbacks are certainly unpleasant I doubt whether in any other situation I should not find them still worse. I believe I must have been cut out for a planter and nothing else. The height of my ambition is to be an independent one'. (Machell, IV, 123/226). See also Machell, 'Journals', IV, 189/12.

48 Machell, 'Journals', IV, 175/324–5.

49 This also includes his ideas about race. During his travels he had made friends with Razzamea, a Muslim from Gujarat, who became his houseguest and co-worker in the indigo factory. When Razzamea ('who I loved as my own brother') dies in Calcutta, Machell mourns deeply and decides to support Razzamea's widow. He comments: 'It is much the fashion in this country to talk of the natives as creatures out of the pale of humanity, and to be hand and glove with a nigger is considered so infra dig and unheard of that none but an eccentric like myself would have ventured to brave public opinion. The white men shrugged their shoulders and the natives opened their eyes. Nevertheless I found a good and gentle heart under the dark skin and loved him for it as well as if his colour had been a shade or two lighter' (Machell, 'Journals', IV, 190–1/14–16).

50 *Report of the Indigo Commission, 1860* (1861).

51 The most influential of these is Dinabandhu Mitra, *Nil Darpan* (Dhaka, 1860, in Bengali); translated as: A Native, *Nil Darpan; or, The Indigo Planting Mirror: A Drama* (Calcutta: C.H. Manuel, Calcutta Printing and Publishing Press, 1861).

52 Blair B. Kling. *The Blue Mutiny: The Indigo Disturbances in Bengal, 1859–1862* (Calcutta: Firma KLM Private Ltd., 1977). The industry survived for another half century in adjoining Bihar. Kathinka Sinha-Kerkhoff. *Colonising Plants in Bihar (1760–1950): Tobacco Betwixt Indigo and Sugarcane* (Delhi: Partridge, 2014).

References

Unpublished material

Machell, Thomas. 'A Rough Sketch of My Life and My Brother Lancelot's, Written for the History of the Machell Family But Considered Too Long for the Purpose'. In Thomas Machell. *'Journals'*, Vol. III, 174–92.

Machell, Thomas. 'Journals of Thomas Machell' (1840–1856) (British Library, India Office Private Papers, Mss Eur B369), 5 Vols.

Published material

Balfour-Paul, Jenny. *Indigo* (London: British Museum Press, 1998).

Balfour-Paul, Jenny, *Deeper Than Indigo: Tracing Thomas Machell, Forgotten Explorer* (Surbiton: Medina Publishing, 2015).

Copies of the Circular Letters Sent on the 13th and 20th of July 1810 by Orders of the Governor General in Council of Fort William to the Magistrates under that Presidency; Ordered, by the House of Commons, to be printed, 27th April 1813 (London: His Majesty's Stationery Office, 1813).

Hammerle, Christa. 'Diaries'. In Miriam Dobson and Benjamin Ziemann (eds.). *Reading Primary Sources: The Interpretation of Texts from Nineteenth- and Twentieth-Century History* (London and New York: Routledge, 2009), 141–58.

Kling, Blair B. *The Blue Mutiny: The Indigo Disturbances in Bengal, 1859–1862* (Calcutta: Firma KLM Private Ltd., 1977).

Kumar, Prakash. *Indigo Plantations and Science in Colonial India* (Cambridge: Cambridge University Press, 2012).

Mitra, Dinabandhu, and Nil Darpan (Dhaka, 1860, in Bengali); translated as: *A Native, Nil Darpan; or, The Indigo Planting Mirror: A Drama* (Calcutta: C.H. Manuel, Calcutta Printing and Publishing Press, 1861).

Phipps, John, *A Series of Treatises on the Principal Products of Bengal. No.1: Indigo* (Calcutta: Baptist Mission Press, 1832).

Report of the Indigo Commission, 1860 (London: The House of Commons, 1861).

Rural Life in Bengal: Illustrative of Anglo-Indian Suburban Life ... letters from an artist in India to his sisters in England [by Colesworthey Grant] (London: W. Thacker & Co., 1860).

Sinha-Kerkhoff, Kathinka. *Colonising Plants in Bihar (1760–1950): Tobacco Betwixt Indigo and Sugarcane* (Delhi: Partridge, 2014).

Van Schendel, Willem. 'The Asianization of Indigo: Rapid Change in a Global Trade Around 1800'. In Peter Boomgaard, Dick Kooiman and Henk Schulte Nordholt (eds.) *Linking Destinies: Trade, Towns and Kin in Asian History* (Leiden: KITLV Press, 2008), 29–49.

Van Schendel, Willem, 'What Is Agrarian Labour? Contrasting Indigo Production in Colonial India and Indonesia'. *International Review of Social History*, 60:1 (2015), 1–23.

Von Greyerz, Kaspar. 'Ego-Documents: The Last Word?' *German History*, 28:3 (2010), 273–82.

3 Multatuli, the liberal colonialists and their attacks on the patrimonial embedding of commodity production in Java

Ulbe Bosma

This chapter details how P.J. Veth, a key person in the liberal opposition (Figure 3.1), used Douwes Dekker's novel to morally discredit the Cultivation System and further his own agenda. Veth's lengthy review of *Max Havelaar* also provides a detailed insight into how commodity production in nineteenth-century colonial Java was embedded in pre-colonial patrimonial structures. However, even more important is that Veth's review uniquely exemplifies the point made in the introduction of this book, that the embedding of commodities was not just an act but an iterative process, a process of permanent readjustment as well, in which metropolitan public opinion played its own powerful role. While the *Max Havelaar* was translated into English as well as many other languages, Veth's influential article never was.

Figure 3.1 Portrait of P. J. Veth[1]

By 1860, the social and moral implications of the way in which colonial commodity production was embedded in Java's rural society had become the subject of fierce debates. Thirty years before, the Dutch colonial government had introduced the Cultivation System, which forced approximately two thirds of Java's population to grow coffee, cane and indigo for the European markets. The system was supervised by colonial civil servants, both European and hereditary Javanese, who all received a share of its profits. The Javanese peasantry, however, was coerced to provide their labour and land against a nominal plant wage, which only in the late 1830s brought real additional rural income.[2] The immense profits from the Cultivation System replenished the Dutch metropolitan exchequer while stories from Java of misery and famine reached the Dutch newspapers. By the mid-nineteenth century, a time when political and economic liberalism became the dominant ideology in Europe, Dutch liberal politicians felt strongly enough to mount fierce opposition to the Cultivation System. They advocated the abolition of coerced labour and the opening up of Java to free enterprise, arguing that this would improve the conditions of the Javanese people and yield even more profits for the Dutch metropolitan economy. They envisioned a new embedding of commodity production, away from the compulsory labour propping up the Javanese patrimonial political structures, and towards one that would attract free entrepreneurs and free labour. In 1870, the liberals won the day and private plantation enterprise began to take large tracts of land into cultivation, both in Java and in Sumatra.

Veth's article in the prominent liberal literary and cultural magazine *De Gids* (*The Guide*) is an excellent source, which brings us to the ideological and moral ramifications of how the Dutch had embedded commodity production in Javanese society, and in particular the mechanisms that had been applied to extract labour and land from the Javanese. Veth's review is a widely circulated key document concerning Dutch colonial policies, written by a prominent liberal expert on the Netherlands Indies. It is also by far the most important review of *Max Havelaar: or the Coffee Auctions of the Dutch Trading Company*, written by former civil servant Eduard Douwes Dekker under the pseudonym Multatuli (Latin: *multa tuli* – 'I have borne many things' or 'I have suffered much'; Figure 3.2[3]). Apart from being an indictment of Dutch colonial exploitation of the people of Java, many Dutch people consider *Max Havelaar*, which was published in 1860, the best Dutch novel ever written. In addition, Veth's review is generally considered as instrumental to the almost immediate success of *Max Havelaar*. Thanks to Veth, liberal parliamentarians embraced the novel to condemn the Dutch Cultivation System for its reliance on coerced labour and for violating the rights of Javanese farmers to their soil in order to produce colonial commodities cheaply.

This chapter first details Veth's political agenda, followed by a brief explanation of the prevailing embedding of commodity production under the Cultivation System. Then, through a close reading of some parts of Veth's lengthy review of *Max Havelaar*, I will show how he presents this novel as an indictment of the Cultivation System. Finally, in order to put Veth's review in a broader historical context, I present his own ideas about how the introduction

Figure 3.2 Portrait of Eduard Douwes Dekker ('Multatuli'), the author of *Max Havelaar*[4]

of a liberal economic order could open up Java – and the Netherlands Indies as a whole – to Dutch investors, thereby generating more wealth for the entire empire. Indeed, Veth was the chief ideologue of modern Dutch imperialism and included *Max Havelaar* in his agenda so effectively that it is still believed today that Multatuli's book was written on behalf of the liberal cause.

Max Havelaar's appeal and Veth's agenda

For Veth and his fellow liberals, the economic development of the Netherlands East Indies should have been based on Western legal premises, such as the independent administration of justice, freedom of movement and respect for property.[5] The liberal politicians – who were a rising political power in the Netherlands after 1848 – needed some ammunition, because colonial affairs continued to be dominated by moderate conservatives or conservative liberals. Veth immediately saw how *Max Havelaar* might serve as a nail in the coffin of an already controversial Cultivation System. He used the opportunity of reviewing this book to demonstrate how commodity production in colonial Java – the richest source of metropolitan wealth in the nineteenth century, accounting for 30 per cent of the annual income of the Dutch exchequer around 1860[6] – was embedded in the patrimonial Javanese society, in servility and ignorance, and was deliberately consolidated by colonial conservatives. The way in which Veth inserted *Max Havelaar* into ongoing colonial debates definitely contributed to the book being widely credited as having hastened the end of the Cultivation System. See, for example, the introduction to the Penguin Classic translation of *Max Havelaar*.[7] Veth's review made *Max Havelaar* the 'bible' for liberal opposition to the Cultivation System, in spite of the fact that Douwes Dekker strongly and publicly resisted being part of any colonial party, although to no avail.[8]

For good reasons, post-colonial authors have singled out *Max Havelaar* as exceptional within nineteenth-century literature on colonialism. Edward Said writes in his *Culture and Imperialism*:

> During the nineteenth century, if we exclude rare exceptions like the Dutch writer Multatuli, debate over colonies usually turned on their profitability, their management and mismanagement, and on theoretical questions such as whether and how colonialism might be squared with *laissez-faire* or tariff-politics; an *imperialist* and Euro-centric framework is implicitly accepted.[9]

One may also argue the reverse and note that Douwes Dekker – or Multatuli, as most people referred to him by his *nom de plume* at the time – was of no use to the liberal colonial agenda, because in political circles he was generally considered to be irrational and too aloof from the political nitty-gritty.[10]

These assessments make Veth's review all the more important. He definitely belonged to Said's mainstream, as he was most interested in issues of colonial management. In the early 1860s, he even wrote manuals on growing tropical crops, rice, coffee, sago and cotton.[11] Nonetheless, he was interested in the moral and political ramifications of colonial commodity production in Java, and the way in which it relied on the cheapest possible way of governing, namely through indirect rule. Veth's review shows that the issue of embedding goes far beyond the question of the correct social and economic conditions for commodity production in Javanese society. The review demonstrates that colonialism is about reshaping these conditions and that in this process, debates on principles regarding property, labour, revenue collection and political accountability all play a role. Though indeed ethnocentric, as Said argues, the discourse about embedding colonial commodity production was not confined to questions of profitability.

It is precisely because of these moral concerns that Veth wanted to draw on *Max Havelaar*, comparing it with *Uncle Tom's Cabin*.[12] *Max Havelaar* might have even greater qualities, I would add, because it is multi-layered and unconditionally sides with the oppressed Javanese. On the other hand, the complex structure of the book and the peculiar setting of Dutch colonial policies, with their heavy involvement in economic life (far more so than, for example, the British in India) and the colonial administration's reliance on local aristocracies, may have stood in the way of reaching a broader international readership. According to the famous Indonesian novelist Pramoedya Ananta Toer, *Max Havelaar* is 'the book that killed colonialism'.[13] However, it killed colonialism only in the particular historical context of Indonesia, where the book was highly popular among the nationalists, particularly during their struggle for the liberation of Indonesia from Dutch rule between 1945 and 1949. Although many well-educated people throughout the world prior to 1940 might have read translations of *Max Havelaar*, it lost its impetus in the second half of the twentieth century, particularly because it was a critique that was embedded in colonial idiosyncrasies. For modern readers, it could hardly serve as a critique of colonialism in general.[14]

While *Max Havelaar* may fall short of being a *j'accuse* against colonialism, it is definitely a *j'accuse* against inhumanity and a fervent argument that truth cannot exist outside humanity and compassion. This is not incommensurable with the objective of its author, the former colonial civil servant Douwes Dekker (Max Havelaar is Douwes Dekker's alter ego in the novel), to seek rehabilitation. Douwes Dekker had resigned from the civil service after having been severely reprimanded by the Governor-General of the Netherlands Indies for daring to propose to send a corrupt Regent, the highest Javanese official in his department, on leave and start an investigation. *Max Havelaar* is the document of a civil servant who felt betrayed by the promises of the new liberal era that had dawned in the Netherlands after 1848. In 1854, the new constitutional regulations for the Netherlands Indies contained clauses about the elimination of personal service and *corvée* that the Javanese had to perform for their own aristocratic rulers and the colonial government. In practice, the colonial government moved slowly and Douwes Dekker was deeply disappointed in his superiors and particularly in the acting Governor-General who was known to be liberal-minded and from whom he had expected support.

For contemporaries who had some knowledge of how the colony was managed, Douwes Dekker's behaviour might have appeared rather naive. However, for Veth, it provided an excellent case to show what was fundamentally wrong in Java, and Veth's opinion mattered in the Netherlands. Being Professor of Oriental Languages at the Atheneaum Illustre (the forerunner of the University of Amsterdam) in 1860, he was an academic and a highly popular publicist in the Netherlands and beyond. According to his biographer, he was one of the founding fathers of the Dutch version of the colonial *'mission civilisatrice'* or white man's burden.[15] He had never been to Indonesia because his fragile constitution prevented this. Veth, the academic figurehead of the liberal camp in colonial affairs, was one of the grand nineteenth-century scholars who absorbed the world in their study room. Nevertheless, although remaining in his study, his voice was still widely heard. Some of his publications had a circulation of ten thousand copies, which made them bestsellers by the standards of their time.[16] Veth's unquestionable authority gave a credibility boost to Multatuli's allegations. The jobless and impoverished former civil servant was extremely grateful for this 'splendid' book review by this 'valiant warrior' Veth, who had professed that 'he would doff his hat in respect if he would meet him'.[17]

No doubt, Douwes Dekker was smart enough to see that Veth was wrapping the book in his own liberal political agenda. However, it must have been apparent that this was a collateral effect of the ambition to stir up debate and to provoke the readership to come forward with evidence and to start a national fact-finding mission; at the end of which, Douwes Dekker was convinced he would be vindicated. I would even argue that he might have anticipated this appropriation when he wrote his book. It is prefigured in the composition of *Max Havelaar*, which resembles a set of Russian *matryoshka* dolls of decreasing size that can be placed one inside the other. The reader will find the evocative story of Saïdja and Adinda – personalising the plight of the Javanese – at the heart of the book, whereas crucial original documents pertaining to Douwes Dekker's own case, are found at the end.[18] The first pages of the book are reserved for a blatant act of appropriation of the *Max Havelaar* manuscript as if the author presaged what would happen with his work. The reader makes acquaintance with 'Droogstoppel', which means 'Drystubble' or 'Dry-as-Dust': a person without imagination. It is a hilarious persiflage of a merchant trading in 'oriental items' who wants to reshape the book into a manual about coffee.

The next, but less imaginative, appropriator was the well-known novelist Jacob van Lennep. Douwes Dekker had asked for his help with the publication of the book. Although politically conservative, and therefore not the most likely promotor of the work, Van Lennep immediately recognised it as a literary masterpiece and facilitated its publication, but how? He replaced all the references to names and locations with dots, published the text in such an expensive edition that only the Dutch elite could afford to read it – hoping that by doing so the political sting would be removed from it – and wrested the copyright out of the hands of the impoverished Douwes Dekker so that the latter could not follow up his initial success with a cheap second edition. Veth's review was the second act of appropriation, less malign, but far more lasting.

Douwes Dekker's objective was to spell out that the Javanese people were severely oppressed, and that his attempt to provide justice had led to his misery. Multatuli (again, meaning 'I have suffered a lot') spoke for both the Javanese and the civil servant, his alter ego Max Havelaar, who he depicted as having a somewhat naive but generous character, expecting that this would raise sympathy among readers. Veth reshaped the message of *Max Havelaar* into a testimony of the moral bankruptcy of the system of commodity production that was embedded in the patrimonialism of Javanese society. Nevertheless, the relationship between the liberals and *Max Havelaar* was not that one-sidedly instrumental; the book also influenced its users. Veth and his fellow liberals did become more radical on colonial issues in the years after 1860 and *Max Havelaar* played a role in that. This is apparent, for example, in another very lengthy article by Veth in *De Gids* of 1866. This concerned the new Cultivation Law put forward by I.D. Fransen van de Putte, Prime Minister and Minister for the Colonies (1863–6 and 1872–4). This law failed to pass through Parliament in the same year, 1866. Veth built a grandiose scholarly and also passionate defence for a political friend in trouble, standing firm for the advance of modernity in

Java, which in his eyes was equivalent to the introduction of a capitalist economy based on property rights and free labour. *Max Havelaar* emboldened Veth and Fransen van de Putte in their quest to root out the Cultivation System.

The mechanisms of the Cultivation System (1830–70)

At this point, it might be helpful to provide a few more words about how colonial rule had organised the embedding of the cultivation of export commodities. The nineteenth-century colonial state had encapsulated the rank and file of the Javanese aristocracy, actually hereditary civil servants of pre-colonial polities, in a system of commodity production that soon came to be known as the Cultivation System. It was introduced in 1830, and encroached deeply and harshly on land tenancy rights, on village structures and on native local government.[19] At the lowest village level (the *desa* in Javanese), the Cultivation System dramatically strengthened the position of the village head, formerly an official who had been elected by the villagers but now became an appointed official. Moreover, it made systematic infringements on the tenancy rights of farmers. Javanese villages were gradually reformed from administrative entities into land and labour recruiting units. Together with the village head, the wealthiest and most powerful villagers became stakeholders, benefitting from the profits of the Cultivation System. This engagement of the *desa* elites in the Cultivation System facilitated its embedding in Javanese society. Thanks to these elites, colonial cash crop production could mobilise an increasing proportion of Javanese rural labour, particularly peasants who did not have enough land to make ends meet: probably half the population in the mid-nineteenth century.[20] Dutch historian Cees Fasseur writes in his reference work on the Cultivation System that its introduction 'led to a strengthening of the village right of control over the cultivated fields of the village, at the expense of individual rights of usufruct and the usage of the land'.[21] At the same time, it put a premium on giving out small plots of *sawah* (irrigated land) to share the burdens of *corvée* and conscript labour. This communalisation or collectivisation of property had nothing to do with egalitarianism, as Veth wrongly claimed: 'Shared ownership of land is communism, and all communism eventually leads to shared misery'.[22] Veth was far off the mark here, because by using the words communism and shared misery, he completely glossed over the actual social inequalities at the village level and the fact that village elites, in particular, profited from the Cultivation System.

By around 1840 the Cultivation System accounted for about 6 per cent of Java's cultivated land (this does not include the extensive coffee lands) and 57 per cent of its population (70 per cent of the agricultural population).[23] Coffee introduced by the VOC (the Dutch East Indies Company) as a forced cultivation was simply subsumed and extended under the Cultivation System, continuing to be the most important export crop of Java throughout most of the nineteenth century, while sugar and indigo were added as forced cultivations. According to government regulations, those who were engaged in the Cultivation System on average had to perform 60 days of cultivation conscription a year, but in practice, this was often more. This also explains why the Cultivation System went through multiple crises, particularly in the course of the 1840s, when the burdens of cash crop production led to food shortages and hunger. As Veth points out in his review, the residents, having a stake in raising the output of the Cultivation System in their administrative units, concealed the facts about shortages of rice in their reporting to the colonial capital Batavia.[24] However, these practices became increasingly difficult to hide from the public after the Dutch Parliament had wrested control over the colonies from the King in 1848. On the eve of the revolution of that year, a government investigation into the occurrence of famine in different parts of Java had already led to the gradual phasing out of indigo production. In the years that followed, increasing reports reached the Netherlands that the people of Java were suffering under the yoke of the Cultivation System.

In terms of embedding the production of cash crops, a historical continuity definitely exists between the Cultivation System and the systems of forced deliveries of labour or commodities that the VOC had imposed on Java. From the seventeenth century onwards, the VOC had used the rights it had obtained via treaties, or as the new sovereign, to conscript labour to build and maintain infrastructure works. A system of contingents for deliveries of cash crops was gradually extended over West Java, which tapped off the existing patrimonial administrative tax system.[25] The regional heads of the waning Mataram Empire, which had ruled most of Java in the seventeenth and early-eighteenth centuries, were ordered to deliver quantities of coffee, and European horticultural experts were attached to these functionaries. Interestingly enough, this was a form of turning the clock back for what was happening in Javanese society as a whole. Here, the monetisation of taxes had already begun under the emperors of Mataram. For the lesser peasants it had always been difficult to pay these taxes or land rents in cash, and hence moneylenders – both ethnic Chinese and wealthy Javanese – came in to provide advances on the crops, against high interest rates of course.[26] It was also one of the major problems of the system of land rent that was imposed during the British interregnum, which was not easy for peasants to pay and in practice, further strengthened the position of the moneylenders. Meanwhile, local officials continued to exact all kinds of compulsory labour from the peasantry.

The hodgepodge of taxes, land rent, bondedness and different *corvées* that existed in early nineteenth-century Java was a disaster in the eyes of the intellectual father of the Cultivation System, Governor-General Johannes van den Bosch (1830–4). However, he did not expect anything like a remedy from the introduction of sound liberal economic principles because in his view these would not work in a Javanese society that was steeped in despotism. At first sight, his own proposal to impose a system of *forced* labour and *forced* cultivation – he literally used these words – could hardly be considered less despotic but its author made it palatable by presenting the Cultivation System as an apprenticeship of sorts: a social remedy against feudalism.[27] When van den Bosch introduced forced cultivation in 1830, he seemed to have declared that it should be applied for just ten years, after which 'free labour' had to become the norm.[28] I have no evidence to corroborate this but what is certain is that the rapid introduction of wage relations in the forced sugar cultivation industry took place from the early 1830s onwards when van den Bosch was still in office as Governor-General. Moreover, wages and monetisation were a basic feature of the Cultivation System. The Javanese cultivators had to pay land rents from their crop payments, and even if the payments were deducted from the rent due, the money circulating in Javanese society still increased considerably.[29] Furthermore, wage labour was already the rule in urban environments and would increasingly replace the role of conscription services in the framework of the Cultivation System in rural Java. It is no distortion of the truth to state that the Cultivation System created the right conditions for a capitalist plantation economy based on wage labour.[30] However, it came at a price, since the *corvée* for local officials, who were crucial to the implementation and maintenance of the Cultivation System, still had not disappeared. At the time of *Max Havelaar*, measures were taken to end these practices but these measures were only the first steps and the Regents – the most senior hereditary native officials, who were adjoined to the Assistants Residents such as Douwes Dekker – were still a powerful factor (Figure 3.3). Against the backdrop of the history of the Cultivation System and the emerging plantation economy, with private plantations already underway, Multatuli rightly pointed out that it was not the principles that were at stake, but the lack of effort by the colonial government to enforce them. While van den Bosch and his successors

Figure 3.3 Regent and Resident in colonial Java[31]

had all insisted that it was the task of the colonial government to protect the Javanese peasants from oppression, the reality was that the peasantry suffered from burdens imposed on them from two sides: from their own aristocracy and from colonial commodity production. Further, as long as the Dutch were dependent upon the same indigenous officials to extract commodities, it was difficult to see how the situation could be changed. This became most clear after the Lebak case, which led to the resignation of Douwes Dekker.

Veth's selections from *Max Havelaar*

Having spelled out Veth's agenda and the way in which the Cultivation System was embedded in Javanese society, we can move on to Veth's review, which is almost 60 pages long and quotes extensively from *Max Havelaar*. It presents three quotations that cover entire pages from the book, namely the description of Java as a patrimonial state analogous to Medieval Europe, the speech of the civil servant *Max Havelaar* to the native heads of Lebak (the department that was assigned to him) admonishing them in a language that tries to appeal to the religious conscience of Christians as well as Muslims to behave as morally responsible administrators, and last but not least the tragic story of the young Javanese couple Saïdjah and Adinda. Moreover, apart from inserting his own comments in the quotations, Veth adds important testimony, particularly in support of Multatuli's moving tale about Saïdjah and Adinda, who were ruined by the district head's repeated theft of their buffalo. Without any hesitation, Veth assigned the latter story a place in the Dutch literary canon, as he predicted that: 'never again an adequate anthology of Dutch prose could appear without the "monotonous story" of what happened to Saïdjah, a story to which we return later on'.[32]

This enabled the Dutch reader to identify with ordinary Javanese, crossing the immense spatial and perceived racial distances, but at same time to be distanced from the 'oriental' political and social structures of Javanese society and in the same breath from Dutch conservatism, which allegedly insisted on perpetuating the lawless conditions of the Javanese:

> It is a mighty protest against the oppression of the Javanese, by the indigenous Regents themselves, it is true, but with a helping hand from the Dutch colonial government. Here, the book not only presents itself as a book, but as an act, an attempt like that of Samson to tear down the temple of Dagon. The book takes its place alongside 'Uncle Tom' and 'Slaves and Freemen'.[33]

A sentence that deserves particular attention is: 'It is a mighty protest against the oppression of the Javanese by the indigenous Regents themselves, it is true, but with a helping hand from the Dutch colonial government'. Whereas Multatuli writes about the improper implementation of rules and regulations, for Veth it is all about deliberate policies, and the Dagon (or Dagan) temple – Dagan was the god of the Philistines – is nothing other than the Cultivation

System itself. The reference to Samson, the biblical figure who paid with his life for the destruction of the temple, is an excellent metaphor for Douwes Dekker's sacrifice by resigning from service and facing social ruin.

Douwes Dekker's resignation as Assistant Resident of Lebak has become a famous trope in Dutch colonial history. It was the consequence of the refusal of his direct superior, the Resident (who, in *Max Havelaar*, was given the name 'Slymering', meaning slimy), to investigate the severe oppression of the Javanese population in the district of the Regent of Lebak. 'Slymering' did not agree with Douwes Dekker's proposal to send the Regent on temporary leave to prevent his interference in the envisaged investigation. Douwes Dekker insisted, however, and requested that his superior should bring the case to the attention of Batavia. Even though the Governor-General did order an investigation, he did not send the Regent away but assigned Douwes Dekker to a post in another Residency, which was held by a relative of the corrupt Regent. The flabbergasted Douwes Dekker resigned, hoping that once he was free of hierarchical constraints he could obtain personal access to the Governor-General and resubmit his case because at that time he believed the latter was an honest man who was being misled by his advisors. The Governor-General was not misled, however, but his hands were tied while the investigation was underway, an investigation Douwes Dekker was unaware of. He therefore conveyed to Douwes Dekker that he had no time to receive him, because he was leaving for the Netherlands. A few months later, the requested report on Lebak drawn up by 'Slymering' came in and some quotations from it were made in the Colonial Report of 1856. Veth used them to refute all attempts to portray *Max Havelaar* as an exaggeration:

> In the Governmental report about the condition and administration of the colonies in the year 1856 the following has been observed: 'After complaints by the native administration a special enquiry was conducted, which revealed that some native officials in Lebak had been guilty of unauthorized requisitioning of labour, money and buffaloes against disproportionate payment or without payment'.[34]

Veth scathingly noted 'Taking away money without payment', what a euphemism (*een gekuischte stijl*)! Veth continued to quote the colonial report that the Javanese civil servants had been fired and the Regent of Lebak reprimanded, which indeed only proved that Douwes Dekker had been correct and that it was incomprehensible for people to speak of exaggeration.[35]

The crux of the matter is that Douwes Dekker had dared to take on a Regent. This explains why the Governor-General had, on the one hand, ordered an investigation and, on the other, conveyed to Douwes Dekker his extreme dissatisfaction for his having:

> Found cause to recommend measures which would have subjected a native Official of the stamp of the Regent of Lebak, a sixty-year-old but still zealous servant of the State, kin to important neighbouring families of Regents and

about whom reports have invariably been favourable, to a treatment that would have meant his complete moral ruin.[36]

It was the Governor-General's decision provisionally to transfer Douwes Dekker to Ngawi, an assignment under probation that robbed Dekker of any further prospects of promotion. It is difficult to see how a colonial civil servant could have accepted such a decision. Nevertheless, the most important ramification of the Lebak case is that it makes abundantly clear that in spite of the formal designation of the Regent as the 'younger brother' of the Assistant Resident, the latter could not do much if the Regent perpetrated gross abuses against his own people. The phrase 'kin to important neighbouring families of Regents', in the letter from the Governor-General rebuking Douwes Dekker, reveals how little room for manoeuvre the colonial government actually had. It had little interest in the fate of an individual Regent, but the fact that he was part of a larger aristocratic network mattered a great deal.

To explain how this anomaly had come into existence, Veth extensively quotes Multatuli. In Veth's own words: 'Most of the fifth chapter of the "Max Havelaar" consists of a masterly exposé of the provenance of the authority of the regents and their relationship with European officials. I can't resist the temptation to quote a few phrases, as a sample'.[37] Accordingly, here follows the crucial quote from Multatuli:

> In each department a native head of high rank, bestowed with the title of Regent, is adjunct to the Assistant Resident. Such a Regent, notwithstanding his position as a salaried civil servant of the colonial administration, belongs to the highest nobility of the country and often to the ruling families, who in previous times had ruled as independent princes in their realms. Thus, with great political insight their old feudal influence, which as a rule in Asia entails considerable leverage and even religious dimensions, is used by placing these heads in a kind of hierarchical construction, at which apex the Governor-General exercises Dutch authority.[38]

Again, the crux of the matter is that within the colonial bureaucracy, the Assistant Resident was the superior of the Regent, but in terms of wealth, power and social position within Javanese society, the European was clearly the junior.[39] What complicated things further, Veth points out, are:

> The vast demands of the Regents, who have to keep up their high rank and status by a spending pattern that sometimes exceeds two hundred or even three hundred thousand guilders per year, which holds them financially in dire straits. The revenues of these heads, which by far, very far, exceed the income of their nominally superior, but relatively poorly paid, Assistant-Residents, consist of the following four categories.[40]
>
> First of all, the monthly payment [by the government], second, a fixed sum as compensation for rights that have been transferred from them to the

Dutch administration, third, a reward that is in proportion to the value of the proceeds of coffee, sugar, indigo, cinnamon etc. in their district and finally the labour and property of their subjects that they put arbitrarily at their disposal.[41]

Veth resumes:

Some further information is given about the latter two sources of income. Skipping over what the author submits about the so-called cultivation bonuses [i.e. their share in the profits made by the Cultivation System in their specific district] and their detrimental consequences, because this issue has been amply illuminated elsewhere, we would like to allow him to dwell on the arbitrary services and proceeds that are imposed upon the population, and that figure so prominently in his book.[42]

However, it is not the evidence submitted by Multatuli that matters here. Rather than presenting all of the facts, what he wanted to accomplish with his novel – which became clear later on from his personal correspondence – was for readers to feel challenged to ponder whether it was true, or just fiction. These facts had been presented before, but without creating a 'shivering through the nation' as the liberal spokesman on colonial affairs, Van Hoëvell remarked in Parliament in September 1860, when he alluded to *Max Havelaar*. Revisiting the existing evidence was what Douwes Dekker had asked for, and that was exactly what Veth did. Of course, Veth chose material that best suited his own argument about the Javanese officials, whose positions were hereditary, who considered themselves backed by the colonial government and who had thrown overboard their last restraint to exploit the Javanese population.[43] Veth presented a number of witnesses – and used the word witnesses deliberately – all of whom testified to the greed and arrogance of the Javanese officials, who were allegedly not interested in providing law and order but just in exploiting the ordinary Javanese. Examples were presented of how Javanese peasants were ordered around to perform all kinds of services for the native lords at any time, who were taking away peasants' property with impunity.

These abuses were not unknown to the Dutch government. The 1850s had seen a series of attempts and new legislation to rein in the power of Javanese officialdom. In order to prevent village heads taking away huge proportions of the crop payments to farmers, in 1851 the government decided that crop payments for sugar, indigo and tobacco cultivation should take place in the presence of Dutch officials. However, many problems continued to exist. According to investigations by representatives of the colonial government, native dignitaries had established their own rights to the fields, collecting a huge share of the crop payments due to peasants.[44] Moreover, the collective contracting of coolie labour also gave village elites power over the village peasantry, a practice that would change only later under the liberal Minister for the colonies, Fransen van de Putte. In addition, the role of the Regents and lower Javanese aristocracy continued to be crucial in assigning the fields to the production of particular cash crops.

The results of these reforms were far from satisfactory. While the colonial government made piecemeal attempts to protect the Javanese farmers, it simultaneously shored up the power of the native elites. Moreover, a highly ambiguous situation had emerged after 1848, when liberals gained increasing influence over colonial affairs, but without being decisive. A crucial article in the colonial constitution of 1854 that was influenced by the new liberal era stated: 'The protection of the native against arbitrariness, regardless from whom it is coming, is one of the most important tasks of the Governor-General. He ensures that civil servants fully comply with the regulations and that all natives will be allowed to submit their litigations.'[45] Nevertheless, this did not change the practice that Regents had become hereditary functionaries, which had been the case before the introduction of the Cultivation System and had been consolidated under van den Bosch.[46] On the contrary, the hereditary position of the Regents was confirmed in article 69 of the colonial constitution of 1854 and would not change during colonial times, although criteria of competence, diligence, integrity and loyalty became additional selection criteria. This mixture of bureaucratic and hereditary principles over time led to the professionalisation of an essentially aristocratic corps.[47] Together with the phasing out of the Cultivation System, it would cause a decline of the power of Regents, but in 1860, the Javanese were more firmly in the clutches of their nobility than ever before.

The theft of buffaloes

Max Havelaar has become so intimately connected to the Cultivation System that the notable fact that the story is located in one of the few parts of Java that were barely engaged in forced commodity production is treated as just a minor detail. Further, one may perhaps argue that it was indeed inconsequential, because the Regent of Lebak was a member of a prominent family and because of that part of the system in which the Cultivation System was embedded. Contemporaries perceived *Max Havelaar* as a potential blow to the colonial system, which explains, for example, the double-dealing by Jacob van Lennep and W.J.C. van Hasselt – the latter a high-ranking civil servant and freemason – who were helping Douwes Dekker get his manuscript published. They contacted the Minister for the Colonies to see whether the publication of this beautiful but potentially dangerous book could be avoided by rehabilitating Douwes Dekker. The Minister seemed wilfully forthcoming to this 'poor man' if the manuscript was withheld from publication. In the ensuing and somewhat murky negotiations, Douwes Dekker named the highest price he could think of: the lucrative appointment as Resident of Pasuruan.[48] Here, the Resident received 25,000 guilders cultivation bonus per year, whereas the Resident of Bantam was given a pitiful 1,300 guilders.[49] It would have been unthinkable to grant such a promotion plus the decoration Douwes Dekker had asked for, as it would have meant a public denunciation of the former Governor-General. The Minister was only prepared to offer another job somewhere in the West Indies.

What emerges from this less palatable sideshow is that Douwes Dekker had succeeded in transforming his personal dossier into something that spoke to Dutch colonial policies in Java in general. He had wrapped these documents in fiction to invite others to submit material in support of his case. The result was the moving tale of Saïdjah and Adinda (narrated in chapter XVII of *Max Havelaar*), from which Veth quoted generously, praising it as a literary masterpiece, a must-read:

> And when you might feel the urge to agree with my judgement on the basis of your own reading, you will experience a staggering admiration for the author and for his ability to arouse your sympathy, while he is transferring you to a world that is alien to you, with people that are hardly moved by the same things as we are; because he has familiarised you so much with this foreign world and has taught you to love these people, whom you have hardly learned to rubricise under the [biblical] expression of your 'neighbour'.[50]

The story of Saïdjah and Adinda presents an example of how the local aristocracy appropriated labour, goods, money and even animals from the peasantry with impunity. One day, the district head took away the buffalo from Saïdjah's father, and a few years later again, and again. Within a decade, the family's buffaloes were stolen three times to be butchered in town; and each new buffalo was weaker and the family poorer and more indebted. Multatuli's account is reproduced in its entirety in the review, but punctuated by comments from Veth, such as when Multatuli writes: 'Later on, Saïdjah's father fled the country fearing retributions for not being able to pay his land rent, and no longer having a pusaka (literally: an heirloom dagger) to buy a new buffalo, because his parents had always lived in Parang Koedjang and thus had not bequeathed him with much.' Here Veth interrupts: 'Note, how the author by the simple word thus, signals, how as a result of the vexations of the already aged regent, prosperity had vanished from the district.'[51] Veth went on to quote the story almost in its entirety, including its tragic and violent end, well aware of the effect this story would have on the readership of *De Gids*, which after all was a literary journal. Veth emphasised in some of his many insertions in Multatuli's text, that the latter presented the theft of buffalo as a matter of fact and the story as fiction. There were many Saïdjahs and Adindas after all, and thus, the reader could conclude, also many thefts of buffalo. The use of fiction here was just to provoke others to corroborate the story – and the widespread theft of buffalo in Lebak had already been confirmed by the investigation of 'Slymering'. In this respect, Veth played Douwes Dekker's game: to wake up Dutch public opinion and make people aware of the widespread injustice in Java.

A new embedding paradigm: the role of the village elites

While Veth successfully used *Max Havelaar* for the liberal cause, the liberals on their part could not escape from the influence of the book. Within a few decades, there would be no civil servant or journalist in the Netherlands Indies who did not take pride in having read the novel and who had not been influenced by it. Moreover, as far as the plight of the Javanese peasantry and the malice of the Javanese aristocracy were concerned, there was not that much disagreement between colonial conservatives and liberals. They were equally concerned about the fact that farmers would be reduced to a single impoverished rural class under a despotic aristocracy propped up by the Cultivation System.[52] However, while there was no difference of opinion regarding the ailment, sharp disagreement existed about the remedy. The conservatives were in favour of strengthening the position of the villages and the European civil service, whereas the liberals were champions of private enterprise.

It is not difficult to prove that the liberal quest for free labour, respect for individual property and the struggle against personal service was emboldened after the publication of *Max Havelaar*. When the liberal Fransen van de Putte became Minister for the Colonies, he read the Lebak files, perhaps initially just out of curiosity; however, he soon found himself ordering a letter to Batavia stating that these extortions were in no way excusable.[53] Actually, he strongly disapproved of the attitude of the acting Governor-General in the Lebak case who had judged that the extortions that had been perpetrated in this case belonged to the usual repertoire of the Regents. Earlier on in his career, Fransen van de Putte had been the administrator and owner of a sugar factory in Java, and in that capacity, he had taken the step of paying wages directly to factory coolies and not via the village elders, as was usual in those days. He knew that otherwise, the rake-off would have been substantial. According to Fasseur, Fransen van de Putte's agenda was to break up the entire village hierarchy to facilitate the advance of the plantation economy.[54] His ideal was to have Javanese land and labour cleansed of feudal structures and customs, and Veth warmly supported him in that respect.

Until 1860, the critique of liberals focused on the position of the Regents, district officials and the village heads: functionaries whose power had grown considerably under the Cultivation System. It was only after 1860 that the question of village communalism versus individual property rights became a hotly contested issue. It meant a shift but also a split in the liberal camp. In the late 1850s, moderate liberal politicians were still speaking about free labour in terms of collective contracting between European entrepreneurs and villages over land and labour. This was an approach that was rejected by Fransen van de Putte because he knew it would further open the door to the exploitation of the ordinary villagers.[55] This was fully consistent with his decision at the beginning of his term as Minister for the Colonies in 1863 to put an end to the practice of collectively hiring coolie labour from the village elite, introduced during the Cultivation System. It was also consistent with another decree, issued on 5 January 1866, at the end of his term, in which the colonial government forbade all personal service by the indigenous population without any exception, either for the Javanese or European heads.[56]

Six years after the publication of *Max Havelaar*, Fransen van de Putte made a bold attempt to bury the Cultivation System, or, at least, half of it because the forced cultivation of coffee – which was of crucial importance to the colonial and Dutch exchequer – was left untouched. His Cultivation Law nonetheless met with stiff resistance in Parliament, where most members perceived it as an attempt to introduce Western institutions into an oriental society. Conservatives claimed that because of the absence of civil registration and land registry, individual property rights could not possibly be administered.[57] This was nonsense, Veth argued in his very lengthy article published in *De Gids* in 1866 in defence of Van den Putte's proposal. First, in the Netherlands these registrations had only been introduced under Napoleon and this late introduction had never been held against individual property, and second, it was the Cultivation System and not the oriental character of Java that had created communalisation and therefore systematically violated the rights of individual farmers:

> Our previous article informed us about the conditions of land ownership in Java, so fragile and miserably arranged, that one can hardly imagine worse a situation. No one dares to call oneself a proprietor of land. Both the owner and the resident farmer hold a title to it, but these are so vaguely delineated that the government, being the strongest party, can afford any arbitrary rulings without the native, who is used to unfair treatment, noticing the injustice. The government considers the rights it has appropriated as an inheritance of the former indigenous princes, obtained by treaty or conquest, without realising that they merited these rights only in their capacity of Mohammedan rulers, which made them non-transferable to an infidel Sovereign. Whereas the Mohammedan heads did not always respect the rights of the people, their European successors trampled upon these rights to the extent that individual land ownership, which widely existed alongside communal property in the past, has disappeared from most of Java. Communal landownership has become the rule, and where individual ownership still exists it is deceitfully taken away from the commoner, whose rights are insufficiently ensured, or because the cultivators are no longer interested in these rights since they are no longer respected and merely entail the burden of cultivation conscription.[58]

Veth went on to argue that the compulsory planting of cane had made much of the *sawah* land (irrigated and often communal village land) practically useless because ownership was burdened with forced labour. He even suggested the expropriation of three quarters of the *sawah* fields that were assigned to cane production, against generous compensation for the population, to relieve the peasantry from the unpleasant and compulsory task of growing cane.[59] It is difficult to believe that he meant this seriously. It was probably an attempt to make the reader think about the fact that asking people to work a substantial part of their time involuntarily led to serious under-productivity, and uncertainty about property rights on land led to underinvestment:

> Where the two requirements: the legal entitlements to the land and free labour are absent, capital is not available, and even if capital was present, it could not be employed. At present capital is wanting in Java for the simple

reason that it goes wherever it is safe. We wish that soon the legislature will remove the hindrances that impede free cultivation and that it will soon provide agriculture with the necessary legal basis without which no cultivation can exist and if so, the moment will follow suit ... upon which the Dutch capitalist will prefer the possession of fertile real estate to Turkish or Austrian bonds.[60]

Fransen van de Putte fought hard for his objective to bring Java under the sway of individual property rights and wage labour, but in 1866 he lost the vote in Parliament and he resigned as Minister. He formed a new cabinet with himself as Prime Minister but lost again. Neither the liberals nor the conservatives in the Dutch Parliament had entirely their way and as a result, the embedding of commodity production shifted halfway between the aristocratic approach of the Cultivation System and the anti-communalist approach of liberal individualism. Although the colonial government recognised individual property rights in land in 1866 – and in the same year detailed registration of landholdings started, followed by an extensive survey of arrangements of landholding in customary law one year later – all these measures would not really change the way in which cash crop production was embedded in Javanese society.[61] Neither would the abolition of the role of Javanese nobility in assigning land to cash crop production make a difference anymore. European private entrepreneurs and the village heads, who had become powerful agents of the Cultivation System, were able to negotiate directly without interference from the Javanese nobility and the European colonial civil servants. In other words, the Cultivation System had been able to embed cash crop production so thoroughly at the village level that, by the 1860s, it had made itself redundant.

Meanwhile, Douwes Dekker had moved closer to the conservative point of view. He had always been suspicious of the combination of private entrepreneurs and local Javanese nobility and village elites, in his eyes a plague worse than the Cultivation System.[62] During a stint in 1857 among tobacco planters in Rembang whose plantations were not embedded in the Cultivation System, he had already noticed that 'in complicity with the Heads they were squeezing the Javanese'.[63] This is exactly what would happen, when finally in 1870, another liberal Minister for the Colonies succeeded in formally terminating the Cultivation System and a number of laws were enacted to change the legal embedding of commodity production in Java.[64] One of these laws was the Sugar Law, which enabled sugar factories to lease land directly from Javanese farmers. Civil servants were no longer involved in assigning land for cane growing. The law contained clauses to prevent abuse, such as that lease contracts needed to be drawn up in the presence of a European colonial official and that the village head was not allowed to receive a bonus for his mediation. However, an investigation into the workings of the Sugar Law in 1877 proved that the Law was barely obeyed. Some measures were taken to counter abuse, but in practice, the sugar factories had assured themselves of the co-operation of the village chiefs, who had a powerful position over many peasants in their village. In districts around sugar factories, almost half of the peasants could not subsist from their land.[65] As late as the 1920s, the village head received 2 to 5 guilders for every bau (0.71 hectares) of land that was leased out to the factory from his village. This was a completely accepted practice and the village heads continued to be much-valued supporters of the sugar factories.

Veth, the beginning of the Liberal Period (1870–1900) and imperialism

The history of nineteenth-century colonial Indonesia is divided into two eras: the Cultivation System (1830–70), followed by the Liberal Period (1870–1900). Whereas the former relied heavily on Javanese patrimonial institutions, the Liberal Period opened the door to direct control over land and labour by colonial enterprise. Liberal colonial politicians had been strident in dislodging colonial commodity production from its patrimonial embedding.

Veth's lengthy review of *Max Havelaar* not only gives us a detailed insight into how commodity production in nineteenth-century colonial Java was embedded in pre-colonial patrimonial structures but also unveils the liberal agenda of re-embedding Java's commodity production for the world market; one that was no longer impeded by patrimonial relationships but governed by the ideology of the free-market economy. Veth's review reveals how the liberals sought public support for changing imperial relations right down to the village level in Java. Veth's review also spells out the daunting task ahead for the liberals, who were mobilising public opinion for their political agenda. The metaphor of Dagan's temple ideally presents the danger of tearing down the edifice in which colonial commodity production was embedded. Eventually, the liberals had to accept that all they could achieve was piecemeal reform. Tearing down the patrimonial state to make room for a new capitalist building was not a feasible option, as they discovered when they took over the reins from the colonial conservatives.

Although the liberals succeeded in excluding the native and European officials from cash crop production, they were unable to prevent the village elites from taking their share. What they accomplished was a travesty of a free-market economy but this rather partial shift of the embedding of colonial commodity production was enough to usher in metropolitan capitalism to exploit the soil and labour of the Dutch East Indies to an extent that had been previously unknown, not only in Java but also in Sumatra. This economic expansion was part and parcel of, and a driving force behind, what came to be known as modern imperialism. Veth had been one of the most eloquent spokespeople against indirect rule in Java and almost in a single breath he became one of the most ardent advocates of bringing the entire archipelago under direct rule and opening it up to metropolitan capital, if necessary by military means. In fact, he became the chief ideologue of Dutch imperialism, but an imperialism that was solidly embedded in local inequalities.

Notes

1. By Jan Veth, 1892.
2. Jan Luiten van Zanden and Daan Marks. *An Economic History of Indonesia 1800–2012* (Abingdon: Routledge, 2012), 53–4.
3. Leiden University, KITLV Collections, reproduced by permission.
4. Leiden University, KITLV Collections, image code 37b630. Reproduced by permission.
5. Paul van der Velde, *A Lifelong Passion. P.J. Veth (1814–1895) and the Dutch East Indies* (Leiden: KITLV Press, 2006), 173.
6. Cornelis Fasseur, *The Politics of Colonial Exploitation. Java, the Dutch and the Cultivation System*, transl. R.E. Elson and Ary Kraal (Ithaca: Cornell Southeast Asia Program, 1992), 150.
7. Multatuli, *Max Havelaar. Or the Coffee Auctions of a Dutch Trading Company*, translated with notes by R.P. Meijer (London: Penguin, 1982), 13.
8. Multatuli, *Nog-eens: vrije arbeid* (1st edition 1870; Amsterdam, E. & M. Cohen, 1917), 10.
9. Edward W. Said, *Culture and Imperialism* (New York: Vintage, 1994), 240.
10. Cornelis Fasseur, *The Politics of Colonial Exploitation: Java, the Dutch and the Cultivation System*. Translated by R.E. Elson and Ary Kraal (Ithaca: Cornell Southeast Asia Program, 1992), 227.
11. Van der Velde, *A Lifelong Passion*, 137.
12. Stowe, Harriet Beecher. *Uncle Tom's Cabin, or, Life Among the Lowly* (Boston: J.P. Jewett, 1852).
13. Pramoedya Ananta Toer, 'The Book that Killed Colonialism: As the West Clamored for Spices, the Novelist "Multatuli" Cried for Justice,' *The New York Times Magazine* (April 18, 1999), 112–4; Carl Niekerk, 'Rethinking a Problematic Constellation: Postcolonialism and its Germanic Contexts (Pramoedya Ananta Toer/Multatuli),' *Comparative Studies of South Asia, Africa and the Middle East* 23:1&2 (2003), 59–60.
14. Niekerk, 'Rethinking a Problematic Constellation,' 60.
15. For the biography of P.J. Veth, see Van der Velde, *A Lifelong Passion*.
16. Van der Velde, *A Lifelong Passion*, 114.
17. Van der Velde, *A Lifelong Passion*, 142.
18. For a discussion on the composition of *Max Havelaar*, see J.C. Brandt Corstius, 'De bouw van de Max Havelaar.' In *Multatuli en de kritiek. Een bloemlezing uit de literatuur over Multatuli*, ed. J.J. Oversteegen (Amsterdam: Athenaeum, 1970), 178–88.
19. Cornelis van Vollenhoven, *Het adatrecht van Nederlandsch-Indië*. Vol 1 (Leiden: E.J. Brill, 1918), 511. See also Fasseur, *The Politics of Exploitation*, 28.
20. Ulbe Bosma, 'The Discourse on Free Labor and the Forced Cultivation System: The Contradictory Consequences of the Abolition of the Slave Trade in Colonial Java, 1811–1870.' In *Humanitarian Intervention and Changing Labor Relations. The Long-Term Consequences of the Abolition of the Slave Trade*, ed. Marcel van der Linden (Leiden/Boston: Brill, 2011), 407. M.R. Fernando, 'Growth of Non-Agricultural Economic Activities in Java in the Middle Decades of the 19th Century.' *Modern Asian Studies*, 30:1 (1996), 77–119.
21. Fasseur, *The Politics of Colonial Exploitation*, 29.
22. Quoted in Van der Velde, *A Lifelong Passion*, 174. The original text by Veth: 'Het gemeentelijk grondbezit is communisme, en alle communisme loopt ten laatste uit op gemeenschap van ellende. Het gelijke deel van allen wordt bij toeneming van het getal der rechthebbenden natuurlijk steeds kleiner voor ieder; maar men gewent zich aan die bekrompenheid, waarin men allen rondom zich ziet verkeeren, en leert niet zijne gedachten te verheffen boven het karig deel aan ieder toegemeten.' P.J. Veth, 'De cultuur-wet,' *De Gids*, 30 (1866) vol. 2: 317.
23. Fasseur, *The Politics of Colonial Exploitation*, 32.

24 P.J. Veth, 'Multatuli versus Droogstoppel, Slijmering en Co: Max Havelaar, of de Koffijveilingen der Nederlandsche Handelmaatschappij, door Multatuli,' *De Gids* (1860), 82.
25 After the Sultan of Mataram, the Susuhunan, had officially handed over the Priangan in West Java to the VOC in 1705, forced cultivation of coffee was introduced. Mason C. Hoadley, *Towards a Feudal Mode of Production: West Java 1680–1800* (Singapore: Institute of Southeast Asian Studies, 1994), 48, 106. See also Jan Breman, *Koloniaal profijt van onvrije arbeid. Het Preangerstelsel en de gedwongen koffieteelt op Java* (Amsterdam: Amsterdam University Press, 2010).
26 Peter Carey, 'Waiting for the "Just King": The Agrarian World of South-Central Java from Giyanti (1755) to the Java War (1825–1830),' *Modern Asian Studies*, 20:1 (1986), 99.
27 J. van den Bosch, *Nederlandsche bezittingen in Azia, Amerika en Afrika in derzelven toestand en aangelegenheden van dit Rijk* ('s-Gravenhage en Amsterdam: Gebroeders van Cleef, 1818) vol. 1, 222.
28 L. Vitalis, *Opmerking omtrent den loop der suiker-industrie in den Nederlandsch O.I. archipel* ('s-Gravenhage: H.C. Susan, C.Hz, 1862), 62–3.
29 See Fasseur, *The Politics of Colonial Exploitation*.
30 I made this argument extensively in Bosma, 'The Discourse on Free Labour'.
31 Pakoe Boewono X, ruler (Susuhunan) of Surakarta (left), with the Resident, W. De Vogel, in 1897. Leiden University, KITLV Collections, image code 7828. Reproduced by permission.
32 Veth, 'Multatuli versus Droogstoppel,' 64. The original text is: 'zeker nooit meer eene bloemlezing van Nederlandsche prozastukken, die weet wat men van haar eischen mag, in het licht zal verschijnen, waarin niet dat 'eentoonig verhaal' van de lotgevallen van Saïdjah, waarop wij later terugkomen, zijne plaats inneemt.'
33 Veth, 'Multatuli versus Droogstoppel.' The original text is: 'Het is een magtig protest tegen de verdrukking der Javanen, door de inlandsche Regenten zelve wel is waar, maar waartoe het Nederlandsch Gouvernement de behulpzame hand leent. En hier vertoont zich dit boek niet meer alleen als een boek, maar als een feit, als eene Simsons-poging om een Dagons-tempel om te rukken. Hier neemt het zijne plaats in naast 'Uncle Tom' en 'Slaven en Vrijen'.
34 The original text is: 'in het Regeringsverslag van den staat en het beheer der Koloniën over 1856 in de volgende woorden is geconstateerd: Naar aanleiding van klagten door het inlandsch bestuur werd een opzettelijk onderzoek gedaan, waaruit bleek, dat sommige inlandsche ambtenaren in Lebak zich hadden schuldig gemaakt aan ongeoorloofde vorderingen van arbeid, geld en buffels tegen onevenredige of geene betaling.'
35 Veth, 'Multatuli versus Droogstoppel,' 251–2, 264–5.
36 Multatuli, *Max Havelaar*, 309.
37 The original text is: 'Het vijfde hoofdstuk van "Max Havelaar" bestaat grootendeels uit een meesterlijk exposé van den oorsprong en den aard van het gezag der regenten en hunne verhouding tot de Europesche autoriteiten. Ik kan mij niet weêrhouden er, als eene proeve, enkele zinsneden uit af te schrijven.'
38 Veth, 'Multatuli versus Droogstoppel,' 73–4. The original text is: 'In elke afdeeling staat een inlandsch hoofd van hoogen rang, met den titel van Regent, den Assistent-resident terzijde. Zoodanig Regent, hoewel zijne verhouding tot het bestuur en zijn werkkring geheel die is van een bezoldigd beambte, behoort altijd tot den hoogsten adel des lands en dikwijls tot de familie der vorsten, die in dat landschap of in de nabuurschap vroeger onafhankelijk geregeerd hebben. Zeer staatkundig wordt alzoo gebruik gemaakt van hunnen alouden feodalen invloed, die in Azië over het geheel van groot gewigt is, en bij de meeste stammen als een punt van godsdienst wordt aangemerkt; dewijl door het benoemen dier hoofden tot beambten eene soort van hierarchie wordt geschapen, aan welker spits het nederlandsch gezag staat dat door den Gouverneur-Generaal wordt uitgeoefend.'

39 Veth, 'Multatuli versus Droogstoppel,' 74–5.
40 The original text is: 'de groote behoeften der Regenten, ten einde hunnen hoogen rang en staat te kunnen ophouden, en waarvan het gevolg is, dat zij soms met een inkomen van welligt twee, ja driemaal honderd duizend gulden's jaars in geldelijke ongelegenheid verkeeren. De inkomsten dezer hoofden, die zeer, zeer verre die van de in naam boven hen geplaatste, betrekkelijk karig bezoldigde Adsistent-residenten overtreffen, zijn volgens onzen schrijver van vierderlei soort.'
41 The original text is: 'Vooreerst het bepaalde maandgeld: vervolgens eene vaste som als schadeloosstelling voor afgekochte regten, die overgegaan zijn op het Nederlandsch bestuur: ten derde, eenebelooning in evenredigheid met de hoeveelheid der in hun regentschap voortgebragtewaren, als koffij, suiker, indigo, kaneel, enz.; en eindelijk de willekeurige beschikking over den arbeid en de eigendommen hunner onderhoorigen.'
42 Veth, 'Multatuli versus Droogstoppel,' 75–6. The original text is: 'Van de beide laatste bronnen van inkomen wordt dan eenige nadere ophelderingen gegeven. Overspringende wat de schrijver de zoogenaamde cultuurprocenten en hunne verderfelijke gevolgen in het midden brengt, omdat dit punt reeds zoo vaak en veelzijdig is toegelicht, willen wij hem omtrent de willekeurige diensten en opbrengsten, van de bevolking gevorderd, die in dit gansche werk zoozeer op den voorgrond treden, nog eenige oogenblikken het woord geven.'
43 Veth, 'Multatuli versus Droogstoppel,' 71.
44 [anon.]'Cultuurmaatschappij Wonolongan (1895–1925),' *Indië*, 9:19 (1925), 314–5, 320.
45 The original text is: 'De bescherming der inlandsche bevolking tegen willekeur, van wien ook, is een der gewigtigste pligten van den Gouverneur-Generaal. Hij zorgt dat de besturende ambtenaren de daaromtrent bestaande of nader uit te vaardigen verordeningen stiptelijk nakomen, en dat den inlanders overal gelegenheid gegeven worde om vrijelijk klagten in te leveren.'
46 Fasseur, *The Politics of Colonial Exploitation*, 50.
47 Heather Sutherland, *The Making of a Bureaucratic Elite: The Colonial Transformation of the Javanese Priyayi* (Singapore etc.: Heinemann, 1979), 35, 41.
48 Dik van der Meulen, *Multatuli. Leven en werk van Eduard Douwes Dekker* (Amsterdam: Sun, 2002; 3rd corrected print), 388–90.
49 Fasseur, *The Politics of Colonial Exploitation*, 47.
50 The original text is: 'En wanneer gij na de lezing u gedrongen mogt gevoelen, om mijn oordeel in het gelijk te stellen, dan zult gij uwe bewondering voor den schrijver nog voelen klimmen, omdat hij zoozeer uwe sympathie heeft weten op te wekken, terwijl hij u verplaatste in eene wereld die u vreemd is, onder menschen die naauwelijks met ons van gelijke beweging zijn; omdat hij u in die vreemde wereld zoo heeft te huis gemaakt, en u die menschen heeft leeren liefhebben, die gij te naauwernood geleerd hadt onder de uitdrukking 'uwe naasten' te begrijpen.'
51 The original text is: 'Eenigen tijd daarna vlugtte Saïdjah's vader uit het land; want hij was zeer bevreesd voor de straf als hij zijne landrenten niet betalen zou, en hij had geene poesaka meer om een nieuwen buffel te koopen, daar zijne ouders altijd in Parang Koedjang woonden, en hem dus weinig hadden nagelaten.' Here Veth interrupts: [Merk op, hoe de schrijver door het enkele woordje dus aanduidt, hoe, ten gevolge der knevelarijen van den reeds bejaarden regent, sedert lang de welvaart uit dat distrijkt geweken was].'
52 Bosma, 'The Discourse on Free Labour,' 412; Fasseur, *The Politics of Colonial Exploitation*, 129.
53 Edgar du Perron, *De man van Lebak: anekdoten en dokumenten betreffende Multatuli* (Amsterdam: Em. Querido, 1937), 410.
54 C. Fasseur, 'Van suikercontractant tot Kamerlid: Bouwstenen voor een biografie van Fransen van de Putte (de jaren 1849–1862),' *Tijdschrift voor Geschiedenis,* 88 (1975), 344.

55 Fasseur, 'Van suikercontractant tot Kamerlid,' 344.
56 Veth, 'De cultuur-wet,' 287.
57 Veth, 'De cultuur-wet,' 78-9.
58 Veth, 'De cultuur-wet,' 475. The original text is: 'Ons vorig artikel deed ons een toestand van het landbezit op Java kennen, zoo onzeker en kwalijk geregeld, dat men zich dien bijna niet erger kan voorstellen. Eigenaar van den grond durft niemand zich noemen. Zoowel de eigenaar als de opgezetene heeft daarop rechten, maar waarvan de grenzen zoo weinig bepaald zijn, dat de regeering, als de sterkere partij, zich de willekeurigste beschikkingen kan veroorloven, zonder dat de aan verdrukking en achteruitzetting gewende inlander die als onrecht gevoelt. De rechten, die de regeering zich toekent, beschouwt ze als de erfenis der voormalige inheemsche vorsten, door verdrag of verovering verworven, zonder te bedenken, dat die rechten den inheemschen Regenten waarschijnlijk alleen toekwamen in hunne hoedanigheid van Mohammedaansche vorsten, en als zoodanig in de oogen van den Mohammedaan niet vatbaar zijn voor overdracht aan een ongeloovigen Souverein. De rechten der bevolking, waarschijnlijk reeds niet altijd geëerbiedigd door hare Mohammedaansche hoofden, zijn door hunneEuropeesche opvolgers geheel met voeten getreden, zoo zeer dat het individueele landbezit, vroeger op vrij breede schaal nevens het gemeentelijke bestaande, in een groot gedeelte van Java schier geheel verdwenen is. Het gemeentelijke landbezit is dus meer en meer algemeen geworden, en waar het individueele nog bestaat wordt het den geringen man vaak door list en bedrog ontfutseld, omdat zijne rechten niet behoorlijk zijn gewaarborgd, of is het voor hem, die er niet in deelt, en toch de cultuurlasten moet helpen dragen, een oorzaak van dubbelen druk.'
59 Veth, 'De cultuur-wet,' 120.
60 Veth, 'De cultuur-wet,' 277. The original text is: 'Waar die twee vereischten: zakelijke rechten op den grond en vrijheid tot arbeid ontbreken, daar is ook geen kapitaal, en al ware er kapitaal, het zou niet aangewend kunnen worden. Op dit oogenblik is op Java geen kapitaal, om de eenvoudige reden dat dit in den regel vloeit naar de plaats waar althans eenige zekerheid bestaat. Mogen derhalve weldra door den wetgever die hinderpalen, welke thans aan de vrije cultuur in den weg staan, worden opgeheven; moge hij weldra aan den landbouw die vereischten schenken, zonder welke geen landbouw kan bestaan, en dan zal ook weldra het oogenblik zijn aangebroken,.... dat de Nederlandsche kapitalist het bezit van vruchtbare landerijen op Java zal verkiezen boven Turksche en Oostenrijksche effecten.'
61 See *Staatsblad van Nederlandsch-Indië* 1866, no. 80, Ordonanncie 23 Julij 1866. See also Handelingen van de Tweede Kamer der Staten Generaal, 1870–1871, 'Model-Dessa Register voor de bijhouding der statistieke opneming bij gouvernementsbesluit van 27 Junij 1866, no. 11 en gewijzigd bij dat van 8 December 1869, no. 23.'
62 It would be, in Multatuli's own words, 'het overleveren van den Javaan aan de hebzucht van avonturiers uit alle windstreken'. See: Multatuli, *Verzamelde Werken: Eerste naar tijdsorde gerangschikte uitgave bezorgd door zijne weduwe. II. Minebrieven. Over Vrijen-arbeid in Nederlandsch Indië. Indrukken van den dag* (Amsterdam: Elsevier, s.a., 4th edition), 91.
63 Van der Meulen, *Multatuli*, 349.
64 One of these was the Agrarian Law, enabling private enterprises to take wasteland for long-term leases of 75 years.
65 Bosma, 'The Discourse on Free Labour,' 409.

References

[anon.] 'Cultuurmaatschappij Wonolongan (1895–1925),' *Indië*, 9:19 (1925), 314–15, 320.

Bosma, Ulbe. 'The Discourse on Free Labor and the Forced Cultivation System: The Contradictory Consequences of the Abolition of the Slave Trade in Colonial Java, 1811–1870.' In *Humanitarian Intervention and Changing Labor Relations. The Long-Term Consequences of the Abolition of the Slave Trade*, edited by Marcel van der Linden (Leiden/Boston: Brill, 2011), 387–418.

Brandt Corstius, J.C. 'De bouw van de Max Havelaar.' In *Multatuli en de kritiek. Een bloemlezing uit de literatuur over Multatuli*, edited by J.J. Oversteegen (Amsterdam: Athenaeum, 1970), 178–88.

Breman, Jan. *Koloniaal profijt van onvrije arbeid. Het Preangerstelsel en de gedwongen koffieteelt op Java* (Amsterdam: Amsterdam University Press, 2010).

Carey, Peter. 'Waiting for the "Just King": The Agrarian World of South-Central Java from Giyanti (1755) to the Java War (1825–1830),' *Modern Asian Studies*, 20:1 (1986), 59–137.

du Perron, Edgar. *De man van Lebak: anekdoten en dokumenten betreffende Multatuli* (Amsterdam: Em. Querido, 1937).

Fasseur, C. 'Van suikercontractant tot Kamerlid: Bouwstenen voor een biografie van Fransen van de Putte (de jaren 1849–1862),' *Tijdschrift voor Geschiedenis*, 88 (1975): 333–54.

Fasseur, Cornelis. *The Politics of Colonial Exploitation: Java, the Dutch and the Cultivation System*. Translated by R.E. Elson and Ary Kraal (Ithaca: Cornell Southeast Asia Program, 1992).

Fernando, M.R. 'Growth of Non-Agricultural Economic Activities in Java in the Middle Decades of the 19th Century,' *Modern Asian Studies*, 30:1 (1996), 77–119.

Hoadley, Mason C. *Towards a Feudal Mode of Production: West Java 1680–1800* (Singapore: Institute of Southeast Asian Studies, 1994).

Multatuli, *Max Havelaar: Or the Coffee Auctions of a Dutch Trading Company*. Translated with notes by R.P. Meijer (London: Penguin, 1982).

Multatuli. *Verzamelde Werken: Eerste naar tijdsorde gerangschikte uitgave bezorgd door zijne weduwe. II. Minebrieven. Over Vrijen-arbeid in Nederlandsch Indië. Indrukken van den dag* (Amsterdam: Elsevier, n.d., 4th edition).

Multatuli. *Nog-eens: vrijearbeid* (1st edition 1870; Amsterdam: E. & M. Cohen, 1917).

Niekerk, Carl. 'Rethinking a Problematic Constellation: Postcolonialism and its Germanic Contexts (Pramoedya Ananta Toer/Multatuli),' *Comparative Studies of South Asia, Africa and the Middle East*, 23:1&2 (2003), 59–60.

Pramoedya Ananta Toer. 'The Book that Killed Colonialism: As the West Clamored for Spices, the Novelist "Multatuli" Cried for Justice,' *The New York Times Magazine* (April 18, 1999), 112–4.

Said, Edward W. *Culture and Imperialism* (New York: Vintage, 1994).

Stowe, Harriet Beecher. *Uncle Tom's Cabin, or, Life Among the Lowly* (Boston: J.P. Jewett, 1852).

Sutherland, Heather. *The Making of a Bureaucratic Elite: The Colonial Transformation of the Javanese Priyayi* (Singapore etc.: Heinemann, 1979).

Van den Bosch, J. *Nederlandsche bezittingen in Azia, Amerika en Afrika in derzelven toestand en aangelegenheden van dit Rijk* ('s-Gravenhage en Amsterdam: Gebroeders van Cleef, 1818), 2 vols.

Van der Meulen, Dik. *Multatuli. Leven en werk van Eduard Douwes Dekker* (Amsterdam: Sun, 2002; 3rd corrected print).

Van der Velde, Paul. *A LifelongPassion. P.J. Veth (1814–1895) and the Dutch East Indies* (Leiden: KITLV Press, 2006).

Van Vollenhoven, Cornelis. *Het adatrecht van Nederlandsch-Indië*. Vol 1. (Leiden: E.J. Brill, 1918).

Van Zanden, Jan Luiten, and Daan Marks. *An Economic History of Indonesia 1800–2012* (Abingdon: Routledge, 2012).

Veth, P.J. 'Multatuli versus Droogstoppel, Slijmering en Co: Max Havelaar, of de Koffijveilingen der Nederlandsche Handelmaatschappij, door Multatuli,' *De Gids* (1860), 58–82, 233–68.

Veth, P.J. 'De cultuur-wet,' *De Gids,* 30 (1866) vol 1, 1–19, 241–90, 475–99; vol. 2, 65–122, 274–332.

Vitalis, L. *Opmerking omtrent den loop der suiker-industrie in den Nederlandsch O.I. archipel'* (s-Gravenhage: H.C. Susan, C.Hz, 1862).

4 Smallholdings versus European plantations
The beginnings of coffee in nineteenth-century Mysore (India)

Bhaswati Bhattacharya

Writing petitions is part of human experience, an age-old practice. As the dispensation of justice and largesse are important parts of administration, authorities in power are vested with the responsibility of paying attention to the grievances, written pleas of their subjects or dependents. These in turn have the right to approach the authorities concerned to implore them to dispense justice or grant a favour.[1] This process of petitioning – requesting a favour, redress of an injustice, or settlement of a dispute – led to the production of historical sources, preserved in the archives of the sovereign/state. Petitions have been studied to analyse the social life of common people, judicial history, the evolution of constitutions, the emergence of early nationalism, and the growth of public sphere.

Natalie Zemon Davis's *Fiction in the Archives: Pardon Tales and Their Tellers in Sixteenth Century France*[2] is a remarkably fine example of the reconstruction of everyday life in sixteenth-century France by means of a critical examination of letters of remission. Such letters or pleas were a common phenomenon in the judicial system in early modern Europe, notably during the late fifteenth and early sixteenth centuries. Written on behalf of the lower classes, usually by notarial and secretarial staff employed by the state, 'Pardon tales' were narrative pleas, a fictional account mixed with judicial speeches detailing the particular circumstances and context in which the crime in question was committed. The purpose of such letters was to draw the attention of the sovereign to the innocence of the petitioner and consequently grant remission or acquittal. By analysing the social customs and cultural practices of the writers and the accused, and situating them in the larger framework of the administrative and judicial practices, Davis dexterously separates the fictional element in the pleas and draws attention to the evidential part of the historical documents.[3] Davis thus demonstrates that the task of the historian is to be aware of the fictional in archival documentation.

The character of petitions is subject to change. In medieval England, even the meanest subject had the right to petition. Pre-1640 petitions were deferential requests and instruments for expressing grievances. They constituted a 'privileged communicative space'. By the mid-1650s, however, a proliferation of petitions in print, which addressed anonymous readers, created the space for voicing public opinion. They were of crucial importance in the emergence of a new political public sphere.[4]

Turning to South Asia we find that petitioning was a political practice already during the Delhi Sultanate (1206–1526), and under the Mughals there existed a 'well-established and sophisticated mechanism to file petitions to superior authorities'. High ranking officials had an office-bearer to receive petitions, prepare summaries, present these petitions to higher authorities and record their decision. Petitions were classified according to the nature of their content and categorized according to the status of the petitioner and the addressee.[5]

The Indian scribes employed by the Mughals were recruited by the East India Company and later by the Imperial Government of India. Government servants, domestic workers, Europeans and natives alike had faith in the efficacy of a written appeal, so the production of petitions became a thriving industry. It gave employment to scribes and translators.[6] In a recent monograph, Bhavani Raman, arguing that bureaucratic institutions and practices are the most durable legacies of the colonial empire, has demonstrated how petitioning became part of the 'papereality' or the reliance on written documents to represent the world in early colonial South India. The colonial government incorporated the pre-existing scribal knowledge and practices, and this led to the growth of 'a new genre that was accessible to means of verification concurrently emerging in metropolitan domains'.[7]

The addressee in the petition has to verify the validity of the claims – the content of the petition before taking a decision on the same. The task of the historian reading a petition in the archive is not entirely dissimilar: s/he has to analyse the viewpoint of the parties concerned and to situate the petition in the larger socio-political and economic framework within which a particular petition is produced. In this way, petitions become a source for reconstructing history.

In Britain, the Petition of Right (1628) was championed by Sir Edward Coke (1552–1634), a distinguished parliamentary adversary to the crown. It set out the rights and liberties of the common subjects as against the prerogatives of the crown.[8] Yet, whereas in the British case the state functioned as norm-giver, in colonial India petitioning by common people was subject to the bias and partiality that was part of alien rule.[9] This chapter takes a close look at a petition submitted by some European planters to the colonial government in India on the issue of tax on coffee.

In a letter of 3 December 1864 one Mr. W. Lonsdale (Secretary to the Mysore Planters' Association in South India) requested the British Commissioner for the Government of the King of Mysore,[10] to forward his petition and the appended memorandum to the Government.[11] Signed by Major-General Coghill Ottley and 21 other members of the Association, the memorandum stated that the signatories represented the coffee planting sector in the Kingdom and wanted to draw the Commissioner's attention to the oppressive nature of the coffee tax levied in Mysore (Figure 4.1).

They referred to a statement released by the office of the Commissioner to the effect that the average yield of the Mysore coffee estates was declared

No. 31. From W. LONSDALE, Esq., Secretary to the Mysore Planters' Association, to the Secretary to Commissioner of Mysore,—dated Munjerabad, the   December 1864.

I HAVE the honour to request, on the part of the "Mysore Planters' Association," that you will do me the favour of forwarding the enclosed letter to the Commissioner of Mysore.

To
    L. B. BOWRING, ESQ.,
        Commissioner for the Government of the Territories of
          His Highness the Rajah of Mysore.

Dated MUNJERABAD, *the* 3rd *December* 1864.

SIR,

WE, the undersigned, being interested in coffee planting, have the honour to bring to your notice the oppressive nature of the coffee tax as at present levied in Mysore.

From our estates as much coffee is yielded as will represent an assessment per acre of sums varying from Rupees (10) ten to (6) six.

If, however, a Statement, which we believe has been officially made, *viz.*, that the average yield of coffee estates is (6) six cwt. per acre, is taken as a basis for calculation, it will be seen that we pay a sum which is equal to Rupees (6) six per acre, and this sum is exactly three times as much as the highest tax which is levied on coffee in any part of India, and six times as much as is paid on the Shevaroy Hills.

Taking into consideration that as the natives at present grow by far the largest quantity of coffee, and that a land assessment would, as is well known, be distasteful to them, we venture respectfully to request that you will make such reduction in the present tax as will place us on a footing with planters in other parts of India.

We have, &c.,

(Sd.)   COGHILL OTTLEY, *Major Genl.*,
                      And 21 *other Members.*
        Signed also in copies by
           MR. MIDDLETON, *and* 7 *others.*

Figure 4.1 Excerpt from the 15-page 'Complaint of Mr. Lonsdale' (1864), as it is preserved in the proceedings of the Government of India[12]

to be six cwt. per acre,[13] and that, at the rate of Re.1 per cwt., they paid the excise duty of Rs. 6 per acre.[14] In their opinion, this was the highest tax levied on coffee in India.[15] As Indians ('natives') also grew coffee in Mysore, the planters demanded a reduction in the tax they were paying. The Commissioner, L. Bowring, forwarded the petition to the Secretary to Government of India, Foreign Department. However, referring to letters that he had received earlier from H. M. Elliot (Superintendent of the Nagar division[16]), D.P. Mackenzie (late executive engineer of Nagar) and Col. J.F. Porter on the question of lowering the duty on coffee in Coorg in 1862, the Commissioner gave a negative advice with regard to the demand of the planters.

The content of the petition, the reports, and the decision of the Commissioner raise several questions concerning the history of the coffee-economy in India. Written in the mid-1860s, the document suggests that by that time both British planters and Indians were already growing coffee in different regions in South India. So, first, when was coffee introduced in India, a country known better for the varieties of tea it grows, consumes and exports? Second, who were the agents behind the process of embedding coffee in Mysore?[17] Was it the Europeans, as suggested in this petition? Interestingly, this is the image imprinted on the popular imagination in India even today.[18] An attempt will be made here to examine if the planters were justified in their complaint that their attempt at embedding coffee in the local economy was being disrupted by local coffee-growers. If it was indeed so, it will be worthwhile to explore the role of the new colonial government by analyzing its role in the way the petition was attended to.

By shedding light on the relationship between the modern agricultural plantation sector, represented by the Europeans, and the traditional economy of the Indian smallholders hinted at in this document, this chapter provides an appreciation of how the crop became embedded in Mysore's economy as well as insights into the roles of colonizers and colonized in the process. Lonsdale's complaint and the proceedings offer an excellent window on the development of the coffee industry in nineteenth-century India. The petition enables us to explore the interaction between the pre-existing village economy and the newly introduced plantation system, and the response of indigenous capital in the face of Western capital penetrating the rural economy. It also helps us to understand why coffee survived in late-nineteenth-century India when coffee production in Indonesia and Sri Lanka was virtually ruined owing to a rust disease that killed coffee plants. We shall begin with a brief introduction to the crop and to the way it came to India.

Coffee: a world commodity in India

Coffea Arabica and *Coffea Canephora* (the former better known as Arabica and the latter as Robusta) comprise the most popular varieties of coffee – the most exported raw commodity after crude oil, traded throughout the world.[19] Until the mid-nineteenth century, the most important variety known and traded was Arabica and this was the species that would be grown in India during the first few decades of commercial coffee production. Robusta (discovered in Belgian Congo) was grown in East African countries, where it had been used in rituals until the late nineteenth century.[20] As the name suggests, the species is more robust and resistant to diseases and pests. It was only after the 1870s when the coffee industry in monsoon Asia had been disastrously hit by the rust disease *Hemileia vastatrix*, that Robusta became popular.

The habit of drinking coffee originated in Ethiopia. In the sixteenth century, it spread through trade across the Gulf of Aden and the Red Sea, and throughout the Ottoman Empire. Indian merchants, Hindu and Muslim, traded to the ports in the Red Sea and the Persian Gulf and it was through these circuits of Indian Ocean trade that coffee entered the Indian market.[21] The elite in Mughal India were familiar with the beverage.[22] Cultivation of the crop in the country seems to have begun in the seventeenth century when, according to a legend, a Qalandar Sufi saint, Dada Hayat (also known as Hazrat 'Abdul Aziz Makki, popularly called Baba Budan or Baba Budhan), while returning from Mecca, smuggled a few seeds and planted them in the Chandragiri Hills in Chikmagalur, Karnataka (South India).[23] As ships carried both pilgrims and traders, commerce and religion were closely intertwined. This was especially noticeable in the case of the annual ships leaving the Indian port of Surat for Mocha, the Yemeni port of disembarkation for pilgrims to Mecca. When the Frenchman Jean de la Roque was purchasing coffee in Yemen for a direct shipment to France, he operated through an Indian intermediary.[24] Thus it was quite possible for an Indian pilgrim to have collected and smuggled coffee seeds out of Arabia, although it is likely that coffee, like other commodities, such as tobacco, circulated with travellers and that more than just one person was responsible for the introduction of coffee production in India. Until the end of the eighteenth century, however, coffee did not feature among the products (areca nut, cardamom, coir and sandalwood) that were exported from Mysore.[25]

The earliest known use of coffee as a brew was for ritual purposes among Sufi saints in Yemen in the middle of the fifteenth century. By the early sixteenth century, coffee was consumed in other parts of Yemen and across the straits to Egypt, from where it spread to the western parts of the Ottoman Empire including the capital Istanbul.[26] The engine behind the migration of the coffee plant across the globe was the drink's steadily growing market in the West. The evolution of coffee from a semi-tropical luxury drink in the seventeenth century to a mass drink in the nineteenth century resulted from the liberalization of the export economy of the Americas and the growth of the demand for coffee among industrial workers in Germany, the Netherlands and the United States. From the late seventeenth century onwards, colonial powers began to grow coffee in their colonies in the Caribbean, Central and South America, Africa and Asia, from where it was exported to Europe.[27] In 1616, the Dutch succeeded in transporting one coffee plant from Mocha to Holland, marking the beginning of Dutch explorations as to how to grow the crop. The Dutch began coffee plantations in Sri Lanka (Ceylon) in 1670 and the first coffee plants introduced to Java were saplings that they had shipped from Malabar (South India) in 1696.[28] Literature points to Muslim pilgrims already having introduced coffee in Indonesia.[29] The increasing demand for coffee in the western world saw the transfer of its production from the Caribbean to colonial Java under the Dutch. By 1726, no less than 90 per cent of the coffee imported to Amsterdam came from Java.[30]

During their brief occupation of Java during the Napoleonic Wars, the British became familiar with the Dutch success in coffee production in Java. Extensive use of fertile virgin land and abundant 'voluntary' labour coerced to produce the crop made the coffee an enormously profitable crop in colonial Java. The

Figure 4.2 Map of nineteenth-century southern India

peasant produce was sold at a fixed price to Dutch burghers who shipped it to the Netherlands.[31]

At least since the late eighteenth century Europeans had made small-scale attempts to grow coffee in different parts of India. In the early nineteenth century William Roxburgh (the superintendent of the Royal Botanic Gardens in Calcutta), his assistant Nathaniel Wallich, and others experimented with the production of coffee in different parts of India.[32] British planters in Sri Lanka already grew coffee. Their profits seem to have inspired the beginnings of the crop in parts of South India where the climate was similar to that on the island. The other major coffee-producing countries in the Empire were British Central Africa and Jamaica.[33]

Coffee is a tropical plant that flourishes best in mountainous regions between the 5th and the 15th degrees latitude, north and south of the equator, or, in other words, in the temperate climate zones in the tropics.[34] Coffee trees and can bear considerable heat provided the climate is proportionately humid.[35] Other important prerequisites are forest land, considerable elevation, shade, moisture and manure. From Chikmagalur, coffee gradually spread to other parts of the southern Indian peninsula. The Western Ghats housed some of the finest coffee districts in Mysore and Coorg, among other areas (see Figure 4.2). At 3,000–6,000 feet above sea level, the hills are at a safe distance from the sea-breeze. The moist, rich red or black clay soil enabled the plant to thrive.

Understanding Mr. Lonsdale's petition

Among the issues raised by Mr. Lonsdale and other petitioners, we are most concerned with their claim that Europeans played the major role in embedding coffee in the local economy – a profitable pursuit that had led to the clearing of forests in the hills of Mysore and Coorg – and that the Indians were awkwardly disrupting the process. The authorities collected reports and views in order to examine the truth of this viewpoint. Their findings made clear that the claim was far from tenable. The real cause of the Europeans' anxiety must have been the stiff competition they faced from Indian smallholders, who supplied the bulk of the Mysore coffee:

> Coffee planting has extended with a rapidity that is a convincing proof that the cultivation is profitable to the native planter, and it is asserted on good authority that a new comer [European] resorting to Manjarabad [a coffee-growing district] would find but little unoccupied land of value, and that he must either content himself with jungles in inaccessible places exposed to the full force of the western monsoon, or must purchase from native proprietors…the great extension of cultivation conveys, to my mind, absolute proof that it is profitable.[36]

This quotation from a report appended to the Petition in question suggests that owning coffee-land was profitable for native proprietors in India. If that indeed was the reality, it would be a scenario different from the one in Java. Although the Dutch did not change the nature of peasant production in Java, the 'Cultivation System' that they had imposed required each peasant to take care of a few hundred coffee plants of which the produce was to be disposed of at a price fixed beforehand. There was a tendency among the villagers to choose land unsuitable for coffee, so productivity was low and the peasant remained passive toward the state-controlled and coercive system that profited only the colonizers.[37]

What had happened in Mysore between the seventeenth century, when coffee seeds had been brought to the region, and the mid-1860s when Lonsdale wrote his application? Coffee production had spread gradually from the Baba Budan Hills (Figure 4.2) to other parts of Mysore but very few details have emerged as to the production, distribution and consumption of coffee for more than two hundred years since it was introduced. This warrants the assumption that coffee – produced locally and distributed through existing trade channels – remained modest enough in scale to have escaped European attention.[38] The first local historical evidence of coffee shows the rulers of Mysore granting special coffee-lands as rent-free land to their favourite lieutenants in return for services rendered.[39] The noted polymath Francis Buchanan, who travelled through South India at the turn of the nineteenth century, saw coffee being cultivated by European officials posted in the region.[40]

The Mysore State used to purchase coffee from the growers, but it was only after the British conquest that the Crown began to claim half the coffee production, a practice that continued from 1799 to 1811. Until 1834, the coffee gardens on the Baba Budan Hills were a Mysore State monopoly with cultivators allowed to keep half the crop.[41] In 1823, the King of Mysore leased out its half share of the Baba Budan produce for 10 years to Thomas Parry of Parry, Dare & Co. of Madras, for an annual sum of Rs. 4,270.[42] During the years that Parry enjoyed the contract, the firm had a virtual monopoly on Mysore coffee; the agreement permitted them to purchase the cultivator's coffee at a price set by the firm, stipulating at the same time that any export of coffee would require Parry's prior approval. In 1838, the contract was replaced by an excise duty of Re.1.[43]

Thus, the State of Mysore gradually recognized the value of coffee and allowed the establishment of large coffee plantations by Europeans. These began during 1834–61 when Mark Cubbon administered Mysore as the Chief Commissioner and Regent of the King.[44] The chapters by Bosma, Saptari and Sinha-Kerkhoff in this volume demonstrate that colonial governments encouraged private Europeans to clear land and grow commercially attractive commodities. We notice the same trend in the case of coffee in India. Mr. Cannon was the first European to establish a coffee plantation in Mysore, south of the Baba Budan Hills, in 1840.[45] Soon a 'coffee rush' ensued. Hugh Francis Clarke Cleghorn, the pioneer of forest conservancy in India, was of the opinion that – by the time Lonsdale and his fellow planters were seeking a reduction in the coffee duty – the influx of merchants and coffee planters as well as an increasing demand for firewood already had a prejudicial effect on the indigenous forests of the neighbouring Nilgiri Hills.[46] The success of coffee in the 1840s and 1850s encouraged the extension of its cultivation in Mysore and other neighbouring districts, as there were constant applications for grants of forest land to open up new plantations. The trend continued into the early 1860s, when European settlers increasingly felled trees in Malabar and Wayanad to clear forests for coffee plantations.[47] Vast areas of forest were cleared by aspiring entrepreneurs lacking in expertiseoften resulting in subsequent abandonment of the land.[48] As coffee needed to be encouraged as 'bona fide cultivation', Cleghorn advised that in order to restrict the destruction of timber, grants of coffee-land should be restricted to places where the plant could be grown with advantage and that the denudation of the higher ridges and slopes of the hills be prohibited.[49] The increase in coffee production during this period is evident from the increase in the government's revenue, especially after the introduction of excise duty on the commodity. Between 1822 and 1861 the annual returns on this account increased by leaps and bounds (Table 4.1).

Table 4.1 Annual revenue from coffee in Mysore, 1822–61[50]

1822–32 (contract system)	Rs. 4,270
1832–37 (contract system)	Rs. 7,472
1838–43 @ Re. 1 per 37.3 kg	Rs. 15,238
1844–49 @ Re. ½ per 37.3 kg	Rs. 26,118
1850–61 @ Re. ¼ per 37.3 kg	Rs. 86,824

This demonstrates the remarkable increase in returns from coffee, especially given the fact that during the early years the excise duty was imposed at one rupee but toward the later years the rate of half a rupee, and then only a quarter of a rupee. Clearly, Mysore was experiencing an astonishing boom in coffee production, resulting from the reduced duty. But there was another factor as well: an increase in the market price for 'native' coffee, which shot up from Re.1 per 37.3 kg to Rs.6–8 per 37.3 kg.[51] What seems to have been even more important, however, is that indigenous farmers grew coffee mostly in forest land where cultivation of coffee was optional.[52] Only a small portion of their farm was under coffee and at the same time they grew betel nut, ginger, plantains, other fruits, turmeric, vegetables, yam and spices.[53] Coffee could be cultivated on smallholdings, like tea and indigo, although the latter crops needed to be processed immediately after harvest and usually require large-scale investments in land, labour and technology.[54] The additional advantage of coffee, especially when processed by the dry method, was that it could be easily stored, giving growers more autonomy vis-à-vis purchasers, as long as producers were not indebted to traders. Peasants and local entrepreneurs often planted coffee in between other cultivated crops; as coffee was by no means the only crop that they depended on, failure of the crop meant a comparatively little loss. Tables 4.2 and 4.3 show that this method suited Indian agricultural entrepreneurs and farmers very well. The prosperity generated by coffee must have inspired them to acquire coffee-growing lands (Table 4.2). As Mr. Lonsdale noted in his complaint, it should be borne in mind that one acre of coffee-land owned by indigenous farmers yielded 186.5 kg of coffee while the same amount of land belonging to European planters yielded at least 932.5 kg of coffee. This clearly indicates that Europeans exploited the land under coffee far more intensively. The European planters took this as proof that Indians did not do their best to grow coffee. D.P. Mackenzie, the engineer with 15 years' experience in Nagar and most probably a planter himself, did not try to mince his words while giving his opinion on the existing system:

> The natives, so far as I can gather, would prefer the halut system [in which an export duty was payable]; it is more consonant with their ideas; it allows them to cultivate as they like, that is, in most instances, not cultivate at all; and it enables them to take up large tracts of land, stick in a few plants here and there for the name of the thing, and thus hold jungle, in the hopes of some day selling it at a profit, and causing in the meantime a loss to the Sircar by keeping *bonâ fide* planters from entering on the cultivation. It is also so far for the benefit of the poorer ryot as, save the expense of planting, he pays nothing to the State until his trees bear. But … this is not cultivation, and as a dose of medicine is given for its good to a child against its will, so I believe that a moderate assessment of say, Rupee one an acre for four years and Rupees two afterwards in perpetuity would make the ryot exert himself, and force him to exhibit, for they well know the profits of the cultivation, an energy of which he has now little idea.[55]

This evidence in support of the petition making a distinction between Europeans as bona fide planters and natives as ignorant of the proper method of cultivation needs critical scrutiny. It expressed the writer's view of 'traditional' vis-à-vis 'modern' agricultural methods. Western planters, generally dependent on monoculture, criticized intercropping. Until the middle of the twentieth century, large landowners throughout northern Europe extended monoculture leading to the emergence of distinct grain regions, vine regions and cattle regions. For example, Languedoc in southern France became identified with a vast monoculture of wine grapes. After the 1860s, the German sugar industry was dependent on the commercial monoculture of sugar beet, replacing cane sugar, in Magdeburg and the lower Rhineland.[56] The use of technically advanced implements and fertilizers increased the productivity temporarily but soon caused havoc as a result of soil erosion and other causes. A classic example is the Irish Potato Famine, caused by a fungus that devastated the highly productive potato monoculture industry, resulting in the death of nearly 1.5 million people.[57]

Intercropping, on the other hand, often reduced the incidence of insects and disease, sometimes raised soil fertility and provided shade, and at all times spread risk. Throughout Central America intercropping of corn, beans and squash was traditionally common.[58] Although some medium-sized planters in central Java, and some large planters in Sumatra, also intercropped coffee, more than 96 per cent of the coffee in Java was grown as a monoculture. The outbreak of rust disease in the late nineteenth century nearly wiped out coffee from the economic geography of the island. Recent researches have claimed that intercropping has an advantage over monoculture because, among other things, the practice makes it difficult for herbivores to find their hosts, helps more efficient use of nitrogen and reduces evaporation.[59]

That Indians owned so much of the coffee-land is an indication that the entry of Europeans into coffee production did not really introduce any major break with the past; when they joined in, the Indians were quick to follow the trend and enlarge their stake in the industry.[61] In Mysore – apart from the small area of Bangalore, where Europeans grew all of the coffee – it was Indians who dominated

Table 4.2 Land under coffee cultivation in Mysore in the early 1860s (in acres)[60]

District	European owned	Indian owned	Total
Bangalore	15	–	15
Kolar	45	59	104
Mysore	764	1,082	1,846
Hassan	21,017	24,708	45,725
Shimoga	142	2,034	2,176
Kadur	4,028	12,647	16,675
Total	26,011	40,530	66,541

Smallholdings versus European plantations 65

the coffee scene. R. H. Elliot observed this on his way from the port of Mangalore to the coffee-growing district of Manjarabad. Almost all farmer families grew some coffee. Once a year they carried the coffee on pack-bullock down the hills to the market in the plain, and they took salt and other items back.[62] This trend continued at least until the end of the nineteenth century, which is evident from the data on plantation holdings in Mysore that James Daniel Moore provided for the period 1862–96.[63] An analysis of the data shows that during this period the number of holdings under European planters increased from 153 (25,444 acres) to 865 (61,955 acres) and the number of those under Indian planters rose from 12,285 (38,247 acres) to 28,116 (102,779 acres). The average size of European holdings decreased considerably, from 165 to 71.6 acres, whereas that of Indian holdings increased slightly, from 3.1 to 3.7 acres. Total acreage increased from 63,623 to 163,734 acres, so the Indians expanded their share from 60.3 to 62.3 per cent, matched by a decrease in the European share from 39.7 to 37.7 per cent. As far as ownership of coffee-growing land is concerned, the Indian share increased by 167 per cent and the European share by 145 per cent.

The information is, however, incomplete because Moore tells us that Indians were buying up tracts of land for coffee but his information does not allow a further breakdown with regard to the actual size of individual holdings. In the context of Sri Lanka, it has been noted that coffee plantations varied in size from a small unit of 20–30 acres to large properties of 1,000 acres and more. Smallholdings were less than 10 acres in size.[64] Therefore, the average size of a coffee holding under Indians in Mysore, as shown above, was much smaller. Similarly, it is not possible to clearly demarcate the boundaries between traditional agriculture and the export-oriented mode of production. What is most important here, however, is the readiness with which the local agriculturalists responded to the expanding opportunities in the coffee economy.

It was generally believed – and the petition upholds this view – that European planters introduced improved methods of cultivation, that Indians were lazy and

Table 4.3 Share of European and Indian planters in the excise duty on coffee in Mysore, 1863–64[65]

District	Excise paid by European planters	Excise paid by Indian planters	Total
Mysore	25	49	74
Hassan	8,864	31,095	39,959
Shimoga	–	1,042	1,042
Kadur	5,892	62,448	68,340
Total	14,781	94,634	109,415
Total	14,781	94,634	109,415

Note: in Rupees (@ Re. ¼ per 92 kg).

unproductive, and that the hard-working Europeans were paying a higher tax. Thus, it was easy to jump to the conclusion, as Lonsdale did, that the Europeans contributed more to the treasury. But contrary to this, and to the claims of Mackenzie and others that the indigenous mode of production was inefficient and ineffective, it was precisely the smallholder sector that provided the lion's share of the duty on coffee in Mysore. Indigenous cultivators contributed as much as 86 per cent of the excise duty (Table 4.3).

It seems that 'neat rows', an obsession of the mathematical mind, were of little concern to the growers. Indian smallholders spaced coffee plants much more closely than estate owners, reducing output per tree, but also reducing labour needs for weeding, while raising output per hectare. This, together with their method of planting coffee together with other crops, proved to be more effective, making further investment in their coffee-growing land unnecessary.[66] In any case, the cause of the European planters' concern is obvious: *Indian smallholders were out-competing large European planters*. In all districts for which data are available, the duty paid by European planters was inconsequential in comparison with that paid by their Indian counterparts.

The European planters' petition thus clearly relates to the discourse on the dual economy, a concept stipulating two distinct economic spheres: one the plantation sector introduced by European capital, and the other the pre-capitalist agricultural sector in which land and labour did not contribute to the accumulation of capital. This concept has been criticized by scholars of South Asia. Ashok Bandarage's work on Sri Lanka and Dick Kooiman's and Barbara Evans's works on South India have emphasized the multiple socio-economic links that connected the plantation sector and smallholder production, the dual forces of the world economy.[67] In Mysore, the smallholders (growing coffee intercropped with subsistence crops) paid more than six times as much duty on coffee as European plantations (growing coffee as a monoculture). This fact puts into question the argument of efficiency resulting from economies of scale, underlines the overlapping spheres of traditional agriculture and modern plantations, and points to the resilience of indigenous capital in the wake of the entry of exogenous capital.[68]

Table 4.4 Loss of forests in some districts of the Western Ghats, Karnataka, 1920[70]

Name of the district	Total area	Extent of forest and scrub	
		Area	Percentage of total area
Chikmagalur	7,184	5,068	71
Hassan	6,818	2,205	32
Coorg	4,098	3,622	88
Shimoga	10,556	6,330	60
Uttar Kannada	10,251	9,134	89

Before we continue with the fate that befell the petition, let us briefly consider the effects of European plantations on the environment. Plantation coffee usually required the clearing of the forest without even planting shade trees, following the practice in Brazil and Sri Lanka.[69] Recent research in land use and environment suggests, however, that the traditional coffee-growing districts in Karnataka – Coorg and northern Karnataka in particular – retained a high proportion of forest shade until at least the beginning of the twentieth century (Table 4.4).

Many smallholders followed a religious practice of preserving patches of forest as 'sacred groves' or *devarakadu*, often as large as 20 hectares.[71] There were also different land tenures with varying rights to the trees growing on them.[72] Still, coffee was grown in some sacred groves. Encroachment on forest land – not only for cultivation but also for extraction of timber for shipbuilding and to make room for railways – began in the nineteenth century and continued unabated during the twentieth century. The result was the destruction of wildlife habitats and forest dwellers' livelihoods.

How Mr. Lonsdale's petition was received

The petition linked up to a discussion about the merits of excise duty versus land tax based on acreage. Both the Commissioner and Elliot stated that the latter had been introduced in Coorg in 1862 (the petitioners did not mention Coorg, but probably had that example in mind) and that this was done because most producers there were Europeans, who purchased land solely for the cultivation of coffee. They were not concerned about returns from any other produce. In Mysore, however, betel nut was extensively grown in the hilly areas where coffee was also cultivated. Betel nut was a luxury article and peasants producing it had to pay twice: an excise duty in addition to the land tax. Moreover, the prevailing rates for this commodity were excessively high compared to those for coffee and, if any reduction in duty had to be considered, that would have to do with betel nut and not coffee.[73]

Mackenzie and Porter both maintained that the planters in Mysore were at a disadvantage compared to those in the territories under the East India Company. Mackenzie admitted that substitution of land tax by acreage for excise duty would immediately result in a considerable loss in revenue for the Government. But he noted optimistically that 'with the present enlightened and liberal policy of the Government of India and with the overflowing treasury of Mysore, I do not imagine that such a loss, even were it permanent, would be thought much of, or allowed to stand in the way'. While Mackenzie pleaded for the acreage as a reward for European capital that improved the country, Porter was against the introduction of acreage as it implied the imposition of an equal tax on all planted lands, even though the yield of coffee-lands varied from estate to estate.[74]

The Commissioner and Mr. Elliot stated that the arguments of Mackenzie and Porter in favour of disadvantaged European planters in Mysore were one-sided. They pointed out that the planters' claim that they were paying a tax that was oppressive did not hold good because the duty of Re. ¼ on 373 kg (or Re.

1 per cwt.) replaced all other demands like house tax, plough tax and income tax and did not amount to more than one-twentieth of the gross produce, or 5 per cent of the lowest selling price of coffee, which was Rs.5 per 37.3 kg.[75] The Commissioner wrote that going by the returns of 1863–4, even lowering the duty by one *anna* (one-sixteenth of a rupee) per 37.3 kg would lead to a yearly loss of revenue worth Rs. 27,000, or almost double the total contribution of the excise duty paid by European planters annually. Although he might still have considered this remission in order to encourage European enterprise in Mysore, he noted – with regard to the planters' claim that the duty they paid amounted to Rs. 6 per acre – that the figures did not match. The total area held by Europeans (Table 4.2) should not be used to calculate how much they paid. Those figures did not tally with the figures for excise duty (Table 4.3) because a considerable portion of the 26,011 acres under European planters comprised plantations that were not yet in production.

Indigenous coffee-growers contributed nine-tenths of the coffee revenue in Kadur and three-fourths in Hassan. The fact that they did not protest against the excise duty demonstrated that this system suited them well because it was flexible: the duty was paid only on the quantity exported and thus could be adjusted according to the actual yield per season. Elliot noted that coffee planters freely admitted that their profit ranged from 40 to 50 per cent; but he had gathered from old coffee hands that a planter could expect a profit of up to 200 per cent in Coorg if he was careful about the plantation labour employed and the other expenditure made. As Mysore coffee was more prized than that of Coorg, and the production cost was lower, it was possible to realize astonishingly high returns from well-managed estates here. These considerations convinced Elliot and the Commissioner that the coffee-growers could bear the existing duty and that there was no need for revision.

Both the government and the planters, however, were guided by the idea of maximum turnover. The Commissioner disagreed with the content of the petition but not because he wanted to protect the indigenous coffee-growers. It simply suited him, for the time being, to leave the excise duty in Mysore undisturbed. But there was no unanimity in government circles: his superior, the Governor-General, wished to modify the system in order to provide some relief to the European planters.[76] An almost universal complaint among European officials and planters was that the excise duty encouraged the 'natives' to stick to the traditional mode of cultivation and go about coffee cultivation as it suited them.

Elliot and Porter agreed that taxing the produce did encourage the peasant to adhere to his 'slovenly style of cultivation'. They were against the introduction of an acreage assessment on coffee-lands but within a decade and a half (in 1879) the excise duty on coffee in Mysore was replaced by land assessment. 'Slovenly' or not, peasant coffee in Mysore survived when it was wiped out in Sri Lanka and Java in the aftermath of *Hemileia Vastatrix*, the rust disease that broke out in 1869. In these regions, coffee gave way to other cash crops, such as rubber and tea. In Mysore, however, 'native' coffee continued to thrive, as Benjamin Lewis Rice, who toured extensively through Mysore as the head of the State Archaeology Department, noted in 1892–3. In Hassan District, coffee was grown on 21,560 hectares – next in importance only to ragi (116,330) and rice (41,715). In Kadur district, there were 543 European planters who owned 13,736 hectares of coffee-land and 11,953 smallholdings owned by Indians, which covered 26,874 hectares and produced 12 million pounds of coffee.[77] In short, the high-altitude coffee-growing districts of Mysore were less affected by the rust disease; at the turn of the twentieth century, Indian producers continued to dominate the coffee economy of Mysore.[78]

Conclusion

This chapter began with a cautionary note that petitions, seeking redress of some grievance, may contain fiction. The historical source on which this chapter is based helps us to explore the role of coffee in the economy of the Kingdom of Mysore from the 1840s onwards. It reveals how coffee production initially brought prosperity to the growers and to the region. After the Europeans began growing coffee on a large scale, there was a 'coffee rush' among the Indian smallholders. The European plantation owners projected a claim that the government was charging them excessively on account of the tax on coffee. Additional reports submitted in the course of the investigation of the claim maintained that the practice of intercropping followed by Indian smallholders obstructed the proper embedding of coffee as an efficient plantation crop. Both the claims proved to be a fiction but the latter gave rise to a myth of European entrepreneurial leadership that still persists in the coffee sector in India.

Other chapters in this volume highlight that colonial states encouraged the production of treasury-friendly cash crops such as coffee, indigo, sugar and tobacco. European entrepreneurs portrayed large-scale plantations as the most treasury-friendly arrangements but this was not always true. In the case of Mysore coffee, Europeans did introduce large coffee plantations but local cultivators were quick to perceive the opportunities that smallholder coffee provided. Going by reports collected in the aftermath of the submission of Mr. Lonsdale's petition, smallholders turned out to be the most significant contributors to the process of embedding coffee in the local economy.

As in the case of faraway Cuba (Jonathan Curry-Machado's chapter in this volume), peasant smallholders in Mysore cash-cropped successfully in combination with other crops. This may have contributed to their ability to withstand the calamity of the rust disease that wiped out coffee elsewhere in Asia. In fact, the scientific, improved methods of plantation agriculture that the Europeans claimed to have introduced seem to have yielded the best results when practiced in combination with traditional agricultural practices. In this, the petition sheds light on the strong multiple links between village agriculture and the plantation sector.

The historical document used as the source material for this chapter is, however, limited in the sense that it informs the reader only about the entrepreneurial aspect of the industry. It demonstrates that there was strong competition between European and local producers and it registers the reactions of state authorities. At the same time, it informs the reader about the role of the state in the development of the industry. But the petition does not offer insights into other aspects that are vital for understanding the process of embedding agricultural commodities into pre-existing agrarian orders, for example, the recruitment and organization of labour in Mysore's coffee plantations.

Acknowledgements

An earlier, larger version of this chapter was published as 'Local History of a Global Commodity: Production of Coffee in Mysore and Coorg in the Nineteenth Century', *Indian Historical Review*, 41:1 (2014), 67-86.

My colleagues of the 'Plants, People and Work' programme and Jon Curry-Machado of the 'Commodities of Empire' programme commented on earlier versions of this chapter. Observations and questions of William Gervase Clarence-Smith helped to clarify some of the issues. The points raised by the peer reviewer of Ashgate were very pertinent. I would like to thank everyone for their comments and suggestions.

Notes

1. Lex Heerma van Voss ed., Petition in Social History, *International Review of Social History*, 46 (2001), Supplement 9, introduction, 1–10.
2. (Stanford University Press, 1987).
3. Cf. Peter Arnade and Walter Prevenier, *Honor, Vengeance and Social Trouble: Pardon Letters in Burgundian Low Countries* (Ithaca: Cornell University Press, 2015).
4. David Zarett, *Origins of Democratic Culture: Printing, Petitions and the Public Sphere in Early Modern England*, (Princeton: Princeton University Press, 2000).
5. S. I. A. Zaidi, 'Introduction', in Majid Siddiqi ed. *British Historical Context and Petitioning in Colonial India*: (New Delhi: Jamia Millia Islamia and Akkar Books, 2005), 9.
6. Chris. A. Bayly, *Empire and Information: Intelligence Gathering and Social Communication in India, 1780–1870*, (Cambridge: Cambridge University Press, 1996), 73–78; Laura Bear, *Lines of the nation: Indian railway workers, bureaucracy, and the intimate historical self* (New York: Columbia University Press, 2007), 114–116.
7. Bhavani Raman, *Document Raj: Writing and Scribes in Early Colonial South India* (Chicago: Chicago University press, 2012), 54.
8. http://www.britannia.com/history/docs/petition.html, accessed on 15.10.2015.
9. Majid Siddiqi, 'The British Historical Context and Petitioning in Colonial India', in Majid Siddiqi ed. *British Historical Context*, 17–41.
10. Mysore was a native kingdom in South India conquered by the British in 1799, following which much of the territory was divided between the British (Madras Presidency) and the Nizam of Hyderabad. The remaining parts were formed into the Princely State of Mysore. A minor prince of the ruling Wodeyar Dynasty was put on the throne under the supervision of an Indian minister while the foreign policy was controlled by the British. Between 1831 and 1880 the British ruled Mysore directly; they exercised their authority through a Commissioner. In 1881 the royal dynasty was put back on the throne and a British Resident appointed at the court, a system that continued until 1947, when India became independent. All coffee-growing districts mentioned in this paper, including Mysore and Coorg, lie in the southern part of the modern state of Karnataka (see Figure 4.2).

Smallholdings versus European plantations 71

11 National Archives of India, Foreign Department: Revenue – A. Fort William, 'Complaint of Mr. Lonsdale against the excise duty on coffee': File no. 212, Proceedings May, no. 32: From the Hon'ble W. Muir, c.s. Secretary to Government of India, Foreign Department, with the Governor-General, to the Commissioner, Mysore, 18 May, 1865. Appended to this file are no. 5271–211, no. 30: From the Commissioner for the Government of the Territories of His Highness the Raja of Mysore to the Secretary to the Government of India, dated Bangalore 12th April, 1865 and no. 31: 'From W. Lonsdale. Esq. Secretary to the Mysore Planters' Association, to the Secretary to Commissioner of Mysore, dated Manjarabad, the [...]December 1864' (15 pages in all); henceforth 'Complaint of Mr. Lonsdale'.
12 'Complaint of Mr. Lonsdale', 4.
13 Units of measurement used in this essay are partly based on the Weights and Measures Act of 1824 and used across the British Empire since 1825. Cwt is the abbreviation of one-hundredweight and is equal to eight stone or 50.8 kg. 1 acre = 0.4046 m². See http://www.metric-conversions.org/area/acres-to-hectares.htm, accessed on 13 February, 2015.
14 Re. = Rupee; Rs. = Rupees.
15 According to petitioners the tax they paid was three times higher than that paid in neighbouring Coorg and six times as high as the tax paid on coffee on the Shevaroy Hills in the Madras Presidency (see Figure 4.2).
16 Not to be confused with Sir H. M. Elliot of *The History of India as it is Told by its Own Historians: The Muhammadan period* (London: Trubner Company, 1867–77).
17 See the introduction to this volume for more on the embedding of cash crops.
18 Personal interview V. G. Siddharth, owner of Amalgamated Bean and Coffee Company and its daughter concern Café Coffee Day, the largest café chain in the country, December 2, 2011. The working class members of the Indian Coffee House Cooperatives, the oldest coffee café chain in the world, cherish the same notion. Peter John, a worker in the Bangalore outlet, would repeatedly point to the framed photograph of Ivor Bull, the English planter who took a pioneering role in forming the consortium – Consolidated Coffee Company – of all British owned plantations in the 1920s, and in setting up the Coffee Cess Committee in 1936 and say, 'The British, and especially He is our God'. See also the blog redscarab of Mallik, Anurag and Priya Ganapathy, 'Berry to brew: the story of coffee' dated 29 September 2014.
19 'Commodity Atlas: Coffee', at http://unctad.org/en/docs/ditccom20041ch5_en.pdf, accessed on 12. 2. 2015. See A. E. Haarer, *Modern Coffee Production* (London: Leonard Hill, 1962), 21–30, for other lesser known varieties of coffee grown especially in different African countries; also R. H. Chenney, *Coffee: A Monograph of the Economic Species of the Genus Coffea L.* (New York: New York University Press, 1925); also Steven Topik, 'The World Coffee Market in the Eighteenth and Nineteenth Centuries, from Colonial to National Regimes', London School of Economics Working Paper no 04/04, 2004.
20 Brad Weiss, *Sacred Trees, Bitter Harvests: Globalizing Coffee in Northwest Tanzania* (Portsmouth, NH: Heinemann, 2003).
21 See e.g. the essays in Michel Tuchscherer (ed.), *Le commerce du café avant l'ère des plantations colonials: espaces, réseaux, societies (XVè–XIXe siècle)* (Cairo: Institut français d'archéologie orientale, 2001).
22 Bhaswati Bhattacharya, *Much Ado over Coffee: A Social History of the Indian Coffee House, 1940–2010*, (New Delhi: Social Science Press, 2016), introduction.
23 The dargah or shrine dedicated to Baba Budan, the oldest Sufi shrine in Karnataka and a shared heritage of the Hindus and Muslims is on the hills since named after him. For more on this, see Yoginder Sikand, 'Shared Hindu-Muslim Shrines in Karnataka: Challenges to Liminality', in: Imtiaz Ahmad and Helmut Reifeld (eds.), *Lived Islam and South Asia: Adaptation, Accommodation and Conflict* (New Delhi: Social Science Press, 2004), 169–75.

24 Jean de la Roque, *A Voyage to Arabia the Happy* (London: G. Strahan.1926).
25 See Ashin Das Gupta, *Malabar in Asian Trade*, (Cambridge: Cambridge University Press, 1967), 106.
26 R.S. Hattox, *Coffee and Coffeehouses*, (Seattle: University of Washington Press, 1986), 17–24.
27 This was not only the case for coffee; for general reasons behind the large-scale migration of plants and plantation system across the globe, see Willem van Schendel's chapter on indigo in Bengal in this volume.
28 William Ukers, *All about Coffee*, (New York: Coffee and Tea Trade Journal, 1922), 36.
29 See e.g. the fictional account in David Liss, *The Coffee Trader* (New York: Ballantine Books, 2003). William Gervase Clarence-Smith has argued that it was from southwest India that coffee spread to different Asian countries, see his 'The Spread of Coffee Cultivation in Asia, from the Seventeenth to the Early Nineteenth Century', in: Tuchscherer (ed.) *Le commerce du café*, 371–81.
30 G.J. Knaap, 'Coffee for Cash: the Dutch East India Company and the Cultivation of Coffee in Java, Ambon and Ceylon, 1700–1730', in: J. van Goor (ed.), *Trading Companies in Asia, 1600–1830* (Utrecht: HES, 1986), 33–50.
31 William J. O'Malley, 'Plantations 1830–1840: An Overview', in: Anne Booth et al. (eds.), *Indonesian Economic History in the Dutch Colonial Era* (Yale: Centre for International Area Studies, 1990), 136–70; W.G. Clarence-Smith, 'The Impact of Forced Coffee Cultivation on Java, 1805–1917', *Indonesia Circle* 64, (1994), 241–64; Jan Breman, *Koloniaal profijt van onvrije arbeid: Het Preanger stelsel van gedwongen koffieteelt op Java* (Amsterdam: Amsterdam University Press, 2010).
32 Bhattacharya, 'Local History'.
33 B.B. Keable, *Coffee: From Grower to Consumer*. Pitman's Common Commodities and Industries (London: Isaac Pitman & Sons, 1900), 52.
34 E. C. P. Hull, *Coffee Production in Southern India and Ceylon* (London: E.F. Spon, 1877), 16–17. A planter with experience in Sri Lanka and South India, Hull suggested that a temperature from 60° to 80° F. in the shade and 100–150 inches of rainfall distributed over twelve months with no month entirely without rainfall suited the coffee plant best; Hull, *Coffee*, x.
35 Hull, *Coffee*, 39, 44–5.
36 'Complaint of Mr. Lonsdale'.
37 M. R. Fernando, 'Coffee Cultivation in Java: 1830–1917', in: W.G. Clarence-Smith and Steven Topik (eds.), *The Global Coffee Economy in Africa, Asia, and Latin America, 1500–1989* (Cambridge, MA: Cambridge University Press, 2003), 157–72.
38 As noted above, the Dutch who exported pepper from Malabar in Southwestern India and sent samples of coffee plants to Java where it became a plantation crop did not mention coffee being produced in India.
39 James Daniel Moore, Jr. 'Plantation Development and Labour Response in Nineteenth-Century Mysore' (Unpublished Ph.D. thesis, University of Pennsylvania 1983), 65.
40 Francis Buchanan, *A Journey from Madras through the Countries of Mysore, Canara and Malabar* (Madras: Higginbotham & Co.), vol. 2, 186.
41 Moore, 'Plantation Development', 68.
42 This amount was Rs. 2,000 less than the annual average of the preceding ten years; Hilton Brown, *Parry's of Madras: A Story of British Enterprise in India* (Madras: Parry's & Co., 1954), 63–64. Thomas Parry died in 1824 but the name of the concern was not changed; in 1833 the contract with Parry's was renewed for five years by the British Mysore Commission for an annual rent of Rs. 7,422.
43 Moore, 'Plantation Development', 70–2, 82.
44 Mysore would be restored to the ruling dynasty in 1881.
45 Lewis B. Rice, *Mysore: A Gazetteer Compiled for Government* (Westminster: Archibald Constable &Co. 1987), vol. 2, 389.

46 H.F. C. Cleghorn, *The Forests and Gardens of South India*, (London: Allen & Co., 1861), 178.
47 Cleghorn, *Forests*, 266. Cleghorn cited W.R. Morgan, in charge of the Mudumalai forests in Tamil Nadu, who observed that an increase in coffee cultivation and the demand for labour (in the plantations) in the Nilgiri district had resulted in a scarcity of labour and an increase in the wages.
48 C.R. Markham noted that in total about 60,000 acres of forest were felled for coffee, tea and chinchona plantations in the Western Ghats. Several thousand acres had been cleared in Manjarabad, Nagar and Coorg, and 16,000 acres had been cleared in Wayanad, more than 9,000 in the Nilgiris, and 600 and 1200 in the Annamalais and in Cochin, respectively; see his 'On the Effects of the Destruction of Forests in the Western Ghauts of India on the Water-Supply', *Journal of the Royal Geographical Society of London* (1866), 180–95.
49 Cleghorn, *Forests*, 16–17, 30–1.
50 John Short, *A Handbook of Coffee Planting in Southern India* (Madras, 1864), 161. The unit of measurement used in the source is 'maund', which equalled 37.3 kg.
51 The returns in the year 1861 were Rs. 68,000 (Rs. 9,000 less than the preceding year) Short, *Handbook*, 160–1.
52 'Complaint of Mr. Lonsdale'.
53 'Complaint of Mr. Lonsdale;' Moore, 'Plantation Development;' 90–6. Jonathan Machado-Curry's chapter in this volume demonstrates how peasants in Cuba also avoided putting all their eggs in one basket. They, too, cultivated multiple crops, so that failure of one crop could be compensated somewhat by the success of another. There was also forest produce to consider. Pepper-vines and other plants, such as cardamom, grew in the wild in the same areas in Mysore in which coffee could be cultivated.
54 Cf. Low technological development did not stand in the way of the phenomenal growth of the coffee industry in Brazil in the nineteenth century. Leslie Bethell, *Brazil: Empire and Republic, 1822–1930* (Cambridge: Cambridge University Press, 1993).
55 'Complaint of Mr. Lonsdale',10; emphasis in original. For a similar statement about the neglected state of indigenous coffee plantations, see Ameer Ali. 'Peasant Coffee in Ceylon During the Nineteenth Century', *The Ceylon Journal of Historical and Social Studies*, 2:1 (1972), 50–9.
56 Tamara L. Whited, Jens I. Engels, Richard C. Hoffmann, Hilde Ibsen and Wybren Verstegen, *Northern Europe: an Environmental History*, (Santa Barbara, CA: ABC Clio, 2005), 106.
57 Matthias U. Igbozurike, 'Against Monoculture', *The Professional Geographer*, 23.2 (1971), 113–17; John P. Holdren and P. R. Ehrlich, 'Human Population and the Global Environment', *Amerian Scientist*, 62.3 (1974) 282–92.
58 Preston Sullivan, 'Intercropping Principles and Production Practices', Appropriate Technology Transfer for Rural Areas, (internet document), http://www.iatp.org/files/Intercropping_Principles_and_Production_Practi.htm, accessed on 15.10.2015.
59 John H. Vandermeer, *The Ecology of Intercropping*, (Cambridge NY: Cambridge University Press, 1992), x.
60 'Complaint of Mr. Lonsdale', 3; 1 acre is equivalent to 0 ha 4046.9m².
61 See Michael Roberts, *Class Conflict and Elite Formation: The Rise of a Katava Elite in Sri Lanka 1500–1931* (Cambridge: Cambridge University Press, 1982) and Dick Kooiman, 'Plantations in Southern Asia: Indigenous Plants and Foreign Implantations', *South Asia: Journal of South Asian Studies*, 15.1 (1992), 53–79, for similar information regarding coffee planting in Sri Lanka and Travancore, respectively.
62 R. H. Elliot, *Written on their Foreheads* (London: Low, Marston, Searle and Rivington, 1879), vol. 2, 46.

63 Moore, 'Plantation Development' (Table 4: 183).
64 Asoka Bandarage, *Colonialism in Sri Lanka: The Political Economy of the Kandyan Highlands, 1833–1886* (Berlin: Mouton, 1983), 66.
65 'Complaint of Mr. Lonsdale', 2.
66 Ibid. Bandarage has argued on the other hand that as coffee was subsidiary to rice cultivation, it was difficult to induce peasants in Sri Lanka to produce a larger quantity of coffee on a regular basis, Bandarage, *Colonialism in Sri Lanka*, 70–72. See also I.H. Venden Driesen, *The Long Walk: Indian Plantation Labour in Sri Lanka in the Nineteenth Century* (New Delhi: Prestige Books, 1997), 14.
67 Kooiman, 'Plantations in Southern Asia' and Barbara Evans, 'From Agricultural Bondage to Plantation Contract: A Continuity of Experience in Southern India, 1860–1947', *South Asia: Journal of South Asian Studies*, 13:2 (1990), 45–69.
68 Bhattacharya, 'Local History'.
69 For the effect of clear felling on ecology and the communities dependent on the forest for their livelihood see Madhav Gadgil and Ramachandra Guha, *This fissured land: an ecological history of India*. (Delhi: Oxford, 1992); Velayutham Saravanan, 'Colonial Commercial Forest Policy and the Tribal Private Forests in Madras Presidency: 1792–1881', *Indian Economic and Social History Review*, Vol. 40.4 (2003), pp. 403–47; for the coffee on the environment in the state of Tamil Nadu in India see Velayutham Saravanan, 'Colonialism and coffee plantations: Decline of environment and Tribals in Madras Presidency during the nineteenth century', *IESHR*, 41.4 (2004), 465–88.
70 C. Nanjundaiah, 'Forests, Environment and Local Community: A Case Study of Coorg (Kodagu) District' (Unpublished Ph. D. thesis submitted to the University of Mysore, 2004), 96.
71 Nanjundaiah, 'Forests'. Madhav Gadgil and V.D. Vartak, 'Sacred Groves of Western Ghats', *Economic Botany*, 30, (1976), 152–60; also M.A. Kalam, 'Sacred Groves in Kodagu District of Karnataka (South India): A Socio-historical Study', Pondi Paper in Social Sciences, no. 21. Institut Français de Pondichéry (1996); S. Menon and K.S. Bawa, 'Deforestation in the Tropics: Reconciling Disparities in Estimates for India', *Peer Reviewed Publications*, no. 12 (1998); http://scholarworks.gvsu.edu/biopeerspub/12. Haarer observed some coffee being grown in Mysore under jungle shade where larger trees were left standing when the area was cleared for planting, Haarer, *Modern Coffee Production*, 394.
72 For example, in Coorg there were seven types of land tenures (granted in return for different kinds of services rendered), five types of lease tenures and seventeen types of forest land tenures. Owners of redeemed land had rights to the trees on the land they had purchased but those owning unredeemed land did not. A.S. Shrinidhi and S. Lele, 'Forest Tenure Regimes in the Karnataka Western Ghat: A Compendium'; Institute for Social and Economic Change, Bangalore, Working Paper 90 (2001); C. Najundaiah, 'Forests, Environment'.
73 'Complaint of Mr. Lonsdale', 2, 5, 12.
74 'Complaint of Mr. Lonsdale', 9–12.
75 Ibid., 1.
76 Ibid., 1.
77 Rice, *Mysore Gazetteer*, vol. 2, 375, see also 423 About 979 acres were under coffee in Shimoga and out of 250 plantations, six were owned by Europeans.
78 Rice, *Mysore Gazetteer*, vol. 2, 328–30, 339. See also Haarer, *Modern Coffee Production*, 387, and Keable, *Coffee from Grower to Consumer*, 53.

References

Ali, Ameer. 'Peasant Coffee in Ceylon During the Nineteenth Century', *The Ceylon Journal of Historical and Social Studies*, 2:1 (1972), 50–9.

Arnade, Peter and Walter Prevenier, *Honor, Vengeance and Social Trouble: Pardon Letters in Burgundian Low Countries* (Ithaca, NY: Cornell University Press, 2015).

Bandarage, Asoka. *Colonialism in Sri Lanka: The Political Economy of the Kandyan Highlands, 1833–1886* (Berlin: Mouton, 1983).

Bayly, Chris A. *Empire and Information: Intelligence Gathering and Social Communication in India, 1780–1870*, (Cambridge: Cambridge University Press, 1996).

Bear, Laura. *Lines of the Nation: Indian Railway Workers, Bureaucracy, and the Intimate Historical Self* (New York: Columbia University Press, 2007).

Bethell, Leslie. *Brazil: Empire and Republic, 1822–1930* (Cambridge: Cambridge University Press, 1993).

Bhattacharya, Bhaswati. 'Local History of a Global Commodity: Production of Coffee in Mysore and Coorg in the Nineteenth Century', *Indian Historical Review*, 41:1 (2014), 67–86.

Bhattacharya, Bhaswati. *Much Ado over Coffee: A Social History of the Indian Coffee House, 1940–2010* (New Delhi: Social Science Press, 2016).

Breman, Jan. *Koloniaal profijt van onvrije arbeid: Het Preanger Stelsel van gedwongen koffieteelt op Java* (Amsterdam: Amsterdam University Press, 2010).

Brown, Hilton. *Parry's of Madras: A Story of British Enterprise in India* (Madras: Parry's & Co., 1954).

Buchanan, Francis. *A Journey from Madras through the Countries of Mysore, Canara and Malabar* (Madras: Higginbotham & Co).

Chenney, R. H. *Coffee: A Monograph of the Economic Species of the Genus Coffea L.* (New York: New York University Press, 1925).

Clarence-Smith, William Gervase. 'The Spread of Coffee Cultivation in Asia, from the Seventeenth to the Early Nineteenth Century', in: M. Tuchscherer (ed.) *Le commerce du café*, 371–81.

Clarence-Smith, William Gervase, 'The Impact of Forced Coffee Cultivation on Java, 1805–1917', *Indonesia Circle*, 64 (1994), 241–64.

Clarence-Smith, William Gervase and Steven Topik (eds.). *The Global Coffee Economy in Africa, Asia, and Latin America, 1500–1989* (Cambridge: Cambridge University Press, 2003).

Cleghorn, H. F. C. *The Forests and Gardens of South India*, (London: Allen & Co., 1861).

Das Gupta, Ashin. *Malabar in Asian Trade*, (Cambridge: Cambridge University Press, 1967).

Elliot, H.M. *The History of India as it is Told by its Own Historians: The Muhammadan period* (London: Trubner Company, 1867–77).

Elliot, R. H. *Written on their Foreheads* (London: Low, Marston, Searle and Rivington, 1879).

Evans, Barbara. 'From Agricultural Bondage to Plantation Contract: A Continuity of Experience in Southern India, 1860–1947', *South Asia: Journal of South Asian Studies*, 13:2 (1990), 45–69.

Fernando, M. R. 'Coffee Cultivation in Java: 1830–1917', in: W. G. Clarence-Smith and S. Topik (eds.). *The Global Coffee Economy in Africa, Asia, and Latin America, 1500–1989* (Cambridge: Cambridge University Press, 2003), 157–72.

Gadgil, Madhav and Ramachandra Guha, *This fissured land: an ecological history of India*. (Delhi: Oxford University Press, 1992).

Gadgil, Madhav, and V.D. Vartak. 'Sacred Groves of Western Ghats', *Economic Botany*, 30 (1976), 152–60.

Haarer, A. E. *Modern Coffee Production* (London: Leonard Hill, 1962).

Hattox, R.S. *Coffee and Coffeehouses*, (Seattle. WA: University of Washington Press, 1986).

Holdren John P. and P. R. Ehrlich, 'Human Population and the Global Environment', *Amerian Scientist*, 62:3 (1974) 282–92.

Hull, E. C. P. *Coffee Production in Southern India and Ceylon* (London: E.F. Spon, 1877).

Igbozurike, Matthias U. 'Against Monoculture', *The Professional Geographer*, 23:2 (1971), 113–17.

Kalam, M.A. 'Sacred Groves in Kodagu District of Karnataka (South India): A Socio-historical Study', Pondi Paper in Social Sciences, no. 21. (Pondichery: Institut Français de Pondichéry, 1996).

Keable, B.B. *Coffee: From Grower to Consumer.* Pitman's Common Commodities and Industries (London: Isaac Pitman & Sons, 1900).

Knaap, G.J. 'Coffee for Cash: the Dutch East India Company and the Cultivation of Coffee in Java, Ambon and Ceylon, 1700–1730', in: J. van Goor (ed.), *Trading Companies in Asia, 1600–1830* (Utrecht: HES, 1986), 33–50.

Kooiman, Dick. 'Plantations in Southern Asia: Indigenous Plants and Foreign Implantations', *South Asia: Journal of South Asian Studies*, 15:1 (1992), 53–79.

Liss, David. *The Coffee Trader* (New York: Ballantine Books, 2003).

Mallik, Anurag and Priya Ganapathy, 'Berry to brew: the story of coffee' dated 29 September 2014 https://redscarabtravelandmedia.wordpress.com/tag/indian-coffee-house/ accessed on 12 February 2015.

Markham, C.R. 'On the Effects of the Destruction of Forests in the Western Ghauts of India on the Water-Supply', *Journal of the Royal Geographical Society of London* (1866), 180–95.

Menon S. and K.S. Bawa, 'Deforestation in the Tropics: Reconciling Disparities in Estimates for India', *Peer Reviewed Publications*, no. 12 (1998); http://scholarworks.gvsu.edu/biopeerspub/12.

Moore Jr., James Daniel. *'Plantation Development and Labour Response in Nineteenth-Century Mysore'* (Unpublished Ph.D. thesis, University of Pennsylvania 1983).

Nanjundaiah, C. *'Forests, Environment and Local Community: A Case Study of Coorg (Kodagu) District'* (Unpublished Ph. D. thesis, University of Mysore, 2004).

O'Malley, William J. 'Plantations 1830–1840: An Overview', in: Anne Booth, W.J. O'Malley and Anna Weideman (eds.), *Indonesian Economic History in the Dutch Colonial Era* (New Haven, CT: Yale Centre for International Area Studies, 1990), 136–70.

Raman, Bhavani. *Document Raj: Writing and Scribes in Early Colonial South India* (Chicago, IL: Chicago University Press, 2012).

Rice, B. Lewis. *Mysore: A Gazetteer Compiled for Government* (London: Archibald Constable & Co. 1987), 2 vols.

Roberts, Michael. *Class Conflict and Elite Formation: The Rise of a Katava Elite in Sri Lanka 1500–1931* (Cambridge: Cambridge University Press, 1982).

Roque, Jean de la, *A Voyage to Arabia the Happy* (London: G. Strahan.1926).

Saravanan, Velayutham. 'Colonialism and Coffee Plantations: Decline of Environment and Tribals in Madras Presidency during the Nineteenth Century', *IESHR*, 41:4 (2004), 465–88.

Saravanan, Velayutham, 'Colonial Commercial Forest Policy and the Tribal Private Forests in Madras Presidency: 1792–1881', *Indian Economic and Social History Review*, 40:4 (2003), 403–47.

Shrinidhi, A. S. and S. Lele, 'Forest Tenure Regimes in the Karnataka Western Ghat: A Compendium'; Working Paper 90 (Bangalore: Institute for Social and Economic Change, 2001).

Siddiqi, Majid. 'The British Historical Context and Petitioning in Colonial India', in Majid Siddiqi, ed. *British Historical Context and Petitioning in Colonial India*: (New Delhi: Jamia Millia Islamia and Akkar Books, 2005).

Sikand, Yoginder. 'Shared Hindu-Muslim Shrines in Karnataka: Challenges to Liminality', in: Imtiaz Ahmad and Helmut Reifeld (eds.), *Lived Islam and South Asia: Adaptation, Accommodation and Conflict* (New Delhi: Social Science Press, 2004), 169–75.

Short, John. *A Handbook of Coffee Planting in Southern India* (Madras, 1864).

Sullivan, Preston. 'Principles and Production Practices', Appropriate Technology Transfer for Rural Areas, (internet document, November 1998), http://www.iatp.org/files/Intercropping_Principles_and_Production_Practi.htm, accessed on October 15, 2015.

Topik, Steven. 'The World Coffee Market in the Eighteenth and Nineteenth Centuries, from Colonial to National Regimes', London School of Economics Working Paper no 04/04 (2004). http://eprints.lse.ac.uk/22489/1/wp04.pdf accessed on February 13, 2014.

Tuchscherer, Michel (ed.) *Le commerce du café avant l'ère des plantations coloniales: espaces, réseaux, societies (XVe–XIXe siècle)* (Cairo: Institut français d'archéologie orientale, 2001).

Ukers, William. *All About Coffee* (New York: Coffee and Tea Trade Journal, 1922).

van Voss, Lex Heerma, ed., 'Petition in Social History', International Review of Social History, 46 (2001), Supplement 9.

Vandermeer, John H. *The Ecology of Intercropping*, (Cambridge: Cambridge University Press, 1992).

Venden Driesen, I.H. *The Long Walk: Indian Plantation Labour in Sri Lanka in the Nineteenth Century* (New Delhi: Prestige Books, 1997).

Weiss, Brad. *Sacred Trees, Bitter Harvests: Globalizing Coffee in Northwest Tanzania* (Portsmouth, NH: Heinemann, 2003).

Whited, Tamara L., Jens I. Engels, Richard C. Hoffmann, Hilde Ibsen and Wybren Verstegen, *Northern Europe: an Environmental History,* (Santa Barbara, CA: ABC Clio, 2005).

Zaidi, S. I. A. 'Introduction', in Majid Siddiqi ed. *British Historical Context and Petitioning in Colonial India*: (New Delhi: Jamia Millia Islamia and Akkar Books, 2005).

Zarett, David. *Origins of Democratic Culture: Printing, Petitions and the Public Sphere in Early Modern England,* (Princeton, NJ: Princeton University Press, 2000).

Zemon Davis, Natalie. *Fiction in the Archives: Pardon Tales and Their Tellers in Sixteenth Century France* (Stanford, CA: Stanford University Press, 1987).

5 'Keeping land and labour under control?'
Reporting on tobacco-shed burnings in Besoeki (Java)

Ratna Saptari

On 9 December 1902, the resident of Besoeki (East Java), Mr. Van den Bergh van Heinenoord, submitted a 16-page report to the Governor-General of the Netherlands Indies.[1] This was a *Mailrapport*, an important type of administrative account meant to update the Governor-General in Batavia (Jakarta) on particular events or incidences occurring in the region under the jurisdiction of a resident.[2] Such detailed reports were different from the *Memorie van Overgave,* another source much used by historians, which is an end-of-term report and gives a general overview of the social, economic and political situation in the residency.

Van Heinenoord's report focused on the occurrence of tobacco-shed burnings in his residency. Since the late nineteenth century, Besoeki had become an important tobacco-producing area, second only to East Coast Sumatra. Tobacco-shed burnings were incidents that caused much consternation to the colonial government and the Dutch planters.[3]

In his *Mailrapport*, Van Heinenoord responded to government concern regarding the frequent outbreak of fires in sheds where harvested tobacco leaves were kept (Figure 5.1).[4] He gave a detailed account of the different incidents and analysed what he saw as the underlying motivations. His report can be divided into four parts: an introduction; the Bondowoso and Djember tobacco-producing regions (including the companies most hit by these fires), the different cases of arson, and recommendations to improve the situation. In his general comments at the beginning and the end of his report, he stated that despite public and secret investigations by European and 'native' officials, and even despite the help of local 'spies', the motivations behind the fires were seldom evident. Although Van Heinenoord himself was quick to state that one of the factors taken into consideration 'is the vengeful and hot-tempered nature of the Madurese'[5] as well as 'existing feelings of enmity among the natives – between the Madurese and the Javanese',[6] he clearly acknowledged that the incidents were too varied in nature to reduce them simply to internal tension within the local population. According to him, the economic and political backgrounds of these incidents were also important factors that should be investigated further.

The report reveals his awareness of the highly diverse combination of factors that could be involved, for which no easy solutions could be found. Unlike

'Keeping land and labour under control?' 79

Figure 5.1 A tobacco-drying shed of the Soekowono company
Source: Besoeki, circa 1905[7]

some of his successors, he steered away from blaming the private estates or trading companies for providing inadequate payment to the farmers or workers. Ultimately, in the short term, pragmatic measures were the only solution to safeguard the sheds, especially increasing the security of the terrain around these sheds, or physically improving the construction of the sheds themselves. Those who succeeded Van Heinenoord as residents of Besoeki showed some variation in their assessments of these incidents in their end-of-term reports but they never failed to mention the factors that should be taken into account to avoid political and social instability.[8]

The first section of this chapter examines Van Heinenoord's report. To place his report within a historical perspective, the following section looks at the social and economic dynamics of tobacco production in the region, particularly regarding competing for access to land and labour between tobacco planters. In contrast to Sinha-Kerkhoff's chapter in this volume (Chapter 6), which focuses on value creation of tobacco through botanical research and scientific experiments in colonial Bihar, my study focuses on the issues surrounding tobacco production and market competition within the local agrarian system. The situation detailed in Bhaswati Bhattacharya's contribution to this volume (Chapter 4) shows a dichotomy between foreign and indigenous producers. Tobacco production in the Netherlands Indies was based on a more complex structure, involving a multitude of actors, who were sometimes competing and sometimes collaborating in order to gain the best advantage. Therefore, this social constellation was more similar to the complexities outlined in Willem van Schendel's chapter on indigo production in Bengal (Chapter 2).

Apart from Van Heinenoord's report, I will also examine other reports and essays that discuss issues surrounding the commoditization of tobacco. Since the production, processing and marketing of tobacco were conducted under politically and economically volatile situations, competition among planters was extremely intense. Agreements between companies were continuously updated and reformulated. For example, the 1914 Rotterdam Agreement was meant to safeguard each company's rights to the land they had rented and to the tobacco grown on their land, and the 1908 Tobacco Ordinance gave private estates the right to cultivate tobacco on their rented land.

Such updating was necessary because agreements and government ordinances were repeatedly being transgressed or ignored, reflecting the unpredictable nature of the tobacco economy with which all actors had to deal. This underlines what Willem van Schendel argues in the introduction to this volume, namely, that processes of embedding commodities were far from assured. The historical documents that underlie this chapter have as their entry point the problems revolving around tobacco production and marketing. They help us to comprehend the way in which officials of the Besoeki residency perceived and dealt with these issues. In the conclusion, we will return to Van Heinenoord's report to reflect on how it may be read on the basis of a broad knowledge of the economic and political background of tobacco as an agricultural commodity.

Reporting on tobacco-shed Burnings in Besoeki residency

Van Heinenoord's report concentrates on two sub-districts of Besoeki residency in East Java. These sub-districts, Bondowoso and Djember, were the most important tobacco-producing areas in the region and they were the worst hit by the shed burnings.[9] According to information on Bondowoso that Van Heinenoord obtained, either through actual surveys, or through rumours circulating in the locality, many factors were thought to contribute to these fires, for example, lack of working capital and low prices in Europe, which also meant that tobacco cultivators were paid low prices; no advances or payment to the peasants who had delivered their tobacco; a foreman (*mandor*) who took some tobacco from the shed to his own house and burned the shed down to create distraction; the possibility that traders in bamboo and *imperata* grass (*alang-alang*), who wanted to sell their products to re-build the sheds, were the culprits; or local farmers who wanted to get out of their twelve-year contracts so that they could plant their own tobacco, which would then be sold to traders offering higher prices.[10]

However, it was especially in the sub-district of Djember that most of the fires occurred and particularly in the 'Old Djember' plantation (LMOD[11]). Again the reasons for these burnings covered a broad range of issues. Mention was made of motives such as the invalidation of a village election result; a 'woman issue', in which a foreman of the plantation was involved; or cases of dismissals (in this case, of two foremen). At one point, in Rambipoedji in the south of Djember, there is a reference to an anonymous complaint against the dealings of a district head, which in the end could not be proven. In the case of the LMOD-owned sheds, the chief administrator of the company saw in these arson cases an attempt by another company to destroy the LMOD through the hands of an employee who at that moment worked for LMOD. But yet again, no direct proof could be found.

In attempting to provide an overview and to simplify the different motivations behind the incidents, Van Heinenoord provided tables in the appendix of his report.[12] The different incidents were classified under a number of headings, which are in themselves worth examining (i.e. 'bad intentions', 'carelessness', 'lightning', 'accident' and 'unclear' (Table 5.1).

Table 5.1 Frequency of tobacco-shed burnings in Bondowoso and Djember, 1898–1902

	Djember sub-district							*Supply shed*
	Drying and packing sheds							
	Bad intentions	Care-lessness	Light-ning	Acci-dent	Unclear	Total	Attempts	
1898	28	5	3	–	1	37	–	–
1899	38	4	1	1	–	44	–	2
1900	34	1	9	1	1	46	–	2
1901	24	5	6	–	–	35	4	10
1902	41	2	3	2	–	48	5	10

	Bondowoso sub-district							*Supply shed*
	Drying and packing sheds[1]							
	Bad intentions	Care-lessness	Light-ning	Acci-dent	Unclear	Total	Attempts	
1898	4	1	–	–	3	8	–	–
1899	9	4	–	–	1	14	1	–
1900	12	2	1	–	1	16	–	2
1901	12	4	–	–	–	16	–	1
1902	11	–	–	–	–	11	–	–

Note
1 In Besoeki, tobacco sheds were often clustered together and not located in a row along the plantation roads, as in Deli, or spread out across the land, as in the Principalities of Central Java. The processes of drying, fermenting and sorting were often done in different parts of the same shed, whereas the packing was often done in a separate shed. Therefore, if mention here is made of 'drying shed,', this refers also to the same sheds where fermentation and sorting is done.

In attempting to explain these incidents, the first two categories ('bad intentions by third parties' and 'carelessness of the estate personnel') were seen as quite significant for both areas. For Djember, the category of 'lightning' was quite prominent. Cases considered as 'accidents' were those in which presumably passers-by or children had caused the fire because these occurred in the middle of the day, which, Van Heinenoord stated, was 'a time that is usually never chosen by arsonists'. However, as we can see in Table 5.1, these cases were few and far between for both sub-districts. And in only a few cases the reason for the fires could not be established; these were noted down as 'unclear'. The predominant occurrence of shed burning fell under the category 'bad intentions by third parties' and in the case of Djember, it almost doubled in 1902 (41 incidents) compared to the preceding year (28 incidents).

This categorization is an interesting process in itself, and one wonders how these diverse incidents were placed in these seemingly well-demarcated categories. For instance, how would one distinguish 'carelessness of the estate personnel' from 'bad intentions by third parties'? In a few of the cases mentioned, the foreman was seen as the main culprit behind the fires and at times it was said that other (competing) companies instigated these fires. In Djember, it was a foreman who wanted to cover up his dishonest practices; in another case, it was a foreman who had been fired.[13] In the estate of the *Besoeki Tabak Maatschappij*, a foreman had sold a lot of tobacco from the shed to 'other parties' and then burned the shed, after which he went on the run. The estate of *Soekokerto-Adjoeng* lost three tobacco sheds because of arson and 'the rancour of the foreman' was mentioned as a possible reason, in addition to his conflict with 'the locals'. However, Van Heinenoord himself added that it was still dubious if these were the real causes of the fires since no proof could be given. In two other cases on the estate of Djelboek, 'the foreman had beaten up two young locals and the fires were retaliation against him'. In the cases where the foremen themselves were involved, these acts seemed to attempt to hide individual malpractices, and whether this came together with the involvement of third parties is often difficult to discern. It was indeed mentioned in one case in the Koning estate (the *Besoeki Tabak Maatschappij*) that coolies 'were paid to induce fire', which refers to a much broader and ever present hazard, which will be discussed below.

Even though it is possible to assume that personal vengeance could be behind these cases, the tobacco sheds became a symbol of the significance of a particular act of arson. An important question to ask is to what extent 'bad intentions' or 'carelessness' could be associated with discontent and resentment against the structural conditions shaping the tobacco economy. For the ordinary person tobacco cultivation and trading ultimately boiled down to the price paid for the tobacco when it was submitted to the sheds, or to the wages received for a certain amount of work. On the other hand, one would also assume that those involved in tobacco production would hardly gain any benefit if the payment for tobacco did not materialize because tobacco sheds filled with tobacco had been burned down. Van Heinenoord did mention a number of cases where

Figure 5.2 Producers, foremen and a supervisor posing in a tobacco field
Source: Soekowono company (Besoeki, circa 1910)[14]

the production relations of the tobacco estates were brought to his attention. In some cases, the main factor considered to underlie these arson cases was 'the limited capital, where initial advances of tobacco deliveries and building material for the barns could not be paid'. In other cases, it was because the local population had already repeatedly expressed their wish to get out of their 12 year contract so that they could plant 'free-man's tobacco' (*vrye tabak*). This would mean that peasants cultivating their own land could sell their tobacco to local merchants and get paid directly for their products – and they could also determine what kind of crop to plant. In the Soekowono plantation, a number of farmers complained that in 1902 only half the rent price of the land had been paid. Even though the farmers had said that they were satisfied with what they received, this situation may have caused discontent (Figure 5.2). Some farmers accused one plantation of breaking its promise because it had not paid them according to the initial agreement for the tobacco they delivered.

Van Heinenoord also added that it was difficult to conclude that arson was resorted to because of farmers' discontent. He based his argument on the fact that in the large plantation of Old Djember 15 barns were burned down (and half of them were filled with tobacco) and the damage totalled around 100,000 guilders. These incidents occurred, he argued, in a situation where the tobacco harvest was good and the tobacco had been paid for. In other areas, where the harvest was not so good and the farmers were not paid, there were relatively few fires. He argued that in general 'it seems seldom mentioned that these fires were because of conflict between the population and the company ... since the latter do not recruit that many workers and the payments of tobacco have so far been satisfactory for the farmers'. He concluded that the factors behind acts of arson were too diverse to find any easy solution. Therefore, the authorities could only prevent or anticipate possible future acts of arson by increasing the security measures on the grounds where these sheds were located – adding security guards, closing off the grounds by strong fencing, or using roof material that did not burn easily. He also added that from the side of the government:

> There is no other policy that can be followed than what we have done so far. This means that in general we have to keep a strong watch over the mixed population among which some bad elements are hiding ... It would be inadvisable, except in situations of (temporarily) extraordinary circumstances to place the burden of guarding the sheds to the local natives; this would create or incite even more animosity against the estate. [15]

It is interesting to note that reports by other (succeeding) residents show different conclusions on these issues. Some residents were more explicit in their reflections on the conduct of private entrepreneurs and the condition of the local farmers. For instance, Van Soelen, the resident of Besoeki, stated in his end-of-term report dated 3 June 1918 that 'a return to the old situation where free tobacco is cultivated and where all kinds of manipulations occur in the buying up of this product' could result in shed burning and stealing. In other words it would lead to 'disorganization and demoralization of the population'.[16] This remark refers to the intense competition occurring between private planters, which consequently meant that more regulation was needed in the kind of land arrangements that entrepreneurs made with local peasants. Another resident who succeeded Van Soelen in that same year, F.L. Broekveldt, did not mince his words when he stated that 'the condition of the native landowner who rents out land to the European tobacco cultures is to be compared with the forced labour in the forced cultivation systems. He gets the land, the seeds and the set price for the delivered product, but all the risks and instability of the company is on his shoulders'.[17]

In order to position these incidents as well as Van Heinenoord's explanations and questions, the sections below will deal with two levels of relationships, which are closely related to each other and which allow a deeper understanding of the tobacco-shed burnings. The first section examines the relationship between tobacco companies and the local population, particularly in the cultivation, processing and transporting of tobacco. The second looks at the relationship between tobacco companies themselves, which greatly affected company-peasant relations.

Land use and land control

For foreign entrepreneurs who wanted to produce agricultural commodities for European markets in the years after the Forced Cultivation (or Cultivation System) period,[18] the main problem was inevitably the question of obtaining land and labour. Even though the colonial state was no longer the main actor regulating the control of land and labour, nevertheless there were different kinds and degrees of regulation. The state was still strongly involved in the regulation of land rights and areas not defined as communal or individually-owned land fell under the direct control of the state. In general one can divide agrarian systems in the Netherlands Indies into four different types, namely a) private lands (*particuliere landerijen*); b) land leases as in the Principalities; c) lease of wasteland and d) short-term leases of native land.[19] Since private lands did not exist in Besoeki, debates between the colonial apparatus and the planters, and to a certain extent the peasants, regarding rights to land revolved around the last two categories (longer-term lease of wasteland and short-term lease of native land). This was because the boundaries between these categories were often debatable (e.g. what was a wasteland and who decided what 'wasteland' was) but also because there were different opinions between government officials regarding the rights of the natives vis-à-vis outsiders. Intensive debates had already occurred among colonial authorities ever since the land rent system was introduced in the early nineteenth century with the introduction of the Cultivation System.[20]

Even during the period of the Cultivation System, there were already indications that private entrepreneurs were allowed some space to be directly involved in obtaining land. The Government Act of 1853 allowed the leasing of 'wild lands' or 'wasteland' and the following Acts of 1854 and 1856 gave the entrepreneur the opportunity to obtain land by two means: a) renting from the government for a period of not more than 20 years, or b) entering into arrangements with the natives to have them grow the products on their land.[21] However, in contrast to the Principalities of Central Java, Besoeki in the mid-nineteenth century was a very sparsely populated area and shifting cultivation was commonly practiced, which meant that no formal property rights of land existed yet.[22] Early notions of property rights were based on who first cleared a forest or virgin land, followed by continued occupation.[23] An illustration of this situation was the case of George Birnie, who became an important figure in establishing the largest tobacco company in Djember. In 1858, he became a government inspector (*controleur*) in Djember. Earlier on he had carried out research on soil and climate conditions in the area and realized that tobacco could grow quite well. Refusing to be transferred to Lampung, South Sumatra, by the resident of Bondowoso, he then resigned as a civil servant and decided to set up his own tobacco company. He established himself in Djember, between the forest area and a village settlement. Broersma, a prolific writer and traveller who wrote an economic and social history of early twentieth century Besoeki, stated that Birnie chose to grow tobacco on dry land first and went to the local population to ask if they wanted to plant tobacco for him. According to him,

Birnie distributed seeds to the local peasants with the condition that the tobacco would be sold at the agreed upon price to the provider of the seeds. Then he started to have the trees cut down and opened up land for the cultivation of tobacco. At that time, a formal contract to rent land or to ask for government permission was not considered necessary. As Broersma reported, 'at that time a request to the government was not needed, one just had to choose a plot and locate oneself there'.[24] The locals could then use the land for the rest of the year for their own plants.[25] He would give them the plants and they would provide him with the harvest for a fixed price per plant.

Other Dutch planters had already made attempts to grow tobacco in the Bondowoso area to the north of Djember. In 1850, C.H. Doup and J.G. Berkholst made direct arrangements with local peasants for the cultivation of tobacco in Soekowono, in Bondowoso. Later, in 1860, their request to rent 30 *bouws* of land situated in six villages in Soekowono was approved by the Dutch colonial government.[26] In 1853, D.J. Uhlenbeck grew what then became the famous Besoeki *Na-oogst* tobacco[27] on land rented from the peasants and he also recruited them in its production. In 1863, he obtained 106 *bouw* of land in Wonosari subdistrict, with government consent.[28] Fransen van de Putte obtained permission in 1857 to rent 60 *bouw* of land from the Dutch government.[29]

The tobacco plantation company NV *Landbouw Maatschappij Oud Djember* (LMOD), headed by George Birnie, established verbal border agreements with the already existing tobacco companies that were located in the more densely populated northern region, to respect each other's territories.[30] According to the 50-year report published in 1909, which recorded the history of the company's establishment, Birnie's own estate in Djember was 'to a large extent based on land that was almost entirely unused land or on land that was only very partially cultivated'.

If we examine other sources, we can see contrasting views regarding the status of land. One example is a text written by 'a local intellectual' of the present period, Jos Hafid, who stated that in various parts of southern Besoeki land chosen for the cultivation of tobacco by European entrepreneurs and LMOD in particular, was already occupied by Madurese and Javanese migrants who had opened up the forests. Thus, he argued that in 1845 in the area of Rambipuji, south of the town of Jember, both Javanese and Madurese groups had opened up the forest land before the arrival of the Dutch planters, totalling an area of approximately 2,465 *bouws*.[31] Hafid argued that these persons were already subject to tax by the Dutch government and that their tax percentage depended on the quality of land, which could be divided into irrigated land and dry land.[32]

Hafid pointed to the disputable status of land claims. According to him, the local population were assumed to all be migrants so that by default they would not have a strong claim to the land.[33] Indeed, this was underlined in the LMOD's 50-year report, which stated that, particularly after the construction of a major irrigation system, people from Madura and central Java started to come in flows. This report pointed out that 'if they came as people without any possessions, within a few years they have become prosperous farmers and they settled also in territories outside the leased lands of the company'. Additionally, it was stated that land outside the leased areas benefitted from the irrigations system as well, and it was calculated that 2000 *bouw* outside company land could take advantage of the water. After 1897, the installation of the Probolinggo-Klakah-Djember-Panaroekan railway line stimulated the arrival of migrants even more, and these migrants came from places further away than Central Java and northern Djember, namely also from West Java. The fear of these unknown elements is often reflected in government reports and other writings on Djember. Thus Broersma states:

> Unfortunately there are many bad elements among them and it is to these elements that the theft of products from the field and from the drying sheds and also the associated arson, can be attributed.[34]

According to Hafid's account, many of the local inhabitants whom Birnie approached to plant their land with tobacco were offered positions as foremen of the tobacco estates. According to him, this was the case with Ki Abdussalam, mentioned earlier, who was offered such a position to compensate for the fact that from the 40 *bouw* of sawah, 10 *bouw* of dry land and 10 bouw of residential land he was afterwards only left with 10 *bouw* of sawah, 5 *bouw* of dry land and 5 *bouw* of residential land, as the rest of the land had to be handed over to the LMOD.

The situation changed even more drastically when the Agrarian Law was introduced in 1870. This Law became a milestone in the development of the market economy and the transformation of the agrarian structures in the colony. The Law declared all land not in private ownership to belong to the state, and a distinction was drawn between 'free' land not subject to native rights (in fact, waste and unoccupied land) and 'unfree' land subject to native rights. The government was empowered to lease 'free' land to Dutch subjects residing in the colonies and to companies registered in the Indies, for a term of not more than 75 years.[35]

After the introduction of the 1870 Agrarian Law negotiations with the Dutch planters were often lengthy and arduous. Hafid mentioned that Ki Abdussalam, who together with his group had opened 275 *bouws* of land in the area of Cangkring, in the southern part of Besoeki, was asked by the local government to surrender the eastern part of his land to the LMOD tobacco estate. He was against this because this land was more fertile than the western part that he was allowed to retain. Birnie himself then approached Ki Abdussalam and, knowing that he was an important figure in the local community, offered him a position as supervisor or *sinder* (*opzichter* or head of the foremen). Another Madurese, originating from the town of Sumenep, however, preferred to leave his hut and land in Cangkring and go back to the northern part of Besoeki, which had been his first stopping point after crossing the channel.[36]

In another report, based on interviews with the European planters in the sub-district of Djember, Carpentier Alting stated that in 1900, of the total irrigated land of the local peasantry that was estimated at 33,094 *bouws*, 80 per cent (or 27,038 *bouws*) was rented by the tobacco companies.[37] Whether through negotiation, persuasion or through other measures, eventually LMOD managed to accrue the largest acreage of land for its tobacco business. According to their 50-year report, by 1893 they had come to occupy 2,600 *bouws* of irrigated land, 15,000 *bouws* of non-irrigated land or tegalan, 16,000 *bouws* of leased land, 150 *bouws* of land with opstal rights and 60 *bouws* of irrigated land with ownership rights. At the same time, LMOD had constructed six fermenting sheds of various sizes, 80 warehouses, 60 housing facilities to accommodate staff employees, and 440 drying sheds.[38]

These figures show the scale on which a company such as the LMOD operated. Probably it is also indicative of their presence that when Van Heinenoord specified the names of the companies that were hit by the shed burnings, as mentioned earlier, this company was on the top of the list.[39] In an end-of-term report by the later resident of Besoeki, J. Bosman, in 1913, reference was made to the fact that land agreements were considered to be an important source of misunderstanding and agitation.[40] Confusion about these agreements, according to Bosman's report, was primarily due to the different views regarding rights and obligations between companies and the locals. Carpentier Alting also stated that, basically, the idea of a rental agreement was that the peasants had to sell the tobacco that they had been asked to cultivate by the renter for a pre-agreed price. In some cases provision of seeds and advance payments were made. Some other planters were much stricter in making agreements with the local landowners in that the peasants had to plant only tobacco for which the planters provided the seeds and they had the cultivation instructions given by the planters.[41]

As far as the land-owning peasants were concerned, they were still in control of their land and were also in charge of the supervision of labour working on their land, so the terms stipulated in the rental agreements did not stop them from entering into trade relations with other figures in the business. The companies could not use deviation from the contract to bring legal action against them because of lack of evidence.

The situation became more complicated when the flow of migrants into the area increased and claims to land were made. The conducive factor was that Besoeki, especially its southern part, was sparsely populated compared to other residencies in central Java and Madura. Since the early nineteenth-century people from Madura, Central and other parts of East Java had already begun to migrate here. Thus in 1847 the Madurese in the Djember sub-district totalled 58,256 people, compared to 657 Javanese; in the northeastern parts of the residency of Besoeki their proportion was much larger; 90,915 as compared to 19,281 Javanese.[42]

Under these conditions, different types of agreements with the local peasantry were made to induce the cultivation of tobacco. If in the reports we see reference mostly to 'land-owning peasants', it should be underlined that the peasantry was not as homogeneous as formally stated. Peasants in the area could already be divided into a) those who were land owners; b) those who were landless c) those who had some degree of control of the means of production and the production process and sold their tobacco to tobacco traders or on the free market. In Carpentier Alting's report, it was stated that among the peasants involved in tobacco cultivation, around 26,619 were landowners; and 15,694 were landless (of which 11,704 were local peasants and 3,990 were migrants from elsewhere).[43]

Calculations regarding the economic benefits that could accrue to the peasants were often made. Thus, Broersma calculated that one could assume that approximately 13,000 trees could be planted per *bouw*, with the realization that around half would survive. The price of tobacco would never be below 20 guilders per 1,000 high-quality tobacco plants. This meant that if around 6,500 plants would succeed, the farmer would get around 130 guilders for each tobacco season. Broersma added that usually the farmer would plant half a *bouw* with tobacco and the other half with rice.[44]

However, these calculations did not take into account the various factors involved in the production of tobacco.[45] Even if the seeds distributed to the peasants were of high quality, the complex process of production – from planting and watering the seedbeds, transplanting the young plants, maintenance and harvesting – was highly labour-intensive, which meant that peasants would not be able to spend their energy on producing staple crops. In the case of limited personnel, control was difficult to implement. Carpentier Alting stated that what the companies could do at best was to regulate the harvesting times when the bottom, middle and top leaves had to be picked.[46] Yet controlling this process was also not easy and ultimately the only way to agree the proper value of the tobacco plant according to company officials would be to pay the peasants based on the tobacco quality.

This was also one of the sources of disenchantment for the peasants, as the tobacco company with which they had a contract would pay high prices for tobacco of good quality and lower prices for poor-quality leaves, rather than pay a standard price for all the delivered tobacco.[47] In some cases, if the tobacco was not up to the required standard, they would not be paid at all.

As mentioned above, after 1870 Besoeki tobacco fetched very good prices in the European market, which meant that a stream of entrepreneurs appeared in the region either to buy up tobacco or to open tobacco companies.[48] This competition allowed peasants also to sell in the free market for prices that were more advantageous than what the companies offered them and this, in turn, stimulated heated controversy among the companies themselves.

Trouble in tobacco lands

With the large demand for dark tobacco in the European market, competition increased among the 'old type' of European planters, who themselves were involved in the process of tobacco cultivation, and the 'new' tobacco merchants, who only bought dried tobacco. The local population had several names for these different types of planters. The old planters were referred to as '*toean ladjoe*' (old master) and the merchants were named as '*toean anjar*' (new master). The latter did not need to invest money in the renting of land, the planting of seedbeds, or the building of drying sheds, and they did not have to supervise the planting. Therefore, they could offer better prices for the tobacco, which was handed over as soon as the money was paid. For the peasant, this was a better deal, since with the old planters they often had to wait until the tobacco had brought a good price in the market. The appearance of these buyers became a source of grievance for the planters who had invested time and money in the setting up of tobacco companies. The situation intensified when in around 1880 a number of employees of Oud Djember decided that they could also enter the tobacco business.[49]

Because of these developments, planters entered into more formal arrangements with the peasants. In 1875 Birnie requested government permission to lease six plots of land (*erfpachtspercelen*), to which soon afterwards were added another six plots.[50] Until 1884, companies did not interfere with cultivation in those areas in which local landowners planted tobacco for the companies. After 1884, the planters began to rent land for periods of five years, in the hope of more direct intervention into the process of cultivation. However, in many cases local peasants who had made rental agreements with one company would rent the same plot of land to another company.[51] Alternatively, they would sell the tobacco in these rented plots to other buyers. Broersma stated that 'the emergence of these unscrupulous buyers made the supply of products highly uncertain. Their manner of "competition" demoralized the population, their sheds were labelled "thief barns"'.[52] According to him, they offered the locals a high price but at the same time the locals had to take most of the risk and, in the end, some suffered under these conditions.

In order to serve the wellbeing of their respective businesses, the six major tobacco companies operating in the regency of Djember finally made an agreement.[53] This agreement, known as the Rotterdam Agreement – signed in Rotterdam on 4 September 1907 – was initially valid for five years. It attempted to ensure the safety of each party's production and trade operations. The terms stated, among others, that they should respect the rights to the rented land that the companies had with local landowners; to introduce as much as possible the same requirements regarding tobacco cultivation, and to refrain from buying tobacco cultivated on land rented by others.[54]

However, these agreements only took care of one side of the coin. On the other side, various factors played a role in impeding the smooth operation of their business. One important factor mentioned by Van Heinenoord was the role of the foremen (*mandor*) who, by default, played an important role in the running of tobacco production and who had some leeway to manipulate the situation to their benefit. Some of these foremen had their land rented out to the estate and, as persons who were responsible for recruiting the labour needed for the production and processing of tobacco, their position was crucial. It was often reported that these foremen would sell or provide high-quality seeds to other cultivators from the local communities, or they would accept 'free tobacco' to be dried in the drying sheds of the companies.[55] Supervision of these foremen by the companies was often difficult because of limited personnel and means of control. Broersma mentioned the LMOD, which in 1884 had five tobacco estates, employed only 60 European personnel, and was surrounded by around 500 foremen and an indefinite number of workers.[56]

So-called 'free tobacco', i.e. tobacco produced by peasants who were *not* tied to the companies under formal contracts (*segel* or sealed), or who did not work on the leased land of the companies was another factor which needed the companies' attention. Since these peasants were not tied to the companies, they could plant tobacco of their own choosing and sell their product to any buyer who offered good prices.[57] Additionally, it was often reported that these land-owning peasants could get quality seeds from their contacts, who worked for the estates. With the help of company personnel, they would even sometimes have their own tobacco dried in the drying sheds of the companies.[58] In order to deal with this situation, it was felt that security had to be improved and, therefore, the category of 'tobacco police' was introduced.

The tobacco police were recruited for the period of planting and harvest. The members consisted of native police officials and European *controleurs*, whom the local government appointed in collaboration with the plantations. The costs were entirely in the hands of the estates. Control checks were to be made at the most important train stations and at various intersections with control posts along the road.[59] These controllers checked whether the amount of tobacco transported tallied with what was stated in the '*vrijmanpippels*' (or *pipils*, pieces of paper with details of the tobacco product, which every tobacco cultivator were required to have). Every 'free cultivator' received a *pippel* on which were written his name, address, number of tobacco plants and amount of dry tobacco leaves. First the tobacco police counted every free-man's tobacco leaf but to ensure the accuracy of the information, the tobacco company also made its own check on the tobacco leaves coming from their territory and then compared this with the list made by the tobacco police. At the control posts, the amounts of tobacco were checked with the *pippels* that had earlier been distributed, to find out whether they were from the same planter. If the inspectors discovered that either the quality or the quantity of the leaves were not in accordance with what was written on the *pippels*, the tobacco would be confiscated and the origins of the tobacco investigated.[60]

This form of strict control, however, could not entirely guarantee that those who worked on the land that the companies controlled were honest in their delivery of the product. Peasants could take advantage of the situation by not delivering the amount of tobacco stipulated in the earlier agreement. There was always a possibility that land-owning peasants might rent the land to two parties at the same time; reports by government officials confirmed this.

The private planters' increasing power in controlling the allocation of capital, land and labour, but also in their conflicts with European tobacco merchants, became a general concern of the colonial government. Even so, within the government perceptions were mixed regarding this situation. There was a debate between those who were for more free market principles (which would guarantee that peasants were paid on the basis of the quality of tobacco sold in the free market) and those who were for tighter control of tobacco cultivation and sale to ensure that good quality tobacco could be linked to particular brands, or particular plantations. Those who were for free market principles pointed to Loemadjang as an example of how the best results could be achieved. This approach was advocated by the traders, who wanted to be able to buy tobacco on the market and not be restricted by various government regulations that put sales of export tobacco in all Besoeki in the hands a few. Descendants of the first planters who 'opened up' Djember were the main proponents of regulation. It is interesting that the rhetoric used in these debates highlighted 'the common good' (*algemeen belang*), which the planters often referred to, and the interests of the 'native population' (*Inlandsche bevolking*), often used by those who were for free market access.[61]

The Tobacco Ordinance of 1908 was meant to protect the rights of the private estates to cultivate tobacco on rented land. It made free cultivation a thing of the past: buyers could no longer buy tobacco from the peasants, quite often at a better price than the plantation owners offered.[62] This seems to be an important factor in the complaints brought forth by the peasants, as they often would prefer to sell to tobacco traders than to the estate owners.

In Besuki, one resident, whose end-of-term report was markedly agitated, was Broekveldt. Written complaints by the *Sarekat Islam* (an Islamic organization) regarding the condition of 'native tobacco' had led to research on tobacco cultivation, carried out by Lieftinck, a member of the *Raad van Indië* (Indies Council).[63] In a provocatively formulated report, he disagreed with the view that companies rented land from the indigenous population. He stressed that most tobacco estates were not companies (*ondernemingen*) at all but just 'buyers'. According to him, the peasants did all the work, brought the tobacco to the sheds, and were paid according to the quality of the produce. If the tobacco was not according to the standards required, they were not paid at all.[64]

Conclusion

Based on Van Heinenoord's classification of the reasons for tobacco-shed burning, apart from accidents and natural causes, we can make two broad distinctions: between what he portrays as intentional and unintentional behaviour, and between actors who were company personnel and 'third party' actors. This reflected the concerns in the minds of government officials as they appear in their writings, both the routine end-of-term reports and reports prepared by special commissions dealing with particular issues. Two aspects are especially striking. First, there was the question of land rights and the rights and obligations of all parties involved. Second, there was the concern of ensuring local security and preventing unknown elements and suspicious characters, thought to be a result of demographic mobility and the entry of migrants into an area.

European planters, on the other hand, had other concerns. If we observe the number of agreements that they made among themselves and the negotiations they performed with the peasants, the major factor for them was to control both the quality of the crop and its marketing.

Explanations of arson could be traced to the consequences of market competition, where 'bad intentions by third parties' were seen as the main reason for these tobacco-shed burnings. This could be interpreted as competition from other companies, which wanted to see a competitor go down. But it could also be a general feeling of discontent regarding the payments for the product, which the peasant producers may have valued more highly. Carpentier Alting's report dealt elaborately with the different expectations of renters and the land-owning peasants who rented out their land. For the tobacco companies, renting land was a means to ensure some form of stability in rights to the product, and not so many rights to the land, because the peasants were still in charge of the actual cultivation of their own lands.

In any case, the primary factors seen as impeding production and business stability were the clashes between the planters and the tobacco merchants and the local peasants' frustrations when payments did not concur with their expectations. In the late nineteenth century and early twentieth century, the issue of workers' conditions were not brought into these discussions; it was only in the 1920s that this became an issue. When the Labour Office started their investigations on workers in certain sectors of the economy, debates ensued as to how to deal with workers' rights and which standards to use. In these debates, more attention was given to workers in the cigarette and tobacco sectors because these absorbed a large portion of the working population.[65] But it is equally important to understand the perceptions of government personnel, their fears and anxieties, and the solutions they deemed important to bring the situation back to a manageable level. In other words, their efforts to re-embed the regular production of tobacco help us understand the ambivalences, doubts and debates among the colonial authorities who were involved in the production of a particular agricultural commodity.

Acknowledgements

The author would like to thank all those who were involved in the 'People, Plants and Work' project, especially Kathinka Sinha and Jean Stubbs, and also Willem van Schendel and Ben White for helping with the editing of this chapter.

Notes

1 Registered under *Nationaal Archief, Den Haag, Ministerie van Koloniën: Mailrapport, Nr toegang* 2.10.36.02. no 1121. I will refer to it below as 'Van Heinenoord's report'.
2 For an extensive discussion on ways of reading such colonial sources, see among others, Stoler, A.L. *Along the Archival Grain: Epistemic Anxieties and Colonial Common Sense* (Princeton: Princeton University Press, 2010); and Ricardo Roque and Kim A. Wagner (eds.) *Engaging Colonial Knowledge: Reading European Archives in World History* (London: Palgrave Macmillan 2011).
3 In East Coast Sumatra tobacco-shed burning was considered as an act of protest of local Karo-Batak chiefs against the Sultan of Deli, who had signed a treaty with the Dutch company to allow it to use the land for 70 to 99 years. See Karl Pelzer, *Planter and Peasant: Colonial Policy and the Agrarian Struggle in East Sumatra, 1863–1947* ('s-Gravenhage: Martinus Nijhoff. KITLV Verhandelingen 84, 1978). The

94 *Ratna Saptari*

discussions regarding these shed burnings are similar to those about incidences of sugar-cane burning in Java. For an analysis of sugar-cane burnings, see Robert E. Elson, 'Cane-Burning in the Pasuruan Area: An Expression of Social Discontent'. In F. van Anrooij et al (eds.) *Between People and Statistics: Essays on Modern Indonesian History* (The Hague, Martinus Nijhoff, 1979), 219–34.

4 The government correspondence to which Van Heinenoord referred was written by the First Secretary on the 14th of November 1902 (missive no. 3906), requesting information regarding the recent shed fires, especially in the sub-district of Djember, and recommendations to improve the situation.

5 Van Heinenoord's report, 2.

6 Van Heinenoord's report, 4.

7 KITLV collections. Reproduced by permission of Leiden University.

8 According to the list of end-of-term reports kept in the National Archives, the residents succeeding Van den Bergh van Heinenoord, who completed his term in 1907, were J. Bosman (1913), B. Schagen van Soelen (1918), F.L. Broekveldt (1919), H. Ph Fesevuur (1922), H.A. Voet (1925) and C.H.H. Snell (1934). See Nationaal Archief, Den Haag, *Ministerie van Koloniën: Inventaris van het archief van de Memories van Overgave, 1852–1962* (1963). Inv. Nr 2.10.39.

9 As early as the 1850s, experiments on tobacco cultivation had shown that tobacco could grow well in these areas. When Besoeki tobacco found a niche in the European markets, particularly for the production of cigars, a flow of Dutch entrepreneurs entered the area, hoping to enter the profitable trade in tobacco, or to establish tobacco plantations.

10 NL-HaNA, Koloniën/Mailrapport no 1121, 2–3.

11 The *Landbouw Maatschappij Oud Djember* (LMOD) or The Old Djember Agricultural Company, was the largest plantation in Djember, owned by the Birnie family. See Elisabeth Birnie. *The Birnies* (Twello: the author, 1992).

12 These tables were handwritten in contrast to the report itself, which is in typed format.

13 These two incidents occurred in the terrain of the Koning estate (Van Heinenoord's report, 6).

14 KITLV collections. Reproduced by permission of Leiden University.

15 *Mailrapport* nr 1121, 15

16 NL-*HaNA, Koloniën / Memorie van Overgave*, Inv. Nr 2.10.39.

17 NL-*HaNA, Koloniën / Memorie van Overgave*, Inv. Nr 2.10.39, Nr 1270/9.

18 See Bosma's chapter in this volume (Chapter 3), which deals with the period of the Cultivation System.

19 Peter Boomgaard and J. L. van Zanden. *Changing Economy in Indonesia. Vol 10. Food Crops and Arable Land, Java 1815–1942* (Amsterdam: Royal Tropical Institute, 1990).

20 This was connected to the idea of whether state revenues should be obtained through tax on irrigated land or through the obligation to provide labour for the cultivation of commercial crops. At the same time there was the question whether protecting the rights of the natives to secure their own subsistence needs was crucial to maintain political stability and economic resilience. See Hiroyoshi Kano. *Land Tenure System and the Desa Community in Nineteenth-Century Java* (Tokyo: Institute of Developing Economies. Special Paper no. 5. (1977), 17–20.

21 Both options were still considered to be a problem for the entrepreneurs, however, because in the first case the duration of the lease was still considered to be too short and in the second case the entrepreneur had too little control over production. See A.J. Vandenbosch. *The Dutch in the Far East* (Berkeley: University of California Press, 1944), 244.

22 Nawiyanto, *Agricultural Development in a Frontier Region of Java. Besuki, 1870– Early 1990s* (Yogyakarta: Galang Press, 2003), 134–5. His discussion is also based on J.W. de Stoppelaar. *Balambangansch Adatrecht* (Wageningen: Veenman, 1927).

23 Nawiyanto. *Agricultural Development*, 136.
24 R. Broersma. *Besoeki: Een Gewest in Opkomst* (Amsterdam: Groesbeek & Nijhoff, 1913), 18.
25 This meant around seven months, since the cultivation of tobacco (not including the processing) would take 4 to 5 months, which includes the gradual process of harvesting. Because of the lesser rains and irrigation compared to the Principalities, agriculture for peasant subsistence was mainly based on maize and soybean. Other crops were not planted because these were considered detrimental for the cultivation of tobacco later.
26 One *bouw* is equivalent to 0.7 hectares. The term *bouw* (or in Javanese, *bahu*) will be retained throughout this chapter as it is most commonly used within the Netherlands Indies context and even until the present period.
27 In Besoeki, *voor-oogst* tabak (meaning literally before the rice harvest), which is for the inner binder leaf of cigars, is planted in January or February and harvested in April or May. The better quality wrapper leaf is given the name *na-oogst* tabak (after the rice harvest) and is grown at the end of June or early July and harvested between October to early December. See O. de Vries. *Tabak* (Haarlem: H.D. Tjeenk Willink & Zoon, 1915), 20; and J.L. Vleming. *Tabak, Tabakscultuur en Tabaksproducten van Nederlandsch-Indië* (Weltevreden: Landsdrukkerij / Dienst der Belastingen in Nederlands-Indië, 1925), 69.
28 The land also for construction buildings for fermentation sheds etc.
29 Broersma. *Besoeki*, 44.
30 In the beginning the plantation experienced some failures; Van Gennep died two years after the establishment of Oud Djember and his shares were bought by the other two partners. In 1874 Birnie bought out Mathiessen from the company and in 1875 placed his cousin, Gerhard David Birnie, in his place, at the moment that George Birnie returned to Holland. Therefore between 1875 and 1890 Gerhard David Birnie was the main figure developing the LMOD. See A.C. Jaeggi. 'De Tabakscultuur van de Residentie Besoeki'. In C.J.J van Hall and C. van de Koppel (eds.) *De Landbouw in de Indische Archipel. Deel II b (Genotmiddelen en Specerijen).* ('s Gravenhage: N.V. Uitgeverij W. Van Hoeve, 1949), 491. Currently the archives of this company are stored in the Deventer Municipal Archives in the Netherlands, and much of the documentation is still being digitalized.
31 Jos Hafid. *Perlawanan Petani. Kasus Tanah Jenggawah.* [Peasant Resistance. The Case of the Jenggawah Lands] (Jakarta: Latin, LSPP, 2001). It is not clear where Hafid obtained his data from but it is curious that he gave very specific figures. He mentions that Ki (the title for a respected Islamic man) Abdussalam opened 275 *bouws* of land; Mbah Budo and her group opened up 400 *bouws*; Ki Muna, 425 *bouws*; Ki Bire, 250 *bouws*, Ki Benjir, 500 *bouws*, Ki Ragil, 90 *bouws*; Ki Wiro and Ki Bongso, who were brothers, 125 *bouws* and Ki Nira Elleng 400 *bouws*. One may surmise that, if the sources for these figures are not stated, this might be a fictitious story and that the stories that he told regarding how they opened up the land are local myths. However, detailed accounts and the processes regarding their experiences in confronting the LMOD, for instance, which are narrated in his book, seem to suggest some certainties. However these are narratives that should be examined further.
32 Hafid. *Perlawanan Petani*, 19–20.
33 Hafid. *Perlawanan Petani*, 26.
34 Broersma. *Besoeki*, 27.
35 Allen, G.C. and Audrey G. Donnithorne. *Western Enterprise in Indonesia and Malaysia: A Study in Economic Development* (London: George Allen and Unwin, 1957), 68. In Java the length of time was more circumscribed because of the predominance of annual crops rather than perennials and because of the density of the population.
36 Hafid. *Perlawanan Petani*, 22.

96 Ratna Saptari

37 'Voordracht in eene onder Voorzitterschap van den Resident van Bezoeki gehouden Bijeenkomst van Tabaksondernemers en Geemployeerden Bij de Tabakscultuur te Bondowoso 16 Februari 1902, 1.
38 Landbouw Maatschappij Oud-Djember. 'Kort Overzicht van Oprichting, Bestaan en Bedrijf der Onderneming 'Oud Djember'. Ter Gelegenheid van haar 50-jarig Jubileum samengesteld., 1859–1909 (1909). Moreover a diversification in business was also practised by LMOD at that time, namely by opening a running coffee warehouse and a transportation company, Panarukan Maatschappij. Birnie was the biggest stock holder of a sugar factory, Prajekan, the owner of Panarukan Maatschappij, and he also owned a marine transportation company and perennial cash crop plantations, such as coffee and cacao.
39 Thus in Van Heinenoord's report it was stated that, in the sub-district of Djember, the ranking of arson cases by company was as follows: Oud Djember (15), Besoeki Tabak Maatschappij (10), C.A. Koning (7) and the rest had had 3 cases or less during 1902. See Van Heinenoord's report.
40 See: *Voordracht*.
41 *Voordracht*, 4.
42 P. Bleeker. 'Bijdragen tot de Statistiek der Bevolking van Java', *Tijdschrijft voor Nederlandsch Indië*. 9de jaargang (1847), 143. See also J. Tennekes. *Bevolkingsspreiding der Residentie Besoeki in 1930* (Amsterdam, TKNAG, 1963).
43 *Voordracht*, 2.
44 Depending on the ecology of the area, the land grown with *Na-oogst* tobacco could be widely spread and interspersed with land grown with other crops (even though they could all be leased or rented by a tobacco company). The cultivation of tobacco is undertaken alternately with other crops, however the different sequences of cultivation vary for every area. Broersma. *Besoeki*, 19.
45 Vleming. *Tabak*, 69.
46 *Voordracht*, 19.
47 *Voordracht*, 22.
48 Thus if in 1860 the price of tobacco was 76 cents per pound, between 1870 until 1873 it reached a peak of 120–60 cents per pound. See Landbouw Maatschappij Oud-Djember. 'Kort Overzicht'.
49 Broersma. *Besoeki*, 28.
50 Jaeggi. *'De Tabakscultuur'*, 488.
51 Jaeggi. *'De Tabakscultuur'*, 488; Broersma. *Besoeki*, 29.
52 Broersma. *Besoeki*, 28.
53 These companies were the Besoeki Tabak Maatschappij; the Cultuur Maatschappij Djelboek; the Landbouw Maatschappij Oud-Djember; the L.M. Soekokerto Adjong; the L.M. Soekowono, and the L.M. Soekasarie. These companies had their head offices in Amsterdam, The Hague, Deventer, Rotterdam, Amsterdam and Soerabaia, respectively. See *Belanghebbenden bij de Tabakscultuur in de Residentie Besoeki thans in het Regentschap Djember, 1907–1932*. Rotterdam: A. Van Hoboken & Co, 1932).
54 *Belanghebbenden*, 8.
55 Broersma. *Besoeki*, 28.
56 Broersma. *Besoeki*, 23. It is interesting to compare this with Deli, which has more complete information on the structures of management. As Jan Breman showed, for one plantation with 280 hectares of land, work in the field would be supervised by one administrator, four assistants, one head foreman, 12 sub-foremen and at least 200 coolies per foreman. Jan Breman. *Koelies, planters en koloniale politiek: het arbeidsregime op de grootlandbouwondernemingen aan Sumatra's Oostkust in het begin van de twintigste eeuw* (Leiden: KITLV Press, 1992), 130.
57 Vleming. *Tabak*, 61.
58 Broersma. *Besoeki*, 28.
59 A company such as the LMOD would transport the tobacco with ox carts from the fermentation sheds to the various train stations, from where the State Rails

transported them to the storage houses of the *Maatschappij Panarukan*. From there boats took the bales to the awaiting ship of the Stoomvaartmaatschappij Nederland, Rotterdam Lloyd, or Ocean, which will take them to Rotterdam and ultimately to the firma Hoboken. This implied that at every check point intensive security control needed to be done. See Landbouw Maatschappij Oud-Djember. *'Kort Overzicht'*.

60 Jaeggi. *'De Tabakscultuur'*, 492–493.
61 This was observed by the retiring resident of Bondowoso, Broekveldt in his *Memorie van Overgave*, 26 February 1919.
62 Broekveldt referred to an article published in the *Javasche Courant* 18 and 22 September 1908 no. 75 and 76, which mentioned this research.
63 This research was conducted between 29 November – 21 December 1917 and the results were reported in Mailrapport no. 1324, 1918 regarding the situation of the *bevolkingstabak* (tobacco not under long-term contract with the plantations).
64 NL-HaNA, Koloniën / Memorie van Overgave, Inv. Nr 2.10.39, Nr 1270/9, 16.
65 See P. de Kat Angelino. *Verslag betreffende eene door den inspecteur bij het Kantoor van Arbeid op de vorstenslandsche tabaksondernemingen gehouden enquête. Publicatie no 5 van het Kantoor van Arbeid* (Weltevreden: Landdrukkerij, 1929); and B. van der Reijden. *Rapport betreffende eene gehouden enquête naar de arbeiderstoestanden in de industrie van strootjes en inheemsche sigaretten op Java*. Publicatie van het Kantoor van Arbeid, no. 9, 10, 11 (Bandoeng: Drukkerij Strafgevangenis *'Soekamiskin'*, 1934–36).

References

Allen, G.C. and Audrey G. Donnithorne. *Western Enterprise in Indonesia and Malaysia: A Study in Economic Development* (London: George Allen and Unwin, 1957).

Belanghebbenden bij de Tabakscultuur in de Residentie Besoeki thans in het Regentschap Djember, 1907–1932. Rotterdam: A. Van Hoboken & Co, 1932).

Birnie, Elisabeth. *De Birnies* (Twello: Birnie, 1992).

Bleeker, P. 'Bijdragen tot de Statistiek der Bevolking van Java', *Tijdschrijft voor Nederlandsch Indië*. 9de jaargang (1847), 143.

Boomgaard, Peter, and J. L. van Zanden. *Changing Economy in Indonesia. Vol 10. Food Crops and Arable Land, Java 1815–1942* (Amsterdam: Royal Tropical Institute, 1990).

Breman, Jan. *Koelies, planters en koloniale politiek: het arbeidsregime op de grootlandbouwondernemingen aan Sumatra's Oostkust in het begin van de twintigste eeuw* (Leiden: KITLV Press, 1992).

Broersma, R. *Besoeki: Een Gewest in Opkomst* (Amsterdam: Groesbeek & Nijhoff, 1913).

De Kat Angelino, P. *Verslag betreffende eene door den inspecteur bij het Kantoor van Arbeid op de vorstenslandsche tabaksondernemingen gehouden enquête. Publicatie no 5 van het Kantoor van Arbeid* (Weltevreden: Landdrukkerij, 1929).

De Vries, O. *Tabak* (Haarlem: H.D. Tjeenk Willink & Zoon, 1915).

Elson, Robert E. 'Cane-Burning in the Pasuruan Area: An Expression of Social Discontent'. In F. van Anrooij et al (eds.) *Between People and Statistics: Essays on Modern Indonesian History* (The Hague, Martinus Nijhoff, 1979), 219–34.

Hafid, Jos. *Perlawanan Petani. Kasus Tanah Jenggawah*. [Peasant Resistance. The Case of the Jenggawah Lands] (Jakarta: Latin, LSPP, 2001).

Jaeggi, A.C. 'De Tabakscultuur van de Residentie Besoeki'. In C.J.J van Hall and C. van de Koppel (eds.) *De Landbouw in de Indische Archipel. Deel II b (Genotmiddelen en Specerijen)*. ('s Gravenhage: N.V. Uitgeverij W. Van Hoeve, 1949).

Kano, Hiroyoshi Kano. *Land Tenure System and the Desa Community in Nineteenth-Century Java* (Tokyo: Institute of Developing Economies. Special Paper no. 5. (1977).

Landbouw Maatschappij Oud-Djember. 'Kort Overzicht van Oprichting, Bestaan en Bedrijf der Onderneming 'Oud Djember'. Ter Gelegenheid van haar 50-jarig Jubileum samengesteld., 1859–1909 (1909).
Nawiyanto. *Agricultural Development in a Frontier Region of Java. Besuki, 1870– Early 1990s* (Yogyakarta: Galang Press, 2003).
Pelzer, Karl. *Planter and Peasant: Colonial Policy and the Agrarian Struggle in East Sumatra, 1863– 1947* ('s-Gravenhage: Martinus Nijhoff. KITLV Verhandelingen 84, 1978).
Stoppelaar, J.W. de. *Balambangansch Adatrecht* (Wageningen: Veenman, 1927).
Tennekes, J. *Bevolkingsspreiding der Residentie Besoeki in 1930* (Amsterdam, TKNAG, 1963).
Vandenbosch, A.J. *The Dutch in the Far East* (Berkeley, CA: University of California Press, 1944).
Van der Reijden, B. *Rapport betreffende eene gehouden enquête naar de arbeiderstoestanden in de industrie van strootjes en inheemsche sigaretten op Java* Publicatie van het Kantoor van Arbeid, no. 9, 10, 11 (Bandoeng: Drukkerij Strafgevangenis 'Soekamiskin', 1934–36).
Vleming, J.L. *Tabak, Tabakscultuur en Tabaksproducten van Nederlandsch-Indië* (Weltevreden: Landsdrukkerij / Dienst der Belastingen in Nederlands-Indië, 1925).

Archival sources and government reports

NL-HaNA, Koloniën/Mailrapport no 1121 ('Van Heinenoord's Report').
NL-HaNA, Koloniën / Memorie van Overgave, Nummer Toegang 2.10.39, inventaris nummer 117, 118, 119.
Voordracht in eene onder Voorzitterschap van den Resident van Bezoeki gehouden Bijeenkomst van Tabaksondernemers en Geemployeerden Bij de Tabakscultuur te Bondowoso 16 Februari 1902.
De Tabaksverordening, benevens eenige andere gewestelijke verordeningen van de Residentie Besoeki, ten dienste van de Tabaksondernemers. 1919.

6 Embedding cigarette tobacco in colonial Bihar (India)
A multi-dimensional task

Kathinka Sinha-Kerkhoff

Introduction

Tobacco plants, initially only found in the Antilles and the more westerly regions of Central and sub-tropical America, have thrived all over the world. The tobacco plant – like sugarcane, as explained by Jon Curry-Machado's chapter in this volume (Chapter 7) – has different varieties.[1] These varieties not only look different from each other, but they also have different uses. The kind of tobacco plant used for the production of smoking tobaccos such as cigars, cigarettes, water pipes (*hookahs*) and *cheroots* (a kind of cigar) is not the same as that used for chewing and sniffing. Even these smoking varieties differ from each other. Tobaccos used as fillers in cigarettes differ from cigar tobaccos or tobaccos used in *hookahs*. Moreover, in order to produce tobacco for varied purposes, different curing systems are required. After harvesting, tobacco is cured to impart the required colour, texture and aroma to the final product. Different methods of curing are adopted for different types of tobacco, depending on quality requirements and the intended use of the final product. Lastly, whereas normally only the leaves of the tobacco plant are used, certain tobacco products make use of tobacco stems and roots, too.

Curing practices also diverge. Ratna Saptari, in this volume, describes the fermenting and drying sheds in Indonesia, which were absent in the state of Bihar in India, where the practice of open air/sun/ground curing was common. What is more, in a country such as India there is also considerable internal division, with certain parts specializing in so-called flue-cured cigarette tobacco (to produce the 'golden' leaf), whereas other soils give off chewing tobaccos only, that is, the 'dark tobacco' described by Saptari.

The most spectacular phase of the tobacco industry – in the sense that it became a global phenomenon – has been the development of the cigarette industry. Cigarette producers now use light coloured leaves that lack gummy substances. The first cigarettes were made from tobacco plants, named Virginia and Burley, cultivated in the USA. These were cured in special chambers known as barns, with artificial heat passing through metal pipes, called flues. Hence, this tobacco became known as 'flue-cured Virginia tobacco' or FCV and was exclusively used as fillers in cigarettes.

Even though cigarette tobacco has become the most popular tobacco variety among cultivators and cigarette smoking the most popular form of tobacco consumption in the world, the cigarette is not omnipresent. Goodman observed that, although Japan and China stood out in Asia as countries 'most thoroughly committed to cigarette consumption', he had noticed that in other parts of Asia 'the progress of the replacement of other forms of tobacco consumption by the cigarettes has been far less complete'.[2]

The Portuguese and, possibly, the Dutch first introduced tobacco cultivation in India during the seventeenth century. From that century onward, chewing tobacco (*khaini*), smoking tobacco for water pipes (*hookahs*), *cheroots* and *bidis* (small hand-rolled cigarettes) became very popular tobacco products. Regular cigarette consumption, however, although high in a few Indian states, remained relatively low in most of the country. And although the states of Andhra Pradesh and Karnataka in southern India specialize in the cultivation of FCV, most of this tobacco is for export outside the country. In general, India figures on the world's tobacco atlas only because of its enormous production of dark, air-cured tobacco that cannot be used as cigarette fillers.[3] The states of Bihar and West Bengal, in the north-eastern part of India, solely produce this kind of tobacco, which is used in water pipes and for various chewing tobacco preparations. Consequently, India rarely figures in histories that describe the coming of the cigarette as the final triumph of smoking.[4]

The story of tobacco experimentation narrated in this chapter illustrates, however, that India became the first country after the USA to develop a kind of tobacco that can be used as cigarette fillers. Moreover, Bihar, a state which now grows no cigarette tobacco at all, became the first region in which this tobacco variety was successfully embedded. We will here analyse this embedding process through an analysis of the title page, two images and a geographical map included in the memoirs of the Department of Agriculture in colonial India, entitled *Studies in Indian Tobaccos*.

At face value, *Studies in Indian Tobaccos* (afterwards: *Studies*; see Figure 6.1) seems to deal only with the technical aspects of embedding 'Types of Nicotiana Rustica, L. and Yellow Flowered Tobacco' in Bihari soil. It comprises 178 pages of text, chemical formulae, images of tobacco fields, different tobacco varieties, various cultivation modes and tobacco experimentation methods in Bihar during the first decade of the twentieth century. I argue, however, that this would be a far too narrow reading. After going through the document, and taking on board the entire spectrum of scientific official reports on tobacco embedding in colonial Bihar, one can conclude that permanent embedding of cigarette tobacco required much more than its technical embedding. Until now it is only scholars with an interest in the history of science who have looked at scientific official reports such as the one analysed here. Historians interested in commodity embedding have largely ignored the scientific technical report, probably because they did not expect economic, political or social aspects to figure in such 'grey literature'. However, a cursory look at *Studies* demonstrates that this is an erroneous assumption. The title page and a few images reproduced here provide the skeleton, if not the flesh,[5]

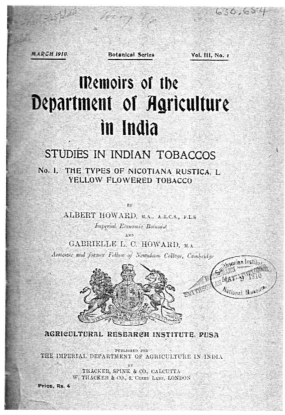

Figure 6.1 Title page of *Studies in Indian Tobaccos*

of the complete Indian cigarette tobacco story narrated in this chapter. These pages give information about the institutional, geographical, scientific, political and economic environment in which tobacco experimentation took place in British India, as well as about those who conducted such experiments around 1910, the year in which the source was published. In other words, our source reveals how cigarette tobacco became embedded in Bihar.

The socio-cultural and political environment of embedding

During the era of so-called high imperialism in Bengal, from 1870 to 1914, European capital, enterprise and knowledge (science) were applied to 'improve' crop-production. Crops were divided into two categories: (1) food and fodder crops, and (2) cash/industrial/commercial crops. Among the latter, cotton, jute and other fibres, tobacco, tea, poppy, indigo and coffee received the attention of British authorities in Bengal and in Britain. What is more, with indigo on its way out (see Willem van Schendel's chapter in this volume (Chapter 2) and coffee not fully a 'European commodity' (see Bhaswati Bhattacharya's chapter (Chapter 4), authorities were looking for substitutes that could be cultivated in India and transported to London.

Thus, they singled out some plants in British India to be transformed into internationally marketable commodities. Tobacco was one of them. Yet, by 1874 Indian tobacco had acquired the unfavourable reputation in the British market of being 'coarse', 'rank', 'ill-flavoured' and in urgent need of improvement.[6] Accordingly, British administrators, eager to get their tobacco imports from the USA replaced by those from their Asian colony, started organized and systematic efforts to improve tobacco cultivation as a cash crop. To this end, the Government of India hired a private business firm, Messrs. Begg, Dunlop and Co. In the village of Pusa, in Bihar, a 'tobacco farm' was established where tobacco was 'grown, cured and manufactured after the American methods' and tobacco cultivation specialists were admonished that,

> [it was] not sufficient to choose what are considered by the ryot good tobacco soils, proper cultivation, &C., it is essential to use other soils and a different culture, to develop qualities different from those at present esteemed in the native commodity. What are considered favourable conditions for the culture of tobacco by the native farmer in India, are in no way an indication of the conditions necessary for ensuring the successful culture of varieties of the European market, and therefore the new trials ought to be made without too much deference to Indian experience.[7]

By 1910, the small tobacco farm at Pusa had been transformed into an Agricultural Research Institute, where two European scientists were deployed to develop such new tobacco qualities. While previous efforts had focused on making Indian tobacco suitable for cigars, now such efforts concentrated on cigarette tobacco, in great demand in the London markets.

Above all, the non-expansion of the tobacco export trade was ascribed to 'the unscientific cultivation and curing adopted in India as compared with America, the Dutch East Indies, &c., where the production is in European hands'.[8] It was thus hoped that the application of 'European capital, energy and enterprise' would improve the quality of Indian tobacco.[9] Yet, the embedding of cigarette tobacco in Bihari soil would, first and foremost, require the fabrication of this desired tobacco variety at Pusa.

Geographical setting

The relationship between Pusa and tobacco research and cultivation, evident from *Studies*, was not new. In fact, the agricultural research institute that the Viceroy of India, Lord Curzon, established in 1904 was located in the same place that the East India Company had selected for a stud-breeding farm that would ensure the indigenous supply of horses (Figure 6.2). The Pusa stud farm had not been successful and was closed down but the estate was still government-owned.

Embedding cigarette tobacco in colonial Bihar 103

Figure 6.2 Map showing the location of Pusa in early-twentieth-century India[10]

From around 1874 onwards, the Government of India had embarked on a mission to make the tobacco of this region (Tirhut in Bihar) an even more profitable crop but now according to colonial requirements. During the next thirty years, successive Lieutenant-Governors of Bengal would be involved in deciding which 'systematic course of experiments for improving both the growth and curing of the plant under State supervision in the districts of Rungpore and Tirhoot' should be adopted. As far as Tirhut was concerned, the Lieutenant-Governor directed that the 'Poosah stud lands, south of the Gunduck', which the Government of India had made over to the Government of Bengal in 1873 for the purpose of experimental tobacco cultivation, 'shall primarily be devoted to this purpose'.[11] Until 1897, the Government of Bengal had leased out the estate to a private business firm. This firm had also been involved in indigo cultivation elsewhere, but the government had vetoed experimentation of this commodity in this part of Bihar. It had instead ordered this firm to undertake tobacco improvement only.

In 1886, Indian Civil Servant W.W. Hunter mentioned that five English and American curers had been employed at the Pusa enterprise because 'an essential condition of success is skilled supervision in the delicate process of tobacco-curing'.[12] Clearly, the colonial authorities at the time ruled that successful embedding of new tobacco varieties around Pusa required not only different soils and seeds but also British, non-Indian skills and knowledge regarding tobacco cultivation and curing.

Institutional setting

In 1871, the Imperial Government established a Department of Agriculture to lessen fears that the Indian economy would not generate the requisite surplus to meet the food and raw material requirements of the motherland, as well as of India itself. This department was 'to take cognisance of all matters affecting the practical improvement and development of agricultural resources of the country'.[13] At a time during which direct state aid for agriculture research was still widely regarded as unthinkable in Britain,[14] the use of science for crop improvement had received great support in India during the 1870s and 1880s. In many ways, agricultural science thus developed and flourished more in British India than in Britain. The scientists employed at the agricultural department included chemists, mycologists and entomologists from outside India. By the turn of the century, Bengal was totally converted 'to the cause of agricultural development' and 'the tendency was for more, and more ambitious, proposals, expressing each official's view of the importance of his field'.[15]

The establishment of an agricultural research institute at Pusa was the outcome of such proposals. In 1898, Lord Curzon had taken over as Viceroy. During his administration, Pusa increasingly became the centre of agricultural engineering. Around Pusa, there had been many British (indigo) planters (see Willem van Schendel in Chapter 2). There was an indigo research centre at Dalsingh Sarai, not far from Pusa. Moreover, Europeans had also been involved in tobacco experimentation under the aegis of the private business firm. In fact, the place had looked like a kind of 'mini British Kingdom' and was therefore thought to be uniquely suitable to carry out crop experimentation applying European capital, skills, science and manpower.

The Imperial Government assigned clear roles to (private) Europeans to enable the embedding of agricultural commodities. In 1904, Lord Curzon sanctioned the formation of an Imperial Research Institute at Pusa (later known as the Pusa Institute) under the direction of a British ex-indigo planter named Bernard Coventry. The powers of the Director of Pusa and the Agricultural Adviser to the Government became vested in one incumbent. Besides, the old Department of Agriculture had employed an Inspector-General of Agriculture, an Agricultural Chemist, a Cryptogamic Botanist and an Entomologist, all of whose duties had been largely advisory. After the establishment of the Pusa Institute, the existing staff of the department was stationed at Pusa, and three additional officers were appointed to deal with three subdivisions: Agriculture, Bacteriology and Economic Botany.

In 1905, the Government of India also decided to develop separate agricultural departments in each of the larger provinces and from that year onwards the organisation of agricultural work in British India followed two mains divisions:

Imperial and Provincial. The Pusa Institute, however, came to house both the Imperial and Provincial departments. In order to coordinate the work of these two departments, the Board of Agriculture, consisting of the staff of the agricultural departments, was also set up in 1905. In the early proceedings of this Board, discussions over research programmes and the approach best suited to the larger problems of Indian agriculture took up much time. In 1908 and subsequent years, interesting discussions took place concerning which plants should be embedded and improved upon, and what would be the best methods of bringing such 'improvements' to the notice of cultivators. Our analysis of cigarette tobacco in Bihar is situated in this period when the Pusa Institute was at its zenith.

In 1919 agriculture in the provinces became a 'transferred subject' and was placed in charge of an Indian Minister responsible to the newly established Reformed Councils composed of a majority of elected unofficial members. Shortly afterwards, the recruitment of officers by the Secretary of State ceased, and the existing European members of the Provincial Departments were given the opportunity to leave India on proportionate pensions. These changes were followed by an alteration in plants selected for embedding or improvement. Consequently, the importance of sugarcane improvement was emphasized more than that of embedding cigarette tobacco in Bihar. Moreover, when a great earthquake in Bihar destroyed a huge part of the Pusa Institute in 1934, the Government of India decided not to rebuild it. Instead, funds were provided for an Imperial Agricultural Research Institute in the capital, New Delhi.[16] It transpired that the departure of Imperial Pusa from Bihar implied the pushing out of cigarette tobacco from the province.

The scientific setting

In 1906, the Imperial Department of Agriculture produced its first annual report (1905–1906). Thiselton-Dyer described it in *Nature* as an 'epoch-making' development. Pusa was called the 'Rothamsted of the East', putting agricultural research in India on a new footing: 'Hitherto fitful and uncoordinated, and always at the mercy of uninstructed and unsympathetic officials', who looked only at 'one cannon of criticism ... the solvency of the annual balance-sheet'.[17] Agricultural research could now proceed in a directed fashion. Through Pusa, it was argued, 'the application of modern scientific methods and knowledge to pressing economic problems' in India could now take place because here 'research is, in fact, directed to practical problems that require early solution, and is not wasted on inquiries which are only of importance from the theoretical standpoint'.[18]

Even as late as 1910, although farming was a very important economic activity in India, the colonial government's interest in agriculture was selective and self-centred. The agricultural science that developed at Imperial Pusa was in the service of exports. It was stipulated that agricultural problems were to be approached by a number of specialists working independently at the institute. The duties of the scientific members of the institute were laid down in an official memorandum on the subject, published by the Inspector-General of Agriculture. These duties not only encompassed research work in laboratories and the experimental farm but also included touring throughout Bihar. For example, the duties of the Imperial Economic Botanist included investigation of the economic uses of agricultural plants, botanical study of the field and garden crops, testing of varieties, transfer of useful varieties from tract to tract, production of new and improved varieties by selection and cross-fertilization, and the testing of 'exotic' plants.

At Pusa, besides major work on fibres, cereals and sugarcane, scientific experimentation with a number of other crops such as indigo, oilseeds, fodder crops, groundnuts, gram and millets was also conducted. Tobacco research was given a prominent place at Pusa between 1905 and 1925. What is more, the task of 'improving' Indian tobacco, that is, making it suitable as fillers in cigarettes, was entrusted to the Imperial Economic Botanist and his 'Associate', that is, Albert and Gabrielle Howard, the authors of *Studies*.

Albert Howard

Albert Howard (1873–1947) is certainly well-known. In fact, this British botanist has become world famous and is now considered by many as the 'father of modern organic agriculture'.[19] Yet, the fact that he was closely connected to tobacco research is not recognized at all. Albert,[20] son of an English farmer, had first been employed in Barbados as Mycologist and Agricultural Lecturer at the Imperial Department of Agriculture in the West Indies. Looking back he wrote about his time: 'In Barbados I was a laboratory hermit [...] but [for] my tours of various islands [...]. This contact with the land itself and with the men practically working on it laid the foundations of my knowledge of tropical agriculture'.[21] After a stint in Kent working with hop growers, Albert was given charge of the Botanical Section of the Pusa Imperial Institute in 1905. Later he remembered: 'On arrival the new institution only existed on paper'. Nevertheless, Albert got an area of about 75 acres of land at one end of the Pusa Estate. During the first few years, Albert experimented with various crops on this land, in particular with tobacco, which it was his duty to improve 'by modern plant breeding methods'. He was expected not only to improve the plant but also to produce new varieties.[22]

Louise Howard, Albert's second wife, later noted that Albert had 'little time for flora with no economic consequence', as 'the true farmer does not care for flowers'.[23] Economic considerations thus inspired Albert to take up tobacco research, among others, and the 'improvement of the crop' was the job at hand. Albert Howard later wrote:

> My main duties at Pusa were the improvement of crops and the production of new varieties. Over a period of nineteen years (1905–24) my time was devoted to this task, in the course of which many new types of wheat (including rust-resistant), of tobacco, gram, and linseed were isolated, tested, and widely distributed.[24]

While at Pusa, Albert conducted numerous tests involving soil aeration, irrigation, pollination and cross-fertilization of species, growing cycles, manuring of crops, harvesting, processing and packing of crops, and he applied these measures to tobacco. He carried out systematic surveys of which tobacco variety was grown, where and how; selected the most promising country types, isolated these, and then followed hybridization of the improved new variety via crossings that did, or did not, conform to Mendelian principles; and lastly, attempted genetic stabilization of hybrid varieties.[25] Albert was considered to be very successful in the field of tobacco improvement at the time but in later life, he (consciously) never referred to his tobacco experiments in Pusa. Yet, as we shall see, he, together with his wife Gabrielle Louise Caroline Matthaei, managed to develop the desired tobacco variety that could be used for cigarettes.

Gabrielle L.C. Howard

Born in London, Gabrielle (1876–1930) was the daughter of Ernst C.H. Matthaei, a Commission Merchant, and of Louise Henriette Matthaei, neé Sueur, a musician. Besides a younger brother, Gabrielle had two younger sisters named Marie and Louise. The latter married Albert after her sister's demise in Geneva in 1930. An excerpt of an obituary in *Nature* (20 September 1930) commented:

> A severe blow has been dealt to the progress of science in India through the death at the age of fifty-three years of Mrs. Albert Howard, which took place at Geneva on Aug. 18 last. Miss G.L.C. Matthaei entered Newnham College, Cambridge, in 1895 and secured the double distinction of a first class in both parts of the Natural Science Tripos. Thereafter she continued to reside at Cambridge, being elected a fellow, and later an associate, of her College. She was fortunate at that time in coming under the powerful influences of Miss Ida Freund and Dr. F. F. Blackman. Her work in association with the latter developed in her capacity for patient pursuit of the elusive in research which was so marked a characteristic of her work to the last [...]. From 1905, when she married Mr. Albert Howard, the scene of her activities shifted to India. With that marriage commenced a comradeship which, if not unique in the annals of science, it at least unique in that it received official recognition from the Government of India, for, in 1910, she was appointed personal assistant to her husband and, in 1913, Second Imperial Economic Botanist. She was also awarded, by H.M. the King, the Kaisar-i-Hind medal of the First Class.[26]

Gabrielle's career was, therefore, remarkable considering that several British women scientists in the late nineteenth and early twentieth century remained 'obligatory amateurs'.[27] What is more, before her marriage with Albert she had already established a name for herself through her research on vegetable assimilation and respiration. This is noteworthy, as at that time in Europe women in agricultural sciences had been an 'anomaly'.[28] Gabrielle and her sister Louise were pioneers in this field:

sisters from a Swiss family of merchants re-settled in London, Gabrielle and Louise successively provided the intellectual and emotional companionship that shaped Sir Albert's explorations and discoveries. Gabrielle married Sir Albert prior to moving to India where they collaborated as research partners for three decades. She co-wrote more than 120 journal articles with him and was co-equal in planning and running their extensive plant breeding and compost research activities. On the eve of their retirement and return to England, Gabrielle passed away and two years later her younger sister, Louise, married Sir Albert.[29]

The anonymous author of Gabrielle's obituary wrote:

'It is not possible, even for one who has had the privilege of sharing in part of the labours of the Howards in India, to apportion merit between the two comrades. Their work stands, and is best left, as a joint record of their devotion to each other and to India'.

Significantly, the writer added:

But Mrs. Howard's association with Pusa introduced a definite economic trend, absent from her earlier work but becoming more and more marked with time. In 1905, the Agricultural Department in India was but recently reorganised and the impetus given by the rediscovery of Mendel's work was still fresh. The earlier papers are tinged by these facts and many plant breeding problems in this new field were brought to solution by these new methods. But even at this period the economic aspect was not neglected.[30]

However, not many seem to have been interested in Gabrielle's legacy. Yet, thanks to her sister Louise, we now know a bit more about Gabrielle's thoughts and work. Not only did Lady Louise Howard review some of Gabrielle's scientific contributions in her biography *Sir Albert in India*, published in 1953, but she also elaborated on Gabrielle's unique position as a married European woman scientist at Pusa, and her 'wider ideas'. After elaborating Albert Howard's scientific contributions, Louise wrote:

In addition to the advantage of arriving with so creditable an achievement to his name, Sir Albert Howard was highly favoured in his marriage. The woman who stood at his side during the long years of research in the East was not only the able housewife, the dignified hostess, and the wonderful companion, but she was also a highly trained botanist, launched on her own career of research at Cambridge, of great intellectual endowment and altogether fitted to be the comrade and inspirer of a pioneer in science, one on a level with himself, as Sir Albert never ceased to emphasize [...]. Her engagement to marry broke off this work to introduce her to years of investigation shared with her husband into the agricultural problems of the East – she came to love India and never felt so well as when she was in that country. She had enormous capacity for patient detail and carried out a very large part of the finer minutiae of plant breeding with her own hands in the area of the Botanical Section at Pusa, at Quetta, and at Indore; with this she combined, what is rarer, a comprehensive insight into and grasp of fundamental principle. Indeed, her mind was masterly and energetic, as was shown in a smaller way in her ability to run her Indian household to perfection in the intervals of her scientific labours, to the astonishment of the ladies of the Station, who prophesied either a complete breakdown in household arrangements or at least sunstroke from so many hours spent in the field.[31]

It was this woman who, along with her husband Albert, embedded a new type of tobacco variety in Bihari soil. Yet, our source also reveals silences. We should realize that at Pusa, European scientists like the Howards never carried out chores such as the collection of plants from the field, preparation of specimens, cleaning, packing, sorting and drawing of sketches, and many other essential tasks for tobacco experimentation. Indians were hired for these jobs. Certainly, tobacco embedding was not an exclusively European business but our source does not mention any names or other information on the Indians so employed.

The Howards and tobacco experimentation at Pusa

For almost 20 years between 1905 and 1924, Gabrielle and Albert worked on tobacco improvement in the 'mini British Kingdom' at Pusa.[32] According to Louise, Gabrielle's 'chosen way of life gave her supreme happiness and her comradeship in investigation with her husband was perfect'. Louise further commented: 'Their combined power of work was colossal nor could the results of their efforts ever be disentangled, as they themselves stated to me on more than one occasion'. Even though Gabrielle was officially known as Personal Assistant and the Second Imperial Economic Botanist to the Government, and Albert as the First Imperial Economic Botanist, these 'rather ugly titles', Louise wrote, had been replaced in popular parlance by the description of the two investigators as 'the Sidney Webbs of India'. In 1921, *The Times* summed up the partnership by stating that 'seldom in the sphere of economic investigation has there been a more fruitful collaboration between husband and wife than that of Mr. Albert Howard, for many years Imperial Economic Botanist at the Agricultural Research Institute, Pusa, and Mrs. Howard'.[33]

The Howards had been asked to develop a kind of tobacco that could be successfully exported. Commenting on the failure of previous attempts to improve the quality of Indian tobaccos, the Howards believed that the introduction of foreign tobacco varieties had been ill conceived, as this had been done without a complete initial sorting and classification of existing types. Instead, the couple proposed a four stage-research: (1) the study of existing Indian tobacco varieties and sorting of types; (2) the isolation of pure cultures of these varieties so as to have appropriate material for trials and hybridization without which no real work could be accomplished; (3) the study of acclimatization of tobaccos from other parts of the world in Bihari soils, and (4) the continuous breeding of plants over a number of generations to study the inheritance of characters, a knowledge of which had to precede systematic crossbreeding needed for plant improvement. The fourth task led to some prolonged and elaborate work on Mendelian principles. The whole work was exceedingly laborious. Every year, thousands of flowers were handled, tied into muslin bags, castrated or hand-fertilized, as the case might be, the inflorescences counted and labelled, buds removed, and so on and everything recorded.

After a few years of work at Pusa and under pressure from the Imperial Department demanding 'concrete results', the couple decided to become more 'practical' and came forward with suggestions and advice as to how to improve Indian tobacco cultivation and curing methods in Bihar.[34] For one, the couple introduced 'furrow irrigation' (see Figure 6.3).

They were, however, careful to see to it that their suggestions never went beyond 'the means of the local planters'. They took great care that the new type of tobacco was embedded not only in the ecological environment in which the plants had to grow but also that it suited the economic and social-cultural environment in which the cultivators worked. Their experiments aimed at developing a variety that would make good cigarette tobacco, even if ground-cured, as was the tradition in Bihar and which was much more economical than flue-curing. After endless experimentation, the so-called Pusa type No. 28 was fabricated by crossing already 'domesticated' plants (Figure 6.4).

Figure 6.3 Furrow irrigation for tobacco as propagated by scientist Gabrielle Howard at the Imperial Institute of Agricultural Research[35]

Embedding cigarette tobacco in colonial Bihar 111

PLANTS OF THE F GENERATION OF THE CROSS TYPE 1 > TYPE 16

Figure 6.4 Cross-bred tobacco plants at Pusa.[36]

This tobacco had the right characteristics to make good cigarette fillings: light colour, fine texture and the necessary elasticity when cut; its flavour and aroma were said to have been fair.[37] The creation of this new tobacco variety had required the use of so-called Indian varieties instead of using 'imported varieties'. The Howards had found that 'the American varieties were not quick growers, an imperative necessity in Bihar where the tobacco must be planted and cut in a few months towards the end of the year'.

> Pusa 28 gives a heavy yield of produce when topped low in the country fashion, and has been taken up by the people for the local trade. When grown on a large scale under estate conditions it has also done exceedingly well, and there has been a demand for its seed not only in Bihar but in other parts of India.[38]

This variety proved popular among Indian cultivators and Albert wrote in his Report of 1912–1913 that the popularity of Type 28 was due to its suitability for widely different soils and climates.[39] In Bihar, the cultivators had been growing the new crop for the Indian Leaf Tobacco Development Company (ILTDC) and were demanding this seed in increasing quantities. Seed distribution had also been carried out by ILTDC through its Dalsingh Sarai Branch. The Howards now wanted to lower the cost of production of this crop. The Imperial Department was also eager to continue experimentation because even the Pusa type No.28 'could not be cured to a really bright colour' and it possessed 'a flavour which makes it unsuitable for use in any but the lowest grade of cigarettes'. This produce was popular among local consumers but it could not be exported to London markets. Experiments at Pusa, therefore, continued and in 1924 it was found that the 'Adcock leaf' did very well in Bihar, provided that certain relatively simple changes in cultivation methods were adopted:

> In Bihar, the prevalence of dust and hot, dry winds in the curing season, were predominant causes of failure in earlier attempts and damp east winds and relatively low temperature at that season were later found to prevent the curing of a good cigarette tobacco. In short, it was found that a good cigarette tobacco could not be cured there unless climatic conditions were under control. Therefore flue-curing was found to be essential for that class of tobacco.[40]

Indeed, during the early 1920s, Pusa experiments in flue-curing gave good results and a large number of flue-curing barns were profitably worked in North Bihar. An extra advantage was that:

> hybrids between the hardy and high-yielding Indian type of tobacco Pusa 28 and Adcock have now been fixed and tested, and that two of these (Pusa H. 142 and H. 177) have given a leaf, the colour of which when flue-cured is quite as good as 'Adcock' or 'Harrison's Special'.[41]

It was also calculated that:

> Including the costs of flue-curing, cigarette tobacco gave a higher profit to the farmer than would have been expected from a crop of country tobacco. On a commercial scale it has been found that a barn with nearly double the cubic capacity of that used in the Botanical Section at Pusa will be more profitable. This necessitates putting two furnaces and a double set of flues into the barn but the amount of leaf cured by this larger barn in course of a season is proportionally greater than the increase in the working expenses. Therefore the cost of curing per lb. of leaf is lowered. The size of the barn is important as the shortness of the curing season limits the amount of curing that can be carried out in a single season.[42]

Apart from proper seed and curing methods, the Howards had also looked into matters of seed supply to the actual tillers of the soil, and into questions of purchase of the crop they produced. The couple seems to have been quite optimistic regarding the future of cigarette tobacco cultivation in Bihar. In their co-authored book *The Development of Indian Agriculture* published in 1929, they wrote:

> With the recent change in fashion from the hookah to the cigarette, combined with the establishment of modern cigarette factories, a demand for a cheap cigarette tobacco has arisen in India. This has been met by the provision of a type known as Pusa 28, a rapid and robust grower which gives a high yield of leaf of good colour, texture and flavour when cured with the smallest

possible quantity of moisture in the country fashion. It is remarkable in its power of adoption to widely different conditions and has done well, not only in Bihar but also in Burma, the Central Provinces, Central India and the United Provinces [...]. With the recent reduction in the customs duties on Empire grown tobacco in Great Britain, the prospects of establishing an export trade in Indian leaf have materially improved. Provided the cultivator can obtain an immediate and adequate reward for increased quality, there seems no reason why this trade should not develop. Leaf with good flavour, texture and colour has undoubtedly been and can be produced in India.

But they cautioned:

The yield per acre however is likely to be less and the cost of production greater than is now the rule with the present coarse types. Moreover, better curing will involve more trouble and considerably more expense than the existing methods. The future therefore will depend on the satisfactory sale of produce off high quality, a problem which still remains to be solved in India. [43]

Even these problems seem to have been resolved because a close relationship had been established between the Indian Leaf Tobacco Development Company (ILTDC) in Tirhut, tobacco cultivators in Tirhut, and the Pusa Institute. The ILTDC, a wing of the Imperial or Peninsular Tobacco Company, purchased the new Pusa seeds from the research institute and distributed them among willing cultivators, providing them with advances to bear the extra costs that cigarette tobacco cultivation entailed. The ILTDC had also started re-drying and flue-curing facilities and, therefore, the permanent embedding of cigarette tobacco in Bihar seemed to be guaranteed.

The end of cigarette tobacco cultivation in Bihar

Owing to the presence of a cigarette factory of the Peninsular Tobacco Company at Munger in Bihar, a cheap type of cigarette could be manufactured by using re-dried tobacco leaf supplied by the ILTDC. This cheap type of cigarette had generated high demand within India – but not in London. The ILTDC was, therefore, eager to purchase the crops raised by *raiyats* (Indian cultivators) from the new seeds fabricated by the Howards at Pusa. There were risks involved in this kind of interdependency. The fortnightly review of the Imperial Department of Agriculture for the West Indies had already warned in 1915 that 'from an economic point of view' there were 'obvious drawbacks to the production of a high grade cigarette tobacco only' because 'the only customer in Bihar for this tobacco is the Peninsular Tobacco Co., as the local dealers do not require this product'. The advice was, apart from the improvement of cigarette tobacco, to pay attention to 'other varieties of tobacco', which was 'a consummation much to be desired'.[44] Likewise a 'Note on Indian Tobacco' cautioned:

The marketing of flue-cured tobacco in India is, however, subject to a very definite limitation. After curing and bulking is completed, it must be passed through large and expensive plants of 're-ordering and drying machines' few of which exist at present in India. Therefore, the sole market for flue-cured tobacco is with the commercial organizations which maintain such machines in India and, for this reason, agriculturists who wish to attempt the production of flue-cured cigarette tobacco, should come to an agreement, with the possible purchasers of their leaf before commencing operations.[45]

These warnings did not prove baseless. The biggest drawback was not so much that the only Bihar customer for the cultivators' cigarette tobacco was a commercial organization, but the fact that this organization was, as Howard Cox skilfully analysed, 'under the control of British rather than Indian capital' because the Government of India had been unable or unwilling to 'help mobilise local capital in the Indian cigarette factory' and local capital had not been forthcoming by itself, in Bihar at least.[46] This dependency of Indian tobacco cultivators on outside 'capital, skill/knowledge and manpower' proved disastrous for the final and permanent embedding of cigarette tobacco in Bihar.

Successful embedding of any plant, the Howards had argued, required an 'agro-ecological approach' in which the plant should remain in central focus. As 'agro-ecologists', the couple did not unanimously oppose new (western) technology or inputs in agriculture but instead assessed how, when and if, new seeds, methods of cultivation and/or curing could be used in conjunction with natural, social and human assets. They proposed a context- or site-specific manner of studying 'agro-ecosystems' and as such recognized that there were no universal formulae or recipes for success and maximum wellbeing of tobacco embedding anywhere in the world. In other words, successful embedding required research on the plant as 'a whole', for example, taking into consideration the ecological as well as socio-cultural and economic environment in which the plant grew. The Howards even came near to arguing that the agro-ecosystem should be studied through an interdisciplinary lens, that is, using natural sciences to understand elements of agro-ecosystems such as soil properties and plant and insect interactions, as well as using social sciences to understand the effects of agricultural practices on the *raiyats*, economic constraints to developing new production methods, or socio-cultural and even political factors that determined agricultural practices among the tobacco cultivators in Tirhut.

The Howards proved to be right: permanent embedding of the new cigarette tobacco plant in Bihari soil was a multi-dimensional task and ignorance of one or more dimensions would foretell the 'death' of the plant. In the case of cigarette tobacco in Bihar, the political embedding of the plant had been ignored. By the time this became evident, the Howards had already left Bihar. During the 1920s and 1930s, the ILTDC faced severe problems that resulted from the civil disobedience movement and, later, the non-cooperation movement, during which the *kisan* movement (peasant movement) gathered strength, demanding a better deal for the *raiyats* in Bihar. What is more, protests against cigarettes played a prominent role during the so-called *swadeshi* movement in vogue around the same time, which negatively influenced the profits of the cigarette factory in Munger. Finally, the ILTDC decided to leave Bihar and concentrate on Guntur in South India where its future looked brighter. Consequently, the demand for cigarette tobacco leaf in Bihar vanished and the *raiyats* gradually discontinued cultivating this tobacco variety because their sole purchaser had left the province. Cigarette tobacco supply decreased to such an extent that the factory in Munger had to purchase its leaf from Guntur instead. Ultimately, 'flue-cured Virginia tobacco' (FCV), exclusively used as fillers in cigarettes, proved a failure in Bihar.

Notes

1. However, Barbara Hahn argues that basically these tobacco varieties are not products of nature but of economic relations as well as continued and intense market regulation. Barbara Hahn. 'Making Tobacco Bright: Institutions, Information, and Industrialization in the Creation of an Agricultural Commodity, 1617–1937'. *Enterprise & Society* 8:4 (December 2007), 790–8.
2. Jordan Goodman. *Tobacco in History: The Cultures of Dependence* (London and New York: Routledge, 1993), 95.
3. Canakapalli Venkata Ram Rao. 'Significance of Tobacco on the Agricultural Economy of India' (Unpublished M.Sc. Thesis, University of Wisconsin, 1952), 2.
4. A notable exception is Howard Cox. *The Global Cigarette: Origins and Evolution of British American Tobacco, 1880–1945* (Oxford: Oxford University Press, 2000).
5. For a much more detailed analysis of this embedding process, see Kathinka Sinha-Kerkhoff. *Colonising Plants in Bihar (1760–1950): Tobacco betwixt Indigo and Sugarcane* (Delhi: Partridge, 2014).
6. 'The Tobacco Industry in India'. *Journal of the Society of Arts*, 22 (July 24, 1874), 790.
7. 'The Cultivation and Preparation of Tobacco in India'. *Journal of the Society of Arts* (July 14, 1871), 658–9.
8. Henry John Tozer. 'The Manufactures of Greater Britain – III. India'. *Journal of the Society of Arts*, (June 2, 1905), 772.
9. Henry John Tozer. 'The Growth and Trend of Indian Trade – A Forty Years' Survey'. *Journal of the Society of Arts*, 49 (March 29, 1901), 349.
10. *Memoirs of the Department of Agriculture in India, Botanical Series*, 3:4 (Calcutta: Thacker, Spink and Co., 1910), facing 218.
11. *The Cultivation and Curing of Tobacco in Bengal* (Calcutta: Bengal Secretariat Press, 1874), 5.
12. W.W. Hunter. *The Indian Empire: Its People, History and Products* (New Delhi and Madras: Asian Educational Services, 2005 [1886]), 499–500.
13. M. J. K. Thavaraj 'Framework of Economic Policies under British Rule'. *Social Scientist* 7:5 (December 1978), 26.
14. Stewart Richards. 'The South-Eastern Agricultural College and Public Support for Technical Education, 1894–1914'. *Agricultural History Review*, 36: II (1988), 172–87.
15. Peter Robb. 'Bihar, the Colonial State and Agricultural Development in India, 1880–1920'. *Indian Economic and Social History Review*, 25:2 (1988), 215.
16. Sir Bryce Burt. 'Agricultural Progress in India during the Decade 1929–1939'. *Journal of the Royal Society of Arts* (February 20, 1942), 205.
17. W.T. Thiselton-Dyer in *Nature*, quoted in R. M. MacLeod. 'Scientific Advice for British India: Imperial Perceptions and Administrative Goals, 1898–1923'. *Modern Asian Studies* 9:3 (1975), 364. Rothamsted is known in England as the oldest

agricultural research station in the world. It was established in 1843 and was the first institution to start long-term field experiments. By 1900, the need for statistical methods was felt, however, and today Rothamsted is also known as the birthplace of modern statistical theory and practice.
18. MacLeod. 'Scientific Advice for British India'. 364.
19. Gregory Barton. 'Sir Albert Howard and the Forestry Roots of the Organic Farming Movement'. *Agricultural History*, 75:2 (Spring 2001), 168–87.
20. For a biography of Albert Howard, see: Louise E. Howard. *Sir Albert Howard in India* (London: Faber and Faber Ltd., 1953).
21. Sir Albert Howard. *The Soil and Health: A Study of Organic Agriculture*. With a new introduction by Wendell Berry (Kentucky: University Press of Kentucky, 2006), 2.
22. E.H. Johnson. 'Review of Crop-Production in India by Albert Howard'. *Economic Geography* 1:2 (July 1925), 266.
23. Thomas F. Gieryn. *Cultural Boundaries of Science: Credibility on the Line* (Chicago and London: The University of Chicago Press, 1999), 236.
24. Howard, *Soil and Health*, 3.
25. Gieryn. *Cultural Boundaries*, 255.
26. 'Mrs. Albert Howard'. *Nature* (September 20, 1930), 445.
27. Marilyn Bailey Ogilvie. 'Obligatory Amateurs: Annie Maunder (1868–1947) and Women Astronomers at the Dawn of Professional Astronomy'. *The British Journal for the History of Science*, 33:1 (March, 2000), 67–84.
28. Heide Inhetveen. 'Women Pioneers in Farming: A Gendered History of Agricultural Progress'. *Sociologia Ruralis*, 38:3 (1998), 265–84.
29. Mark Keating. 'History of Organic Agriculture Series – Part 1'. *Organic Agriculture: Its Origins, and its Evolution over Time*. http://cookingupastory.com/organic-agriculture-its-origins-and-evolution-over-time. Accessed 17 November 2011.
30. 'Mrs. Albert Howard', 445. Most likely, the author was Mr. H. Martin-Leake, Sc.D., formerly Director of Agriculture, United Provinces, who also worked in Bihar for some time and was a close friend of the couple.
31. Howard. *Sir Albert Howard in India*, 21.
32. A detailed discussion of the couple's labour carried out during those twenty years can be found in Albert Howard and Gabrielle. L. C Howard. *The Development of Indian Agriculture: India of Today, Vol.VIII* (London: Humphrey Milford/Oxford University Press, 1929). See also: Albert Howard. *Crop-production in India: A Critical Survey of its Problems* (London: Oxford University Press, 1924).
33. Howard, *Sir Albert Howard in India*, 22.
34. For example, Albert Howard, and Gabrielle L. C. Howard. 'The Improvement of Tobacco Cultivation in Bihar'. *Pusa Bulletin*, 50 (1915), IV–20; Albert Howard. 'The Improvement of Crop Production in India'. *Journal of the Royal Society of Arts*, 68:3530 (1920), 555–64; and Gabrielle L. C. Howard and Kashi Ram. 'Studies in Indian Tobaccos. No. 4. Parthenocarpy and Parthenogenesis in Two Varieties of Nicotiana tabacum L. – var. Cuba and var. Mirodato; & No. 5. The Inheritance of Characters in Nicotiana rustica L'. In *Memoirs of the Department of Agriculture in India, Botanical Series, Agricultural Research Institute, Pusa*, 13:1 (Calcutta: Spink and Co., 1924).
35. A. Howard and G.L.C. Howard. *Studies in Indian Tobaccos: No. 1. The Types of Nicotiana rustica, L. Yellow Flowered Tobacco. Memoirs of the Department of Agriculture in India. Botanical Series*, 3:1 (Calcutta: Thacker, Spink & Co, 1910), Plate I.
36. F_3 generation of cross type 1 ´ type 16. Illustration in Howard and Ram. 'Studies in Indian Tobaccos', n.p.
37. This fabrication process can be followed through a review of the *Reports of the Agricultural Research Institute and College, Pusa* (Calcutta: Superintendent Government Printing) for the period between 1907 and 1929.
38. 'Note on Indian Tobacco Prepared by the Agricultural Expert to the Imperial Council of Agricultural Research, India' (n.p.: n.d.), 12–6.

39 *Report of the Agricultural Research Institute and College, Pusa* (Calcutta: Superintendent Government Printing, 1912–13, 1914), 34.
40 *Scientific Report of the Agricultural Research Institute, Pusa (1924–1925), Including the Reports of the Imperial Dairy Expert, Physiological Chemist, Government Sugar Expert and Secretary Sugar Bureau* (Calcutta: Government of India 1925), 3.
41 F. J. F. Shaw and Kashi Ram. 'Production of Cigarette Tobacco by Flue-curing'. *Pusa Bulletin,* 187 (1928), 187.
42 Shaw and Ram. 'Production of Cigarette Tobacco', 187.
43 Howard and Howard. *The Development of Indian Agriculture*, 42–3.
44 'Note on Indian Tobacco', 251.
45 'Note on Indian Tobacco', 15.
46 Howard Cox. 'International Business, the State and Industrialization in India: Early Growth in the Indian Cigarette Industry, 1900–19'. *Indian Economic and Social History Review*, 27:3 (1990), 312.

References

Barton, Gregory. 'Sir Albert Howard and the Forestry Roots of the Organic Farming Movement' *Agricultural History*, 75:2 (Spring 2001), 168–87.
Burt, Bryce. 'Agricultural Progress in India during the Decade 1929–1939' *Journal of the Royal Society of Arts* (February 20, 1942), 202–23.
Cox, Howard. *The Global Cigarette: Origins and Evolution of British American Tobacco, 1880–1945* (Oxford: Oxford University Press, 2000).
Cox, Howard. 'International Business, the State and Industrialization in India: Early Growth in the Indian Cigarette Industry, 1900–19' *Indian Economic and Social History Review*, 27:3 (1990), 289–312.
Gieryn, Thomas F. *Cultural Boundaries of Science: Credibility on the Line* (Chicago. IL: The University of Chicago Press, 1999).
Goodman, Jordan. *Tobacco in History: The Cultures of Dependence* (London and New York: Routledge, 1993).
Hahn, Barbara. 'Making Tobacco Bright: Institutions, Information, and Industrialization in the Creation of an Agricultural Commodity, 1617–1937' *Enterprise & Society* 8:4 (December 2007), 790–8.
Howard, Albert. 'The Improvement of Crop Production in India'. *Journal of the Royal Society of Arts*, 68:3530 (1920), 555–64.
Howard, Albert. *Crop-production in India: A Critical Survey of its Problems* (London: Oxford University Press, 1924).
Howard, Albert. *The Soil and Health: A Study of Organic Agriculture.* With a new introduction by Wendell Berry (Kentucky: University Press of Kentucky, 2006).
Howard, Albert, and Gabrielle L. C. Howard. *Studies in Indian Tobaccos: No. 1. The Types of Nicotiana rustica, L. Yellow Flowered Tobacco. Memoirs of the Department of Agriculture in India. Botanical Series*, 3:1 (Calcutta: Thacker, Spink & Co, 1910).
Howard, Albert, and Gabrielle L. C. Howard. 'The Improvement of Tobacco Cultivation in Bihar'. *Pusa Bulletin*, 50 (1915), IV–20.
Howard, Albert, and Gabrielle L. C. Howard. *The Development of Indian Agriculture: India of Today, Vol.VIII* (London: Humphrey Milford/Oxford University Press, 1929).
Howard, Gabrielle L. C., and Kashi Ram. 'Studies in Indian Tobaccos. No. 4. Parthenocarpy and Parthenogenesis in Two Varieties of *Nicotiana tabacum* L. – var. Cuba and var. Mirodato; & No. 5. The Inheritance of Characters in *Nicotiana rustica* L.' In *Memoirs of the Department of Agriculture in India, Botanical Series*, 13:1 (Calcutta: Thacker, Spink and Co., 1924).

Howard, Louise E. *Sir Albert Howard in India* (London: Faber and Faber Ltd., 1953).
Hunter, W.W. *The Indian Empire: Its People, History and Products* (New Delhi and Madras: Asian Educational Services, 2005 [1886]).
Inhetveen, Heide. 'Women Pioneers in Farming: A Gendered History of Agricultural Progress' *Sociologia Ruralis*, 38:3 (1998), 265–84.
Johnson, E.H. 'Review of Crop-Production in India by Albert Howard' *Economic Geography*, 1:2 (July 1925), 266.
Journal of the Royal Society of Arts, 'The Tobacco Industry in India', 22 (July 24, 1873), 790.
Keating, Mark. 'History of Organic Agriculture Series – Part 1' *Organic Agriculture: Its Origins, and its Evolution over Time*. (2009) http://cookingupastory.com/organic-agriculture-its-origins-and-evolution-over-time. Accessed 17 November 2011.
MacLeod, R.M. 'Scientific Advice for British India: Imperial Perceptions and Administrative Goals, 1898–1923', *Modern Asian Studies* 9:3 (1975), 343–84.
Memoirs of the Department of Agriculture in India, Botanical Series, 3:4 (Calcutta: Thacker, Spink and Co., 1910).
Nature 'Mrs. Albert Howard'. (September 20, 1930), 445–6.
'Note on Indian Tobacco Prepared by the Agricultural Expert to the Imperial Council of Agricultural Research, India' (n.p.: n.d.).
Ogilvie, Marilyn Bailey. 'Obligatory Amateurs: Annie Maunder (1868–1947) and Women Astronomers at the Dawn of Professional Astronomy'. *The British Journal for the History of Science*, 33:1 (March, 2000), 67–84.
Rao, Canakapalli Venkata Ram. 'Significance of Tobacco on the Agricultural Economy of India' (Unpublished M.Sc. Thesis, University of Wisconsin, 1952).
Reports of the Agricultural Research Institute and College, Pusa (Calcutta: Superintendent Government Printing, 1907–1929).
Richards, Stewart. 'The South-Eastern Agricultural College and Public Support for Technical Education, 1894–1914'. *Agricultural History Review*, 36: II (1988), 172–87.
Robb, Peter. 'Bihar, the Colonial State and Agricultural Development in India, 1880–1920'. *Indian Economic and Social History Review*, 25:2 (1988), 205–35.
Scientific Report of the Agricultural Research Institute, Pusa (1924–1925), Including the Reports of the Imperial Dairy Expert, Physiological Chemist, Government Sugar Expert and Secretary Sugar Bureau (Calcutta: Government of India 1925).
Shaw, F. J. F., and Kashi Ram. 'Production of Cigarette Tobacco by Flue-curing'. *Pusa Bulletin*, 187 (1928), 187.
Sinha-Kerkhoff, Kathinka. *Colonising Plants in Bihar (1760–1950). Tobacco Betwixt Indigo and Sugarcane* (New Delhi: Partridge, 2014).
Thavaraj, M. J. K. 'Framework of Economic Policies under British Rule'. *Social Scientist* 7:5 (December 1978), 13–44.
The Cultivation and Curing of Tobacco in Bengal (Calcutta: Bengal Secretariat Press, 1874).
Tozer, Henry John. 'The Growth and Trend of Indian Trade – A Forty Years' Survey'. *Journal of the Society of Arts*, 49 (March 29, 1901), 333–54.
Tozer, Henry John. 'The Manufactures of Greater Britain – III. India'. *Journal of the Society of Arts*, (June 2, 1905), 752–80.
Watson, F. 'The Cultivation and Preparation of Tobacco in India'. *Journal of the Society of Arts* (July 14, 1871), 658–9.

7 Cuba, sugarcane and the reluctant embedding of scientific method
Agete's *La Caña de Azúcar en Cuba*

Jonathan Curry-Machado

This chapter uses as its main source Fernando Agete's *La Caña de Azúcar en Cuba* (*Sugarcane in Cuba*) – an expansive, two-volume report into the state of sugarcane farming in Cuba and its short fallings, in the mid-twentieth century.[1] A report on this scale was unprecedented in Cuban history, and what it reveals is not only the well-known dominance of sugarcane within the island's agricultural economy but importantly the ongoing difficulty in persuading the island's cane farmers to adopt more rational, scientific methods in their farming practice.

Based upon a fairly exhaustive survey of Cuba's sugar plantations, and commissioned by the Cuban Ministry of Agriculture, Agete's report provides an extraordinary wealth of material detailing the state of Cuban cane agriculture in the early 1940s. It was written with contemporary local concerns in mind, and perhaps because of this, the result was a text of significant value to historians – though one which has received limited circulation, originally published in Spanish and aimed specifically at a national audience of cane cultivators and sugar producers. The scope of the report is so comprehensive that it appears to leave out no grain of detail. Extensive tables provide full information about the sugar factories operating in the island in the first half of the twentieth century, the quantities of each variety of cane these grew, the comparison between provinces and over the years, the productivity of different soils and cane types, and even climatological information. Every variety of sugarcane employed in Cuba (even if in insignificant amounts) is described fully, with its origins and detailed diagrams, along with cultivation and production data gathered from farmers and factories. Maps show the location of central sugar factories, and the genealogy of the cane varieties is explained. The report includes a full description and assessment of the island's soils, and their suitability for agricultural uses (as well as their misuse by planters); and every aspect of cane farming – from land preparation to harvesting, including machinery and animals employed – is discussed in full, with regional variations described and critiqued. Finally, the report examines the illnesses and pests to which sugarcane in Cuba fell victim, and concludes with a brief exposition of the fabrication of the sugar itself (although the industrial aspect is really outside the text's remit); while amply illustrating all the sections with photographs taken in the Cuban field.

As with any text, it is the product of its historical moment, and the context in which it was written. For this reason, it offers many insights into the concerns that were around regarding the scientific backwardness of Cuba's agriculture, and the longer-term implications that this was likely to have. At many points within the report, Agete makes reference to the difficulty of persuading most Cuban agriculturalists to adopt more rational approaches, and he indicates the effect that this was clearly having on the future sustainability, and diversity, of the island's farming. It is also a rich source of descriptive material relating to how farmers prepared their land and cultivated their crops – showing how this varied from region to region. This is an aspect that often remains invisible from the historical record, so it is of immense value to the historian to have, in a single publication, so much material to draw on.

However, Agete's report did not emerge in isolation. The early years of the twentieth century saw an increasing concern in Cuba to systematically describe and quantify the island's agriculture. From 1906, the Secretariat of Agriculture, Industry and Commerce (*Secretaría de Agricultura, Industria y Comercio*) began to publish a monthly Official Bulletin (*Boletín Oficial*), which collated reports on a wide variety of farming concerns, along with extensive data. This contributed to the development of an island-wide network of experts and informants, which ultimately would provide the infrastructure that enabled Agete to produce his study. This was furthered in 1940 when the *Secretaría* became the Ministry of Agriculture. The publication of the *Boletines* coincided with the establishment in 1905 of the International Institute of Agriculture (IIA) in Rome, which sought to collect agricultural statistics and data about scientific developments in farming as well as agricultural pathogens from around the world. This led to the first world agricultural census being published in 1930. With Cuba very much under the political and economic tutelage of the United States in this period – and the latter at the forefront of the collation and publication of agricultural data – it is not surprising that a similar concern developed in the island, particularly as this built on an indigenous history dating from the late-eighteenth century of promoting the study and development of the island's agricultural economy. Agete's report was itself published in the immediate aftermath of the IIA's conversion into the United Nation's Food and Agriculture Organisation.

As Director of Cuba's Experimental Sugarcane Station (*Estación Experimental de la Caña de Azúcar*), at a time when Cuba's once pre-eminent sugar industry and trade was suffering the impact of global competition, Agete was better placed than most to appreciate the dangers faced by the island's sugar sector should it fail to adapt. His familiarity with developments elsewhere in the world, as well as the access to plantations and mills that his employment by the Cuban government provided him, gave him an overarching perspective that was very different to the somewhat short-sighted views of many Cuban sugar planters. However, his report – although surpassing other sources for the period in the amount of data – remains limited by the somewhat varied response from the island's sugar producers to his survey. While most seem to have been happy to provide information regarding the cane varieties employed, a number ignored

Agete's requests resulting in notable gaps in the figures, and only a rather more limited number provided more expansive detail concerning soils and methods. Agete's own background as an agronomist also meant that most of his attention was devoted to the agricultural side of the industry, with only a somewhat cursory look given to the manufacturing aspects. There is also no indication to what extent the data provided is limited to that relating to lands planted under the direct control of the sugar factories. At this time a lot of the island's cane was grown on independent or semi-independent farms, to then be sold to the mills. With Agete's survey targeting the mills rather than the multitude of cane farmers, it is possible that much of this cane is missing from his figures.

While this affects the accuracy of any statistical or geographical analysis, nevertheless Agete's report is a very interesting source. Not only does it illustrate just how embedded certain varieties of sugarcane were in Cuba, it also shows the slow process by which newer varieties were introduced. In this chapter, 'reluctant embedding', not just of improved cane but also of a more scientific approach to its cultivation, is explored.

Cuban cane

Although sugarcane had been cultivated in Cuba since shortly after the island's conquest by the Spanish in the early sixteenth century, the spread of sugar plantations was rather slow – with farmers showing a preference for tobacco and coffee, and with many parts of what continued to be a rather sparsely populated island given over to livestock, or exploitation of the extensive and officially protected forests.[2] However, when revolution in the neighbouring French colony of Saint-Domingue (Haiti), at the end of the eighteenth century, removed from the world market the most important sugar producer of the period, Cuban planters were perfectly placed to take advantage of the opportunity, and did so with alacrity.[3] Not only did sugar plantations begin to extend the area cultivated with cane, but the island's mills introduced the latest developments in steam-powered machinery, such that by the mid-nineteenth century Cuba's sugar industry had become the world's most advanced.[4]

Sugar had for many centuries been traded internationally as a luxury commodity, but by the mid-nineteenth century its consumption had become popularized, and an important source of energy for growing urban and industrial populations, thereby resulting in a massive expansion of world demand.[5] From the seventeenth century, the Caribbean had been at the centre of global sugar production; but since sugarcane is a crop that, if proper care is not taken, results in rapid soil exhaustion, it was cultivated on an ever-shifting frontier. The extensive tracts of unexploited fertile land (with expansive forests for fuel) available in Cuba appeared, in the nineteenth century, to offer the prospect of limitless expansion. With world sugar prices high, those who established sugar mills could make considerable profits, and as a result, sugar came to dominate both the island's agriculture and its export economy. It also resulted in Cuba becoming the world's most important producer of cane sugar, with 42 per cent of global sales by 1870,[6] a position that it still held in the 1920s – though from then on it found itself becoming overtaken by other producers.[7]

During the first period of expansion of the Cuban sugar industry in the nineteenth century, plantations and mills were vertically integrated businesses. That is, they consisted of a sugar factory surrounded by cane fields, under single ownership and control.[8] However, increasing costs and debts – accentuated by the island's wars of independence (1868–78, 1878–79 and 1895–8) – as well as the ever present problem of labour shortage compounded by the eventual abolition of slavery (1886), prompted a radical change in the production system. Sugar processing and cane cultivation became separated, with a reduced number of mills taking on the role of central sugar factories (*centrales*), purchasing an expanded quantity of cane from dedicated cane farms (*colonias*). This 'central' system became the basis for the ongoing expansion of the Cuban sugar industry into the twentieth century – as well as its spread to other places, such as Puerto Rico and the Dominican Republic.[9] While by 1862 the number of sugar mills in the island had reached 1,473,[10] there were fewer than 200 left by the time of Agete's report. Nevertheless, total annual Cuban sugar production surpassed the five-million-tonnes mark in 1925, ten-times higher than its level in the 1860s.[11]

Ignoring Reynoso

Agete's report needs to be seen in relationship to another text, written some 80 years earlier and dealing with the same concerns for embedding scientific method into the cultivation of sugarcane. In 1862, the Cuban chemist and agronomist, Álvaro Reynoso, published his *Essay on the Growing of Sugarcane*.[12] Quickly translated into the languages of other sugarcane-growing countries, this became one of the most influential texts in the development of a more scientifically rational, and agriculturally efficient, approach to farming a crop whose produce had become the world's most important traded food commodity. In his text, Reynoso detailed every aspect of the process of preparing the land and cultivating it, recommending a move away from the rapidly land-exhausting techniques generally employed in Cuban sugarcane farming. He argued for the intelligent use of appropriate fertilizers and irrigation as a means of improving yields, while at the same time ensuring future agricultural sustainability.

Reynoso's *Essay* was written at a time when sugar was increasingly dominating Cuba's land and economy, and there were already danger signs looming. Rapid soil exhaustion led to sugar planters having to look to the exploitation of virgin lands to maintain yields, and the generalized deforestation of the island was already well under way. But 'economic rationality…trumped agricultural rationality',[13] and Reynoso's ideas were on the whole ignored. Cuban planters tended to argue that his proposal was too complicated, utilizing too much labour in an island that suffered from chronic labour shortage. There was a feeling that so long as there was plenty of underexploited land available, Cuba's sugar industry would be secure, without any need to waste time and resources, or even thought, for the adoption of a sounder scientific approach. Thus even while the island's sugar industry adopted the most advanced milling and processing technology available, putting great effort into ensuring the quality and quantity of the end product, improvements in the cultivation of the raw material came only slowly – and often reluctantly.

For this reason, Reynoso's *Essay* proved considerably more influential on the other side of the world, in Java – where the sugar industry was also rising, by the late-nineteenth century becoming second only to that of Cuba (and even surpassing it when the independence war brought a sharp, albeit temporary, drop in Cuban production).[14] A Dutch translation of the *Essay* was published in 1865; and in Java, Reynoso's various methods were employed to great effect, in the successful attempt to raise land yields. In fact, Java became a leading centre for the development of, and application of agricultural science to, sugarcane farming, with the Dutch colonists bringing with them a familiarity with, and sensitivity to, scientific practice quite divergent from that of the Spanish in Cuba. This was seen not only in the maximizing of soil productivity – on an island where land scarcity was of greater concern than labour scarcity – but also in the development of cane varieties, irrigation, fertilization and the treatment of crop pests.[15] It was partly awareness of the success that Reynoso's ideas had in Java and elsewhere, and their limited application in Cuba, that prompted Agete to try to push Cuba's recalcitrant sugar industry in a more scientific direction.

However, while there may have been issues around the embedding of sugarcane cultivation in Javanese rural society – with its well-established populations, and food-based agricultural systems[16] – lightly populated Cuba had no such problems. Cane farming seemed to spread inexorably down the island, and there seemed to be little challenge to sugar's dominance of the island's farming, industry and economy. By 1920, 92 per cent of Cuba's export earnings originated in sugarcane;[17] by 1926, 12 per cent of the island's total land surface was planted to cane (although less than two-thirds of this was actually harvested);[18] and as Figure 7.1 (collated from data provided by Agete's report) shows, in 1940 although sugar production on the island was already in

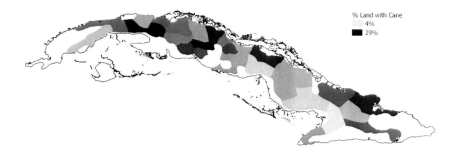

Figure 7.1 Concentration of cane cultivation in Cuba, 1943 (proportion of land planted to cane)[19]

decline, cane was being cultivated down the entire length of the island. In some districts, more than a quarter of all land was sown to this one crop. When the large amounts of exhausted land caused by earlier cane plantings are taken into consideration, along with land that was not suitable for agriculture, there can be little doubting the epigram that 'without sugar there is no country.'

Of course there had been challenges to this: the persistence of slavery into the 1880s as the prime means of providing labour for Cuba's sugar plantations generated considerable social tensions and fragility; the establishment of extensive sugar latifundia in the early twentieth century in the East of the island, often under the control of US corporations, entailed the appropriation of much land from peasant farmers;[20] and throughout the history of the rise of the Cuban sugar industry, voices had warned of the dangers of allowing untrammelled advance of this one crop at the expense of a more diverse and sustainable approach to the island's agriculture.

It was this latter concern that really defined the intellectual context both of Reynoso's essay and Agete's report. During the nineteenth century, and into the twentieth, many prominent commentators – above all those with some scientific knowledge and training – sought to temper the apparently unbridled spread of the sugar industry, suggesting an alternative vision to that of cane monoculture with all its attendant problems. This project of '*Cuba pequeña*' ('Little Cuba') perceived the possibility of the island's agriculture developing on the foundations of a strong smallholding peasantry, with commercial farming (whether of sugarcane, tobacco, coffee, or a potential range of other crops) combined with the diversified and plentiful cultivation of food crops and rearing of livestock. Far from being driven by a romantic belief in an idyllic agrarian society (though certainly such comparisons with the brutal environmental and social impact of the sugar-plantation economy were by no means lacking), this was based on sound scientific principles and an awareness that only through the application of experimentally proven methods would the island's agriculture (and the rural society that depended upon this) prove ultimately sustainable.[21]

But what attempts there were to limit cane's domination of the island did not prevent Cuba from becoming the world's single most important producer of sugar and maintaining this position into the 1930s. So buoyant did Cuba's sugar industry appear that, despite growing warnings, most planters continued to trust the natural benefits of virgin lands, fertile soil and climate.

By the 1930s, though, warning signs abounded that this unthinking approach was jeopardizing the island's leading position. The reduction in Cuba's share of the world sugar market obligated a restriction in production. But the extensive approach to land use on the cane plantations, coupled with the reluctance to relinquish what had been such a potentially wealth-generating crop for so long, limited the possibility of switching to alternative crops and land uses. While the island really needed a trimmer, more efficient sugarcane sector as part of a more diversified agricultural plan, the continuation of the old practices and the resistance to the adoption of more scientific methods (which were being successfully employed by Cuba's leading competitors, such as Java or Hawaii) prevented this from occurring. Thus, three-quarters of a century after Reynoso wrote his famous essay his prescripts were still worryingly ignored in the land of his birth, and it was this that prompted Agete's survey and report.

The report was primarily written as a resource for all those involved in Cuba's sugar industry – from field to factory – but above all those involved in the large-scale cultivation of sugarcane that so dominated the Cuban landscape, and which had done so much to limit the diversity (and, it was increasingly feared, the sustainability) of the island's agriculture. Not only does it inform, but also indicates ways in which farming could be improved – showing not only what the state-of-the-art was and suggesting this as best practice, but also the areas that would greatly benefit from the adoption of experience-based reforms, employing rational, scientific methods rather than basing decisions upon commercial expediency and short-term profits (as had been too often the case in the Cuban sugar industry).

However, what cane farmers were being asked to do was to give up their decades-long favouring of short-term economic advantage, in order to pursue a strategy the benefits of which might only be felt in the long term. Although some key plantations were quick to see the importance of such arguments and led the way in the use of scientific experimentation and application, most only did so as it became evident that they were facing declining profits and reduced competitiveness. It is this 'reluctant embedding' that this chapter explores, through the various examples revealed by Agete's report: first, in the transferring and establishment of new cane varieties (often in response to the epidemics of pests and diseases that themselves spread globally and became embedded); second, in the slow development of specifically Cuban cane hybrids, adapted more closely to local conditions; and third, in the adoption of scientific approaches at all stages of cane farming. It is above all in this that the need to rationalize cane cultivation in order to make possible a diversification of Cuba's agriculture (the vision of '*Cuba pequeña*') can be seen.

Transferring varieties

The first main section of Agete's report concentrates, with expansive detail, on the range of cane varieties used in Cuba's sugar industry. Amidst all the data, what is of particular importance is what this shows of the process, and progress, of embedding new varieties of cane; and of how successive generations of cane hybrids became adopted as a result of the embedding of cane pathogens (pests and diseases) that accompanied the global spread of new varieties.

From the advent of cane cultivation in Cuba in the sixteenth century, through to the end of the eighteenth, a single variety of cane, which eventually became known as Creole due to its local ubiquity, predominated. While this had taken readily to conditions on the island, and had proved to be both relatively free from pests and diseases and easy to process in the primitive mills of the period, its low yields limited its usefulness when the Cuban sugar industry took off from the late-eighteenth century, and planters needed to boost their production.

From the 1790s, the higher yielding Otaheite variety – obtained from the Pacific islands and already planted in several other sugar colonies – quickly replaced the Creole as the cane of choice on the more commercially-oriented Cuban estates.[22] It spread through the island as the cane fields gradually extended eastwards from Havana and was accompanied by the development of new sugar-milling and processing technologies during the early to mid-nineteenth century, bringing Cuba to global sugar pre-eminence.[23]

By the mid-nineteenth century, Otaheite was the dominant variety throughout the world. However, this contributed to it becoming vulnerable to the 'global exchange of sugar pathogens' that resulted from the combination of extensive monoculture, the global transfer of plant specimens and improved transport links. In effect its success had become its downfall: with the tendency towards large-scale monoculture, based upon this single variety, making crops increasingly susceptible to pests and diseases.[24] Improved global transportation and the accelerating transfer of plant specimens around the planet further facilitated this.[25] Otaheite crops became infected with disease, and as elsewhere, this made it necessary in Cuba to adopt other varieties. Although it was not until after 1885 that experimentation began in a systematic way, by the mid-nineteenth century Java had already become prominent in the global transfer of new cane varieties. Cinta (or Batavian) cane became established on a small scale in particular in Eastern Cuba, though not as a commercial crop; likewise, Javanese Black Cheribon (known as 'Morada' in Cuba) was present from as early as the 1820s, but although it continued to be found into the twentieth century this was generally as a border crop to protect cane fields from livestock. In the late 1850s, cane was imported into Mauritius from Java as possible replacements for the ailing Otaheite. Amongst these were some samples of a variety known as White Priangan.[26] Having encountered rapid success in Mauritius, it found its way to the Caribbean. Although some sources, including Agete, claim that samples reached Cuba as early as 1796 or 1820, it would be from the 1860s that it became widely adopted in Cuba as a replacement for Otaheite, under the name of 'Cristalina'.

Despite the problems with Otaheite, Cuban planters were already demonstrating the tendency to resist change that would characterize the island's cane agriculture into the twentieth century. In part, they were able to be conservative since there was still such a quantity of unexploited land available. As yields declined, both due to soil exhaustion and crop diseases, plantations could move to virgin soils with high fertility, thereby masking this effect. However, Cristalina was not just resistant to the epidemic affecting Otaheite. It also proved to grow well in exhausted soils, was relatively easy to cultivate, drought-resistant, and responded well to the 'ratooning' methods (whereby the lower part of the cane was left in the ground upon harvest and allowed to grow again for further seasons) favoured in Cuba over labour-intensive replantings.[27] As a result, by 1880 Cristalina had become the island's primary variety; and as Agete's report demonstrates, this was a dominance it maintained well into the twentieth century. In 1916, 127 out of 177 Cuban sugar estates were growing nothing other than Cristalina, 48 combining it with other varieties, and just two persisting with Otaheite.[28] In the 1920s, the Puerto Rican Commissioner of Agriculture and Labor commented, following a visit to investigate Cuba's sugar industry, that 'the Cristalina seemed to be the universal and only variety known';[29] and as Agete's report shows, this overwhelming dominance continued into the early 1930s, representing more than 89 per cent of cane grown in Cuba.

But there was now another cane pathogen that had taken on pandemic proportions in the global sugar industry: the mosaic virus. This seems to have originated in Java and quickly spread from there around the world accompanying the many Javanese cane varieties that were being circulated. It seems to have entered the Americas through Argentina, eventually reaching the Caribbean, to devastating effect in Puerto Rico in 1917.[30] This obliged Puerto Rican planters to actively seek canes resistant to the disease; and from the mid-1920s, the Experimental Stations at Río Piedras and Mayagüez, along with the Fajardo and Aguirre sugar factories, carried out experiments to obtain a locally successful variety through hybridization. Known as 'Mayagüez', a number of these were introduced into Cuba after 1930, though only one of these (MPR 28) was cultivated in any great quantity, and then only for a couple of sugar factories. Mosaic also reached Cuba by 1915, and by the 1920s it had become generalized throughout the island's plantations. However, Cuba's crops did not appear to be anywhere near as affected by it as those of Puerto Rico, and planters believed that their Cristalina cane was mosaic-resistant, with any drop in yield due to problems of soil exhaustion and the need for better irrigation rather than a disease that would force them to change their long-established crops.[31] As with the earlier reluctance to replace Otaheite, the process of accepting the need for new varieties to replace Cristalina was slow to spread. Even in 1946, when Cristalina's national share had been reduced to just a quarter of all cane, Fernando Agete was able to write that:

> it is so linked to our sugar industry, so rooted amongst us, that it continues to be very hard for our landowners and sugar farmers to grow accustomed to the idea of doing without it, others continue cultivating it, even if as just part of their crops, and many hope that it will make a come back in its own right, with its well earned fame for magnificent variety.[32]

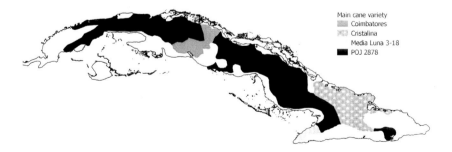

Figure 7.2 Main sugarcane varieties used, 1943[33]

Cristalina's share had reduced dramatically as it became indisputable that Cuba's sugar industry was suffering from mosaic, and it was conceded that new cane varieties were needed. Samples from other key sugarcane-growing areas were introduced, in particular through the Experimental Station at Santiago de las Vegas, and a few key sugar factories. From these centres, particularly promising varieties spread elsewhere, with a small number taking on commercial significance as an alternative to Cristalina.

The data provided by Agete enable us to identify the main sugarcane varieties used in each sugarcane-cultivating district (see Figure 7.2). By the 1940s, all sugar factories in the West had abandoned Cristalina as their main crop, and only in the East of the island did this once ubiquitous variety continue to dominate, where the largest of the island's sugar factories controlled vast swathes of virgin land and the natural fertility of the soil (not yet exhausted by over-cultivation) countered any reduction in yields that mosaic might have brought.

In the centre of the island, there was widespread acceptance of cane varieties originating in the Indian experimental station at Coimbatore. Developed to be particularly strong in soil and climate conditions adverse to other varieties, these spread through the cane lands where the soils were rather rocky and dry, and Cristalina and other popular varieties proved difficult to cultivate. Coimbatores could also be found in small quantities elsewhere in the island, on land that was otherwise not suitable for cane, and two varieties in particular (Co 213 and Co 281) became the third and fourth most cultivated canes in Cuba by the 1940s. However, Agete's data shows that most of this was in a crescent of cane-cultivating lands arcing through the centre of the island.

While the global transfer of cane varieties from Java had spread pathogens such as mosaic, the disease itself helped stimulate the continuing experimentation with hybridization in Java, in the search for strains that would prove to be not only high-yielding, but also resistant to this, and other diseases and pests. In 1887, the Pasuruan Experimental Station was established in East Java (POJ), and a programme of cane hybridization began. Over the coming decades, an increasing amount of money was invested in this endeavour;[34] and by the 1920s, numerous commercially viable varieties had been developed and spread around the cane-growing world, including Cuba. The first recorded arrival of a POJ variety in Cuba came in 1917 (POJ 36), and many others followed it in the following years. However, despite their increasingly wide adoption in other sugar-producing countries, the deep-seated resistance to agricultural change amongst Cuba's planters meant that by 1931 only 3 per cent of Cuba's cane was POJ. This was in stark contrast to Cuban eagerness to introduce new technology into sugar processing, with the island leading the world on the manufacturing side of the sugar industry since the mid-nineteenth century. Unlike in Java, there was a tendency to avoid investment in agricultural improvements, preferring short-term economic expediency over possible long-term advantages. But the organization of the Cuban sugar industry also slowed the introduction of new varieties. From around the 1880s, sugar manufacture had become concentrated in a reduced number of large sugar factories, with the cultivation of cane separated and handled by cane farms (*colonias*). Although in many respects the factories held either direct or indirect control over these farms, the system was based upon contracts between the central factory and the cane farmers (*colonos*). These established a fixed amount of refined sugar per weight of raw cane, and payment was based on this calculation. Since the formula had been worked out for expected yields of Cristalina, a change to a new, untried variety tended to generate suspicion on both sides: any difference in expected yield would benefit one to the detriment of the other. By the 1920s, this was just one aspect of the increasingly difficult relationship between *colonos* and sugar factories.[35]

Nevertheless, the need to change became increasingly necessary as mosaic along with other factors brought ever decreasing yields through the 1920s and into the 1930s in many sugar-growing areas. At the same time, other countries were threatening to displace Cuba from its decades-long predominance. One of the POJ varieties became particularly important in this, representing a global shift on a par with Otaheite and Cristalina before. In 1921, the mosaic-resistant and high-yielding POJ 2878 resulted from a providential hybridization and following extensive testing in Java it was put to commercial use in 1926. Along with a number of closely related POJ hybrids, it was extraordinarily successful, and within four years, nine-tenths of Java's cane fields were under it. While still being tested, samples were taken elsewhere, including Louisiana and the Caribbean, where it was readily adopted. Agete's report shows how in Cuba, POJ 2878 displaced Cristalina in most cane-growing areas during the 1930s. By 1938, a majority of Cuba's sugar came from POJ varieties, and this had reached 63 per cent by 1943. While sample crops of a wide range of POJs could be found around the island, it was POJ 2878 that clearly dominated. The first samples had been sent to the Experimental Stations at Santiago de las Vegas and Central Baraguá, and from these two sites spread all over the island. By 1938, 38 per cent of Cuba's cane was POJ 2878, reaching 46 per cent in 1940, and over 51 per cent in 1943 (Figure 7.3).

This change was closely related to soil exhaustion and the decreasing yields from Cristalina, which is evident from the fact that the dominance of POJ 2878

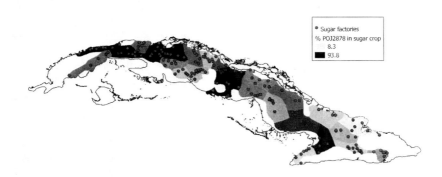

Figure 7.3 Sugar factories, and concentration of POJ 2878 cane in the sugar crop, 1943[36]

130 Jonathan Curry-Machado

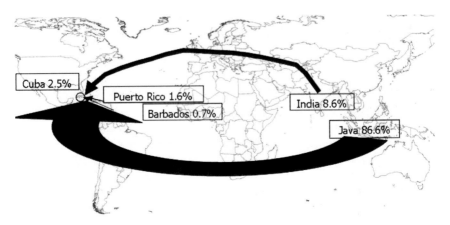

Figure 7.4 Origin of cane varieties grown in Cuba, 1943[38]

was greatest in the three western provinces, where the sugar industry had been long established and long exhausted its possibilities for expansion, and only four factories had not made this their primary crop by 1943. Beyond the central Coimbatore belt, POJ 2878 also out sowed other varieties. Only in the east did this still run second to Cristalina, amounting to just a quarter of production – though here too, some districts were already embracing the change (see Figure 7.2). POJ 2878 was set to dominate Cuba's sugar industry until another shift in cane varieties occurred in the 1960s when longer harvests demanded the cultivation of a range of cane that would guarantee a harvestable crop over a longer period than had historically been the case. The spread of mechanization to cutting also made it necessary to have cane bred not just for its high yield and disease resistance, but also for its straightness and homogeneity in height. By 1973, only 8 per cent of Cuba's cane was still POJ 2878; and by 1980, it had apparently disappeared.[37]

Agete's report shows that although Cuba's sugar industry was leading the world – in terms of quantity produced, and in technological advances in the manufacturing process – the island's agriculture was overwhelmingly dependent upon cane varieties developed elsewhere. As Figure 7.4 shows, in 1943, 95 per cent of cane grown on the island's plantations originated in Asia, the vast majority of this from Java. Indeed, since Cristalina was itself a cane of Javanese origin, this dominance became established from the 1880s. Despite hybridization taking place in the experimental stations of Barbados and Puerto Rico – and in Cuba itself, as the following section discusses – Cuban planters continued to favour the globalized Asian commercial varieties.

Local hybridization

Agete's report shows the reluctant but ultimately implacable transfer to Cuba of new cane hybrids, developed in Java – in particular, POJ 2878. But at the same time, it expresses the need for the island to adopt a similar approach to development of locally-specific hybrids as was exemplified with great success by Java, and could be seen in other cane-growing countries that threatened to out-compete Cuba:

> All this has led us to reaffirm our opinion concerning the necessity for a labour that should have been performed many years ago, tending towards an improvement of the cultivation of the cane, in the same way as was brought about, with success, in the industrial sector, but which was considered unnecessary by those who are accustomed to sowing a piece of cane to harvest, without effort, a full plant…We feel the need to obtain Cuban cane varieties in Cuba, to be a question of fundamental importance…[39]

Following the end of the Cuban War of Independence in 1898, the island's sugar industry (along with much of its agriculture) was greatly reduced, as a result of the devastation and depopulation caused by the hostilities. Before the war, in 1895, over one-third of the world's traded sugarcane came from Cuba, but in just three years this had fallen to a mere 8 per cent, and production stood at a quarter of its pre-war level.[40] Other producers, notably Java, had stepped into the breach and taken advantage of Cuba's woes to further their own sugar industries. The post-war period brought Cuba firmly under US tutelage, and North American investors and planters were able to consolidate their dominance over the island's sugar industry and trade. But a boost was also given to those who had been arguing against the current since Reynoso's time for the need to adopt a more scientific approach to cane cultivation. Edwin Atkins, the North American owner of the Soledad mill near Cienfuegos, 'was convinced that the production of new sugarcane varieties could take place in Cuba, in the same way as the Dutch were doing in Java';[41] and he cooperated in the establishment on his estate of the Harvard Botanical Station for Tropical Research and Sugarcane Investigation in 1901. Within two years, 51 cane varieties were being tested by the Station, including a new Cuban variety named 'Harvard.'[42] Atkins reported that tests demonstrated this to be 'a very good cane, of great commercial value', with high sucrose content and purity.[43] Harvard cane also produced more seeds than Cristalina and showed better cold resistance; and the Station continued to develop varieties, to the extent that by 1912 they had 30 worthy of exhibit at the Second National Cuban Exhibition in Havana.[44]

But no other Cuban varieties were displayed alongside them, and despite the good results obtained in tests, Harvard cane did not succeed in becoming commercially accepted elsewhere on the island. Agete shows that by 1938, other than the Soledad that maintained some samples, only the Boston and Algodones factories in the East made any use of Harvard, and then only in relatively small quantities. By 1943, no Harvard varieties were to be found anywhere at all.

Over the decades following the Harvard Garden experiments some other places attempted to develop Cuban varieties, but again Agete's report reveals that these were of limited success. The Banes hybrid cultivated by the Central Boston had low sucrose levels. The Cuban Sugar Club – one of the key importers of new foreign varieties – experimented with its own Baraguá hybrid, but in a half-hearted fashion and with appropriately unsatisfactory results. By the 1940s, the Baraguá itself had no plantings of Cuban varieties. The Central Palma had rather better results with their crossing of Java and Barbados canes, but even on the Palma these did not become anything other than small experimental crops. In the West, the Central Mercedita over a period experimented with obtaining their own varieties, but these efforts had no perceivable impact and were discontinued. A similar story can be seen with the canes obtained at San Manuel – belonging to the Central Chaparra in the East.

Such experimentation was carried out, in rather more systematic fashion, from about 1914 by the Experimental Agricultural Station at Santiago de las Vegas, committed to the belief that Cuba should be developing varieties to fit its specific local conditions. Many hybrids resulted from this, and their performance studied not just on the Station but also on a number of plantations around the island. This work became intensified in the 1940s, with the establishment of the Sugarcane Experimental Station (*Estación Experimental de la Caña de Azúcar*), under Agete's direction. However, with POJ 2878 so dominating the Cuban sugar industry, these attempts at creolizing the crop did not result in any commercial acceptance. The only two varieties that made any headway at all were C35 and CH 64(21). The former was being planted in 20 places on the island by 1927, though not in large quantities; and it had apparently disappeared by the 1940s. The latter seems to have had greater success in South Africa, where it was introduced to control mosaic.[45]

Agete's report shows that there was one clear success story for Cuban cane varieties. From around 1930, a hybridization campaign was begun on the Central Isabel in the Manzanillo region in south-eastern Cuba, crossing POJ 2878 with the Barbadian variety Santa Cruz 12/4. This gave birth to a new family of canes, which became known collectively as 'Media Luna'. ML 3-18 proved to be particularly successful, becoming extensively adopted in most of the sugar estates neighbouring the Isabel. It was found to have good results both agriculturally and industrially – maturing early, resistant to drought and resulting in high sucrose yields and purity. It also resulted in a useful bagasse that could be used as fuel, as well as cattle forage, and by 1943 it had become the ninth most-grown variety in Cuba. Ten sugar factories across the easternmost province were growing commercially viable crops from ML 3-18 (though only two, the Niquero and the Soledad, produced a majority of their sugar from it). It could also be found in smaller quantities elsewhere on the island.

Apart from the conscious hybridization of new varieties, there were other means by which locally-specific cane varieties might emerge. Sometimes the cane would mutate, resulting quite accidentally in strains with new characteristics, which might prove an improvement in local conditions. One Javanese variety, in particular, was prone to this (POJ 2714), and resulted in two mutated versions in Cuba – so-called 'Sports'. These were named after the factories where they emerged: San Cristóbal and Baraguá. The former became the primary crop employed by the factory that discovered it, though did not

Table 7.1 Numbers of sugar factories in Cuba, with Cuban cane varieties grown in related farms, 1943

	Cuban-owned		Foreign-owned		Total	
	No.	%	No.	%	No.	%
No Cuban cane	55	57.9	18	34.6	73	49.7
Less than 13 ha. (experimental crop)	9	9.5	3	5.8	12	8.2
13 to 67 ha. (test crop)	9	9.5	15	28.8	24	16.3
67 to 268 ha (small crop)	10	10.5	10	19.2	20	13.6
268 to 671ha. (medium crop)	5	5.3	1	1.9	6	4.1
More than 671 ha. (large crop).	7	7.4	5	9.6	12	8.2
Total	95		52		147	

extend much beyond. The Sport Baraguá, on the other hand, was introduced by farms supplying 21 sugar factories around the island, though only two of these grew it any large quantity.

Nevertheless, half of all sugar factories in Cuba had land on which at least a small number of Cuban cane varieties was being grown by the 1940s, and more than a quarter – while generally not using these varieties as their primary crop – had plantings of sufficient size (more than 67 hectares) to perhaps warrant being considered commercially relevant (Table 7.1). These were almost equalled in number by those with smaller plantings – either little more than experimental (less than 13 hectares) or as test crops (between 13 and 67 hectares).

But who were the planters that were showing themselves most willing to experiment with, or adopt Cuban cane varieties, rather than just accept the commercial standard? Of the eight factories where new Cuban varieties were developed, six were owned by US citizens or corporations. Of the other two, it was a descendent of British migrant families that had been prominent in the development of the sugar industry in Eastern Cuba (Richard Beattie), who was behind the development of the Media Luna strains. Only the San Cristóbal was Cuban-owned – and their contribution to improved local varieties was the result of a fortuitous mutation rather than conscious effort. Table 7.1, which draws on the detailed data provided by Agete, shows that foreign-owned sugar factories were substantially more likely to be trying Cuban varieties than were the Cuban-owned – a majority of whom showed no interest at all. Particular interest also seems to have occurred in loose local clusters (Figure 7.5), with a rather higher rate of adoption towards the east of the island in comparison to the

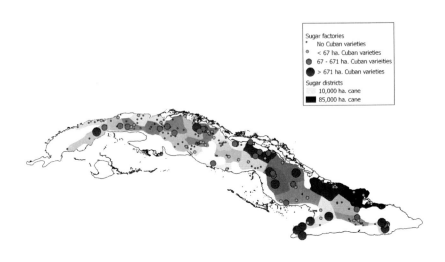

Figure 7.5 Sugar *centrales* with Cuban cane varieties, and total land with cane in district (1943)[46]

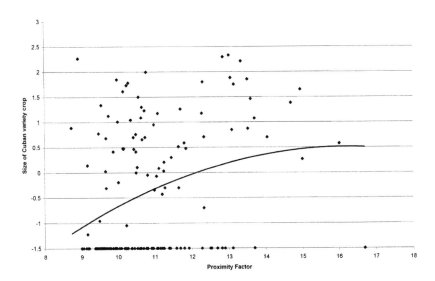

Figure 7.6 Relationship between amount of Cuban cane varieties grown for a sugar factory, and proximity to other Cuban cane-variety crops[47]

west and centre (where only two factories reported very extensive plantings of Cuban varieties). However, the areas with the highest levels of sugar production – dominated by the largest, overwhelmingly US-owned sugar factories – had very little interest. Since this was also the area where Cristalina persisted longest (Figure 7.2), no doubt this was very much related to the large amount of highly fertile virgin lands being newly planted with cane, bringing higher than average yields and less necessity to experiment with new varieties.

The example of the adoption of Media Luna canes around Manzanillo, and the apparent clustering elsewhere would suggest that the willingness of a sugar factory to adopt a Cuban cane variety, either to test or for a part of their crop, was related to the proximity of other factories already making use of these varieties. In Figure 7.6, Cuba's sugar factories have been plotted according to the amount of Cuban-variety cane that Agete's report shows that they were themselves growing, and a 'proximity factor' obtained from the sum of Cuban cane produced in all other factories, in inverse relationship to how far away they were. That there are values spread widely around the graph reflects the presence throughout the island of at least small quantities of Cuban cane. However, if a trend line is plotted, that this slopes upwards suggests that the closer a factory was to another crop of Cuban variety, the more likely it was that they might also consider such a crop themselves. Put another way, the further a farm was from other farms cultivating Cuban hybrids, the less likely it was that planters would consider this to be a viable option for their own crop.

This 'proximity effect' is not surprising. Behind most decisions made in the Cuban sugar industry was the economic imperative – this was big business, and the primary concern of planters was to maximize their profits while minimizing their risks. While in the long term this contributed to the resistance to the introduction of scientific best practice, planters nevertheless made evidence-based decisions. While only a handful of sugar factories were prepared to invest time, land and energy to the investigation and development of locally improved hybrids, when it became clear that another plantation was finding some success with a new variety – particularly if on land similar to their own, and close enough for ready communication and exchange of samples between them – then they would be more prepared to plant at least a part of their crop with this same variety.

The complete agriculturalist and the forlorn hope of Little Cuba

There was much more to the science of effective and rational agriculture than the appropriate choice of cane variety or development of hybrids suitable for local conditions. Agete, openly following the path shown by Reynoso 80 years earlier, explored every aspect of cane cultivation, providing indications of what best practice should be, with not infrequent reference to the general backwardness in Cuba in the application of such methods.

Agete realized it was of fundamental importance to have a complete understanding of the variations in soil from one district to another, and the impact that this might have upon agriculture and the ability to grow good crops. It was empirically well known that some kinds of soil were more fertile, and farmers knew from practice that some soils were better for certain crops rather than others. But the only existing scientific study of Cuba's soils in their entirety at that time was made in 1927 by H. H. Bennett and F. V. Allison under the auspices of the Tropical Plant Research Foundation. While very detailed in its description of the different kinds of soil, it only provided a quite general indication of the zones where each soil might be found.[48] Agete understood that this was a factor that should also affect the choice of cane variety to be used:

> Some have a superficial root system and, therefore, suffer a great deal in dry lands that do not conserve moisture well. Others, on the other hand, possess a deep radicle system, and they adapt best to friable lands that offer no resistance to the penetration of their roots; but not to those that at a small distance from the surface have an impermeable rocky layer that blocks the growth of the roots and which, by detaining the water in its filtration, lead these to rot.[49]

It was also crucial to better understand the relative fertility of each soil, as a result of ongoing cultivation. Yet in Cuba, the only method employed by most farmers was to classify their soils, not with the characteristic-based detail provided by Bennett and Allison (and expanded on by Agete), of which they generally appeared ignorant, but simply according to colour. Instead of 90 different types of soil, they only perceived it as black (*negro*), brown (*mulatto*) or red (*colorado*) – hardly a basis for a rational use of land. Indeed, the history of the expansion across the island of cane cultivation is littered with examples of the effect of poor choice of land on which to plant. This had resulted both in considerable deforestation, and loss of land to other agricultural uses, for minimal or no gain. Inappropriate soil produced weak crops, resulting in abandonment and (increasingly) invasion of the land by opportunistic invasive plants – such as the *marabú* (sicklebush, *Dichrostachys cinerea*) that was introduced in the nineteenth century as an ornamental plant but which quickly took a hold and rapidly spread through poorly treated and over-exploited canefields.[50]

A proper understanding of the soil was not only necessary to ensure that the right crop or variety would be planted in the right place. Unless the properties of the land were fully appreciated, it would be impossible to apply fertilizers in a rational way. The lack of particular nutrients could hardly be determined purely through observation of the earth's colour. But Agete discovered that throughout Cuba, planters appeared to think that applying any fertilizer would do, with effects that were often worse than useless – since using the wrong fertilizer could lead to the soil becoming exhausted even faster. On many plantations, increased productivity was sought through the sowing of more vigorous varieties – but again, though bringing short-term improvements, this tended to exhaust the land all the faster.[51]

Agete showed that while Cuba's soil had become generally deficient in key nutrients, it was above all nitrogen that was lacking. Yet the most commonly applied chemical fertilizers were primarily phosphorous-based. In this, as in other agricultural matters, the Cuban sugar industry was out of step with its main competitors (such as Java) – where the conclusion had already been reached, through experimentation and analysis, that better results could be obtained for sugarcane crops from nitrogen-based fertilizers. In this, Cuban planters revealed not only their worrying lack of concern for the application of best scientific practice, but just how closely tied they were to, and influenced by, commercial interests. It seems that the widespread use of inappropriate fertilizers was the result of vigorous marketing on the part of the fertilizer manufacturers, seeking to push their phosphorous-based products.[52] A clear majority of sugar factories showed such little concern for the question of fertilization that they did not bother to report upon the practice in their own fields when requested to provide details of their operations. By 1946, only twelve factories (out of 161) showed signs of paying attention to the analytical approach recommended by Agete. While several others were applying chemical fertilizers, this often seems to have been more with the blind hope of improvement, rather than expectation based on scientific method. For example, the Jobabo in Oriente 'had tried diverse bands, formulas and quantities, without having obtained definitive results with any of them';[53] while the Manuelita in Las Villas 'had tried several, but had not been able to obtain one that was appropriate to their agricultural conditions.'[54]

Reynoso had stated that 'cane is a plant requiring irrigation.' This was ever to the fore in the agricultural practice of the sugar industry in Java (the Dutch being, after all, global experts in the development of irrigation systems). Yet 80 years after Reynoso's essay, Cuba's farms continued to be overwhelmingly dependent on the vagaries of rainfall.[55] In 1946, only 27 of Cuba's 161 sugar factories gave any indication that they were at all engaged in the irrigation of their crops, and less than half of these were doing so in anything like a comprehensive and systematic way.[56]

Agete, in line with Reynoso, made recommendations covering all aspects of the farming of sugarcane. Yet as with his predecessor, he seems to have been largely talking to deaf ears. The production of sugar in Cuba was overwhelmingly an industrial affair, and – with some notable exceptions – the sugar factories showed little interest in encouraging, or themselves leading, a more rational and scientific approach to the cultivation of the crop upon which they depended on. Industry publications, such as the *Gilmore Cuba Sugar Manual*, vividly demonstrate this imbalance, by on the one hand providing extensive detail of the factory machinery and methods, and on the other, continuing to relegate agricultural data to an afterthought – and in many cases, not even that.[57]

Those who supported pursuing an agricultural approach along the lines suggested by Reynoso and Agete were keenly aware of the primacy of the economic argument amongst cane planters and sugar manufacturers. With few exceptions, they based their decisions upon short-term commercial considerations, with the over-riding concern for maximizing their profits. For this reason, to argue from the perspective of scientific rationality, or in terms of generalized and (in present-day parlance) sustainable improvement of Cuba's agriculture and rural economy was unlikely to be heeded. Therefore, appeals were made to the sense of impending doom faced by the island's sugar industry as, by the 1930s, it was becoming very clear that Cuba's dominant position in global production was coming under sustained attack, and the island found itself slipping into the wake of rising competitors.

However, such reasoning (exemplified by Agete) was, in reality, a front – expressed in terms of the self-interest of sugar agri-business – for an alternative vision of what Cuba's agriculture could, or should, be. Since the rise to dominance of sugarcane in the early- to mid-nineteenth century, a minority of voices – generally led by the most scientifically informed of Cuban opinion makers – expressed serious concerns about the island following a monocultural path. Cuba's sugar industry had taken advantage of the underexploited, highly fertile land. Visitors to the island in the mid-nineteenth century remarked upon 'how rich must be the resources of the soil, that can sustain, without exhaustion, this lavish and unceasing expenditure of its nutritious elements';[58] but by the start of the twentieth century, 'passed…is that happy age in which with pride we could say that Cuba was the promised land, in which it was sufficient to cast the seed over the terrain in order to harvest shortly afterwards flavoursome, exquisite and abundant fruits.'[59] While increasingly foreign-dominated vested interests pushed the industrialization of sugar production forward, and with it increasing domination of land by cane fields; others perceived how Cuba, despite the island's agricultural potential, was failing to feed itself. They conjured up an alternative picture of '*Cuba pequeña*,' Little Cuba, in which a diversity of agricultural wealth and plenty would be made possible by building upon the foundations of a strong peasantry.[60] Rather than all becoming oriented towards an untrammelled sugar industry, they believed that a strong sugar industry could be maintained in the midst of a diverse range of other crops – which would reduce the island's dependency upon a single crop, and ensure that the population could feed itself without the increasing reliance on expensive food imports.

This was not a vision that excluded sugar. On the contrary, it formed the basis of the arguments, from Reynoso to Agete, in favour of a more scientific approach to cane cultivation, carried on as part of a richer, diversified farming practice. But most sugar plantations had been developed, and continued to be exploited, with very little attempt to combine it with other crops. As Agete wrote:

> The mills, created exclusively for the exploitation of cane, with their great sugar transactions, have not concerned themselves with crop diversification, which would make crop rotation possible. The available virgin lands made them think of nothing other than the destruction of forests to extend the cane. Sugar was all.[61]

Not only did the sugar plantations themselves fail to combine cane with other land uses (beyond some minor growth of food crops for domestic consumption, and some land for the pasturing of the estate's livestock), they increasingly ensured that much of the prime agricultural land in their vicinity (an ever-widening area thanks to the transport provided by the island's extensive and growing railway network) was also grown to cane. Throughout Agete's report into cultivation methods, the concern is expressed that failure to develop successful Cuban canes, or to introduce proper irrigation, or to use fertilizers in a rational way based on soil analysis, meant that a far greater area of land was devoted to sugarcane than was really necessary. Whereas on Java, and other sugar-growing territories, an attempt was made to intensify cultivation, to make fuller use of available land – in Cuba, the mentality continued to persist that the island had an inexhaustible supply of land that could be expanded into indefinitely. But if local cane varieties – with improved and reliable yields and resistant to prevalent cane pathogens – proven by practice, could be introduced (rather than simply the most viable of the commercially available varieties), along with ongoing experimentation for further improvements, then the necessary amount of cane to guarantee sugar-production levels could be grown on a smaller area, thereby freeing land for other crops and uses. If proper soil analysis were to be made of all lands, planters could ensure that cane would only be grown where most appropriate, leaving other lands free for diversification of output. Rather than blindly fertilizing with whatever product was being sold commercially, planters could use carefully balanced fertilizers appropriate for their lands, thereby maintaining and improving yields rather than overcoming declining yields by expanding the fields. If plantations took the trouble of installing proper irrigation, they would not need to force more land than was necessary to be planted to cane in order to counteract the risk of drought reducing their crop.

But failure to adopt the practices recommended by Agete, and Reynoso before him, meant that far more cane tended to be grown than was necessary, in order to ensure supply. This had consequences that went far beyond the ability of the Cuban sugar industry to sustain itself, and withstand the challenges of global competition. In the wake of the inappropriate and unthinking expansion of cane fields, soil exhaustion resulted in the now denuded land becoming taken over by opportunistic invasive plants. The lack of attention to crop diversification saw the island become increasingly less capable of providing for its own food needs, and dependent upon foreign imports – to be paid for from the proceeds of a sugar industry that by the 1930s was suffering from ever decreasing prices. And displacement of once self-sufficient cultivators, to make way for the vast extension of inefficiently and unscientifically planted cane, saw Cuba's rural society become radically disjointed: 'The small Cuban landowner, independent and prosperous... is gradually disappearing. The farmer is becoming a member of the proletariat, just another laborer, without roots in the soil, shifted from one district to another.'[62]

Conclusion

When Fernando Agete wrote his report, he was already Director of the Experimental Cane Station located within the Experimental Agricultural Station of Santiago de las Vegas, near Havana. This latter had been founded in 1904 and was to play an important part over the coming years as a centre for research into improving the island's agriculture. However – despite developing under US tutelage, and for all that it engaged in cane research – its direct impact upon the Cuban sugar industry, as this went through rapid expansion during the first decades of the twentieth century, was minimal. The outlook of the Station was clearly one of supporting, through the promotion of scientific method and practice, the development of diversified agriculture, favouring not only the large, commercial sugar interests but also small farmers. Thus despite its North American inspiration, the Station – and those involved in it – was above all concerned that Cuba's developmental path be a more self-sustaining one, in line with the vision pushed by proponents of '*Cuba pequeña*' (Little Cuba) since the early-nineteenth century. It was a vision that, as exemplified by Agete and Reynoso, sought to marry scientific advance and best farming practice, in a way that would enable not only the continuing benefit of a vibrant export-oriented agriculture but also a cohesive rural society in which large plantations and smallholdings would mutually benefit one another.

But, with a few prominent exceptions, those who sought to develop and embed a more scientific approach were not the leading players in the Cuban sugar industry. Just as in the nineteenth century, the availability of under-utilized land encouraged planters to simply expand their holdings, rather than make more efficient use of those they already had. Why invest time and resources in more scientific approaches if they could simply farm virgin soils, which would offer naturally high fertility, and then move on elsewhere once the inevitable soil depletion had occurred? The Cuban sugar industry thus continued to exist as a continually extending frontier. The impact of the War of Independence (1895–8) furthered this since it removed many peasants from the land – and sugar interests were much better placed to obtain the necessary investment to lead the way in the post-war reconstruction. Therefore, much land that had previously been given to other crops became swallowed up by sugarcane.

An underlying cause of the 'reluctant embedding' of the scientific method in cane agriculture was that, from the outset, Cuban sugar had been industry-driven. It owed much of its nineteenth-century rise to the introduction of the latest advances in milling and steam technology – and not to the improvement of the agricultural side. This continued into the twentieth century; and the post-1880 separation of cane fields from sugar factories, far from enabling a change in attitude, served to harden this prejudice. Many cane farms may have been nominally independent, but most in one way or another remained tied to the large central sugar factories. Rather than factories serving the needs of farmers to process their crops, farmers were beholden to the needs of the factories, which remained the most financially lucrative segment of the sugar sector. Unless the sugar factory showed a concern for embedding scientific practice in cane farming, it was hard for individual cane farmers to make this step themselves. But the factories and their owners tended to be more embedded in commercial and industrial networks, paying at best secondary attention to the agricultural – with possible fluctuations in crops guarded against by quantity sown, rather than by quality of method.

It was this that also contributed to the apparent conservatism of the Cuban sugar industry with respect to cane varieties. Once a particular variety had become firmly embedded (as with Cristalina in the late-nineteenth century), and was proving its commercial worth, it would take a great deal to convince Cuban sugar producers to switch to another, albeit better, hybrid. Even in the face of evidence that the mosaic virus was having a serious detrimental impact on yields, it took several years for most planters to adopt resistant varieties; and when they did, they opted not for hybrids developed for local conditions, but the most commercially proven of those coming out of Java. It was commercial practice, not scientific or agricultural, that was embedded in the Cuban sugar industry – the guarantee of profits today, rather than long-term rural and farming sustainability. But while this made the fortune of those who controlled sugar production and trade, the failure to embed a more scientific approach to the cultivation of cane furthered the process of disembedding food-crop-producing smallholders. A combination of factors related to the sugar industry (the desire amongst smallholders to share in the financial gains offered by sugar, acquisition of arable land by large sugar interests, or pressure exerted upon farmers by the sugar factories that dominated local economies to turn a larger part of their crop over to cane) in many districts compounded further the tendency already seen in the nineteenth century away from agricultural diversity, food security and rural sustainability.

Agete's report may have highlighted just how little had changed qualitatively in Cuba – despite the quantitative advances – in the 80 years since Reynoso wrote his famous *Ensayo*. It also shows its limitations as a source in that – despite the perspective from which Agete came – the survey upon which it was based relied upon information provided by the sugar factories, rather than going to the farmers themselves and learning directly from them. However, the critique that Agete made struck a chord at the highest levels of the Cuban polity – coinciding as his report did with Cuba losing ground to other sugar producers, and with a rural population that had become increasingly proletarianized by the sugar industry, dependent upon food imports, and radicalized by the social tensions that this generated. An immediate response of the Cuban government was to sponsor the establishment of a new Experimental Cane Station at Jovellanos, right in the heart of Cuba's sugar lands, in 1947 – with Agete as a key protagonist. This presaged the changes that would come 12 years later, following the island's political and social revolution, when Cuba's agriculture (though its dependence on sugar would not be broken until the end of the twentieth century) ceased to be beholden to powerful corporative sugar interests, and applied agricultural scientific research was at last given the opportunity to come into its own.

Notes

1. Fernando Agete y Piñero. *La Caña de Azúcar en Cuba* (Havana: Ministerio de Agricultura, 1946).
2. Julio Le Riverend. *Historia Económica de Cuba* (Havana: Editorial de Ciencias Sociales, 1967); Reinaldo Funes Monzote. *From Rain-Forest to Cane Field in Cuba* (Chapel Hill: University of North Carolina Press, 2008).
3. Manuel Moreno Fraginals. *The Sugar Mill: The Socio-economic Complex of Sugar in Cuba* (New York and London: Monthly Review Press, 1976); Roland T. Ely. *Cuando reinaba su Majestad el Azúcar* (Havana: Imagen Contemporánea, 2001[1963]).
4. Jonathan Curry-Machado. *Cuban Sugar Industry: Transnational Networks and Engineering Migrants in Mid-nineteenth Century Cuba* (New York: Palgrave Macmillan, 2011).
5. Sidney W. Mintz. *Sweetness and Power: The Place of Sugar in Modern History* (New York: Penguin, 1985).
6. Moreno. *The Sugar Mill*.
7. Antonio Santamaría García. *Sin Azúcar no hay País: la industria azucarera y la economía cubana (1919–1939)* (Seville: CSIC & Universidad de Sevilla, 2001).
8. Moreno *The Sugar Mill*.
9. Alan Dye. *Cuban Sugar in the Age of Mass Production: Technology and the Economics of the Sugar Central, 1899–1929* (Stanford: Stanford University Press, 1998); Fé Iglesias García. *Del ingenio al central* (San Juan: Editorial de la Universidad de Puerto Rico, 1998).
10. Levi Marrero. *Cuba: Economía y Sociedad (Vol. 10)* (Madrid: Playor, 1984), 278.
11. Moreno. *The Sugar Mill*.
12. Álvaro Reynoso. *Ensayo sobre el cultivo de la caña de azúcar* (Havana: Artes Gráficas, 1963[1862]).
13. Stuart McCook. *States of Nature: Science, Agriculture, and Environment in the Spanish Caribbean, 1760–1940* (Austin: University of Texas Press, 2002), 23.
14. Ulbe Bosma and Jonathan Curry-Machado. 'Two Islands, One Commodity: Cuba, Java and the Global Sugar Trade (1790–1930).' *New West Indian Guide* 86:3–4 (December 2012), 237–62.
15. Ulbe Bosma and G. Roger Knight. 'Global Factory and Local Field: Convergence and Divergence in the International Cane-sugar Industry, 1850–1940.' *International Review of Social History*, 49 (2004), 1–25; Harro Maat. *Science Cultivating Practice: A History of Agricultural Science in the Netherlands and its Colonies, 1863–1986* (Dordrecht: Kluwer, 2001).
16. Ulbe Bosma. 'The Cultivation System (1830–1870) and its Private Entrepreneurs on Colonial Java.' *Journal of Southeast Asian Studies* 38:2 (2007), 275–92.
17. Santamaría. *Sin Azúcar no hay País*, 399.
18. Santamaría. *Sin Azúcar no hay País*, 73.
19. Based on data from Agete, *La Caña de Azúcar*.
20. Oscar Zanetti and Alejandro García et al. *United Fruit Company: un caso del dominio imperialista en Cuba* (Havana: Editorial Ciencias Sociales, 1976).
21. Leida Fernández Prieto. *Cuba Agrícola: Mito y Tradición, 1878–1920* (Madrid: CSIC, 2005); Leida Fernández Prieto. *Espacio de poder, ciencia y agricultura en Cuba: el Círculo de Hacendados* (Seville: CSIC and Universidad de Sevilla, 2008).
22. McCook. *States of Nature*, 79–80.
23. Curry-Machado. *Cuban Sugar Industry*.
24. A. C. Barnes. *The Sugar Cane* (Aylesbury: Leonard Hill, 1974), 306.
25. McCook. *States of Nature*.
26. Noel Deerr. *The History of Sugar* (2 vols) (London: Chapman and Hall, 1949).
27. Fernández. *Cuba Agrícola*, 172.
28. Rafael Martínez Viera. *70 años de la Estación Experimental Agronómica de Santiago de las Vegas* (Havana: Academia de Ciencias de Cuba, 1977), 31.

29 McCook. *States of Nature*, 100.
30 McCook. *States of Nature*, 87–8.
31 McCook. *States of Nature*, 98–9.
32 Agete. *La Caña de Azúcar*, 75.
33 Based on data from Agete, *La Caña de Azúcar*.
34 Wim J. van der Schoor. 'Pure Science and Colonial Agriculture: The Case of the Private Java Sugar Experimental Stations (1885–1940).' In Yvon Chatelin and Christophe Bonneuil (eds.) *Nature et Environnement. Nature and Environment. Vol. 3 of Les Sciences hors d'Occident au XXe siècle. 20th Century Sciences beyond the metropolis* (Paris: Orstom Éditions, 1995), 14.
35 McCook. *States of Nature*, 101.
36 Based on data from Agete. *La Caña de Azúcar*.
37 Brian H. Pollitt. 'The Technical Transformation of Cuba's Sugar Agroindustry.' In Jorge F. Pérez-López and José Alvarez (eds.) *Reinventing the Cuban Sugar Agroindustry* (Oxford: Lexington, 2005), 48.
38 Based on data from Agete. *La Caña de Azúcar*.
39 Agete. *La Caña de Azúcar*, 47.
40 Manuel Moreno Fraginals. *El Ingenio*, Vol. 3 (Havana: Editorial Ciencias Sociales, 1978), 38.
41 Pedro M. Pruna Goodgall. *Historia de la Ciencia y la Tecnología en Cuba* (Havana: Editorial Científico-Técnico, 2005), 205.
42 McCook. *States of Nature*, 58.
43 Agete. *La Caña de Azúcar*, 26–7.
44 Robert Grey. *Report of the Harvard Botanical Gardens, Soledad Estate, Cienfuegos, Cuba (Atkins Foundation), 1900–1926* (Cambridge: Riverside Press, 1927), 3–9.
45 Agete. *La Caña de Azúcar*, 56.
46 Based on data from Agete. *La Caña de Azúcar*.
47 Log factor of area plotted against log2 of quantity of Cuban cane varieties related to each factory divided by square of distance. Based on data from Agete. *La Caña de Azúcar*.
48 H. H. Bennett and F. V. Allison. *The Soils of Cuba* (Baltimore: Monumental, 1928).
49 Agete. *La Caña de Azúcar*, 238.
50 Funes. *From Rain-Forest to Cane Field*.
51 Agete. *La Caña de Azúcar*, 239.
52 Agete. *La Caña de Azúcar*, 401.
53 A. B. Gilmore (ed.). *Manual Azucarero de Cuba* (Havana and New Orleans: Gilmore, 1946), 340.
54 Gilmore. *Manual Azucarero*, 114.
55 Agete. *La Caña de Azúcar,* 407.
56 Gilmore. *Manual Azucarero*.
57 Gilmore. *Manual Azucarero*.
58 Benjamin Norman. *Rambles by Land and Water* (New York: Paine & Burgess, 1845), 52.
59 Francisco Cruz. *Primer informe anual de 1904–1905* (Santiago de las Vegas: Estación Central Agronómica, 1905), 27.
60 Carlos Venegas Fornías. 'Estancias y sitios de labor: su presencia en las publicaciones cubanas del siglo XIX.' *Colonial Latin American Historical Review*, 81:3–4 (2001), 27–59.
61 Agete. *La Caña de Azúcar*, 337.
62 Fernando Ortiz. *Cuban Counterpoint: Tobacco and Sugar* (New York: Random House, 1970), 53.

References

Agete y Piñero, Fernando. *La Caña de Azúcar en Cuba* (Havana: Ministerio de Agricultura, 1946).
Barnes, A. C. *The Sugar Cane* (Aylesbury: Leonard Hill, 1974).
Bennett, H. H., and F. V. Allison. *The Soils of Cuba* (Baltimore, MD: Monumental, 1928).
Bosma, Ulbe. 'The Cultivation System (1830–1870) and its Private Entrepreneurs on Colonial Java.' *Journal of Southeast Asian Studies* 38:2 (2007), 275–92.
Bosma, Ulbe, and Jonathan Curry-Machado. 'Two Islands, One Commodity: Cuba, Java and the Global Sugar Trade (1790–1930).' *New West Indian Guide* 86:3–4 (December 2012), 237–62.
Bosma, Ulbe, and G. Roger Knight. 'Global Factory and Local Field: Convergence and Divergence in the International Cane-sugar Industry, 1850–1940.' *International Review of Social History* 49 (2004), 1–25.
Cruz, Francisco. *Primer informe anual de 1904–1905* (Santiago de las Vegas: Estación Central Agronómica, 1905).
Curry-Machado, Jonathan. *Cuban Sugar Industry: Transnational Networks and Engineering Migrants in Mid-nineteenth Century Cuba* (New York: Palgrave Macmillan, 2011).
Deerr, Noel. *The History of Sugar* (2 vols) (London: Chapman and Hall, 1949).
Dye, Alan. *Cuban Sugar in the Age of Mass Production: Technology and the Economics of the Sugar Central, 1899–1929* (Stanford, CA: Stanford University Press, 1998).
Ely, Roland T. *Cuando reinaba su Majestad el Azúcar* (Havana: Imagen Contemporánea, 2001[1963]).
Fernández Prieto, Leida. *Cuba Agrícola: Mito y Tradición, 1878–1920* (Madrid: CSIC, 2005).
Fernández Prieto, Leida. *Espacio de poder, ciencia y agricultura en Cuba: el Círculo de Hacendados* (Seville: CSIC & Universidad de Sevilla, 2008).
Funes Monzote, Reinaldo. *From Rain-Forest to Cane Field in Cuba* (Chapel Hill, NC: University of North Carolina Press, 2008).
Gilmore, A. B. (ed.). *Manual Azucarero de Cuba* (Havana and New Orleans: Gilmore, 1946).
Grey, Robert. *Report of the Harvard Botanical Gardens, Soledad Estate, Cienfuegos, Cuba (Atkins Foundation), 1900–1926* (Cambridge: Riverside Press, 1927).
Iglesias García, Fé. *Del ingenio al central* (San Juan: Editorial de la Universidad de Puerto Rico, 1998).
Le Riverend, Julio. *Historia Económica de Cuba* (Havana: Editorial de Ciencias Sociales, 1967).
Maat, Harro. *Science Cultivating Practice: A History of Agricultural Science in the Netherlands and its Colonies, 1863–1986* (Dordrecht: Kluwer, 2001).
Marrero, Levi. *Cuba: Economía y Sociedad (Vol. 10)* (Madrid: Playor, 1984).
Martínez Viera, Rafael. *70 años de la Estación Experimental Agronómica de Santiago de las Vegas* (Havana: Academia de Ciencias de Cuba, 1977).
McCook, Stuart. *States of Nature: Science, Agriculture, and Environment in the Spanish Caribbean, 1760–1940* (Austin, TX: University of Texas Press, 2002).
Mintz, Sidney W. *Sweetness and Power: The Place of Sugar in Modern History* (New York: Penguin, 1985).
Moreno Fraginals, Manuel. *The Sugar Mill: The Socio-economic Complex of Sugar in Cuba* (New York and London: Monthly Review Press, 1976).
Moreno Fraginals, Manuel. *El Ingenio*, Vol.3 (Havana: Editorial Ciencias Sociales, 1978).
Norman, Benjamin. *Rambles by Land and Water* (New York: Paine & Burgess, 1845).
Ortiz, Fernando. *Cuban Counterpoint: Tobacco and Sugar* (New York: Random House, 1970).

Pollitt, Brian H. 'The Technical Transformation of Cuba's Sugar Agroindustry.' In Jorge F. Pérez-López and José Alvarez (eds.) *Reinventing the Cuban Sugar Agroindustry* (Oxford: Lexington, 2005).

Pruna Goodgall, Pedro M. *Historia de la Ciencia y la Tecnología en Cuba* (Havana: Editorial Científico-Técnico, 2005).

Reynoso, Álvaro. *Ensayo sobre el cultivo de la caña de azúcar* (Havana: Artes Gráficas, 1963[1862]).

Santamaría García, Antonio. *Sin Azúcar no hay País: la industria azucarera y la economía cubana (1919–1939)* (Seville: CSIC & Universidad de Sevilla, 2001).

Van der Schoor, Wim J. 'Pure Science and Colonial Agriculture: The Case of the Private Java Sugar Experimental Stations (1885–1940).' In Yvon Chatelin and Christophe Bonneuil (eds.) *Nature et Environnement. Nature and Environment. Vol. 3 of Les Sciences hors d'Occident au XXe siècle.20th Century Sciences beyond the metropolis* (Paris: Orstom Éditions, 1995), 13–20.

Venegas Fornías, Carlos. 'Estancias y sitios de labor: su presencia en las publicaciones cubanas del siglo XIX.' *Colonial Latin American Historical Review*, 81:3–4 (2001), 27–59.

Zanetti, Oscar and Alejandro García et al. *United Fruit Company: un caso del dominio imperialista en Cuba* (Havana: Editorial Ciencias Sociales, 1976).

8 Globalization's agricultural roots
Some final considerations

Marcel van der Linden

> 'The great benefit resulting from colonies is
> the cultivation of staple commodities
> different from those of the mother-country.'[1]

Our lives have become unimaginable without plants that at one time existed only in quite different parts of the world. Rice, maize, potatoes, tomatoes, cassava and countless other crops have spread all over the world and are important ingredients in the daily nutrition of hundreds of millions, or even billions, of people. Natural rubber enables car transport on all continents, and cotton and flax are indispensable in the textile industry.

Over the centuries, plants have travelled widely. Frequently, such relocations have taken place without any human intervention. For example, sweet potatoes appear to have originated in the Americas and were transported to Africa, presumably by sea currents.[2] Conversely, coconut and kapok trees are thought to have reached South America from Africa without any human intervention.[3] More recently, when plant transfers *did* come about through human intervention, such action was often unintentional, for example, because the construction of canals and bridges removed longstanding distribution barriers, or because species came along with human travellers, their means of transportation, or the plants and animals that accompanied them.[4] It is assumed that seeds of several African crops, such as oil palms, were brought to the Americas in this way, as a side effect of the slave transports.[5]

In many cases, humans also *deliberately* transported plants from one area to the next, for example, because of their value as food, medicine, or decoration – frequently for a combination of these reasons. Strategic considerations sometimes came into play as well. Already around 2800 BCE, the Chinese Emperor Shen Nung dispatched collectors to remote areas to gather plants with a medicinal or agrarian value.[6] In the early centuries CE, sandalwood trees were transported from Indonesia to India, across about five thousand kilometres, where they were used to build Hindu temples, incense burners, and the pyres on which the Brahmans were cremated.[7]

Early on, Europeans engaged in deliberate transfer as well – they brought back plants from Asia and Africa to Europe. Bitter oranges, citrons and lemons came from Asia and are known to have been cultivated in the Mediterranean since antiquity. Sugarcane, basil, musk, melons and watermelons are believed to have arrived somewhat later on from the East as well while cress found its way to Europe from Africa and the Near East.[8] Sugar beets originated in the southern Himalayas and the Middle East but are thought to have arrived in Europe over two thousand years ago.[9] During the early centuries of Islam, plant transfers appear to have increased, driven by initiatives by peasant growers and rulers who longed for these exotic crops in their botanical gardens.[10] Such international transfers concerned mainly – though not exclusively – plants that were edible and could be stored for extended periods: cereals (rice, wheat, maize, rye, barley, oats and millet) and leguminous plants containing protein (peas, beans and lentils).[11]

Some efforts to transfer plants, however, were economically motivated. For example, in the fifteenth century, Japanese traders sold so much Southeast-Asian pepper in Korea that the Koreans thought it was a Japanese product. Therefore, in the 1480s, King Songjong repeatedly asked the Japanese envoys to provide him with pepper plant seed, so that the crop might be grown in Korea.[12] Actually, black pepper came from southwest India (Malabar) and was subsequently, in the fifteenth century, transferred to Sumatra to meet the immense Chinese demand.[13]

After 1500, and especially from 1600, long-distance plant transfers increased rapidly. The 'discovery' of the Americas and the circumnavigation of Africa greatly promoted the transfer of crops from one continent to another. Intentional and unintentional transcontinental translocations of plants between the 'Old' and the 'New' Worlds started with the Columbian Exchange – the exchange of crops between Europe and the Americas. The Magellan Exchange – the exchange of crops between the Americas and Asia – soon followed.[14] Table 8.1 depicts these exchanges.

Crops were deliberately distributed as commodities, as diplomatic gifts or as food products for settlers. In the sixteenth century, the Spanish and Portuguese took important plants from the Americas to China, including groundnuts, which were cultivated around Shanghai from the 1530s; the sweet potato, which was first mentioned in Yunnan in 1563 and gained popularity as a good alternative to the Chinese taro; and maize in the seventeenth century.[15] Products that the Portuguese brought from Brazil to South and Southeast Asia included the cashew nut, pineapple, sweet potato, cassava, groundnut and chilli pepper. They also tried to cultivate the same food plants on small farms in Angola from around 1629.[16]

All these transfers had major consequences. Consumption patterns changed in most parts of the world. American chilli has become 'the world's most used spice'[17]; and potatoes, maize and rice have become staple foods way beyond their areas of origin. Demographic trends were entirely altered as well. Africa experienced considerable population growth after 1600, despite the export of countless slaves to other parts of the world. It owed this population growth to the introduction of maize, which replaced the traditional sorghum; and cassava (manioc), which replaced the yam. The new crops enabled expansion to previously uninhabited areas.[18] In China, the new crops led to 'a true agricultural revolution' and strong population growth in the eighteenth century.[19]

Table 8.1 The Columbian and Magellan exchanges of crop species

From Old to New World		From New to Old World	
banana	olive	arrowroot	paprika
barley	onion	avocado	peanut
black pepper	pea	beans	pecan
buckwheat	peach	capsicum pepper	pineapple
cabbage	pear	cashew nut	potato
citrus	rice	cassava	rubber
coconut	rye	chilli pepper	squash (inc. pumpkin)
coffee	sorghum	kina (cinchona)	sunflower
egg-plant (aubergine)	soy	cocoa	sweet potato
garlic	spelt	cranberry	tobacco
lentil	sugar beet	guava	tomato
lettuce	sugarcane	maize (corn)	vanilla
nutmeg	turnip	okra	
oats	wheat	papaya	

Sources: Van der Weijden et al. Biological Globalisation, 26; Stanley B. Alpern. 'The European Introduction of Crops into West Africa in Precolonial Times', History in Africa, 19 (1992), 24–31

The global triangle

Intercontinental agricultural entanglements are longstanding and we have been aware of them for quite a while. For example, when German historian and playwright Friedrich Schiller was granted a chair at the University of Jena in 1789, he stated in his inaugural address that 'the most remote regions of the world contribute to our luxury'. After all, he continued, '[t]he clothes we wear, the spices in our food, and the price for which we buy them, many of our strongest medicines, and also many new tools of our destruction – do they not presuppose a Columbus who discovered America, a Vasco da Gama who circumnavigated the tip of Africa?'[20]

Nevertheless, quite some time passed before professional historians began to consider these global connections in their research – and any interest taken in entanglements was more likely to address industrial and military than botanical and agricultural aspects. This may have been because since the days of Marx, capitalism has been associated with factories and industries. The overwhelming majority of studies on the capitalist production system focus on urban merchant capital and its gradual transformation into manufacturing and later industrial production.

In recent decades, however, it has become increasingly clear that this interpretation of the past merits review. Since the 1970s historians' renewed interest in rural cottage industries has enhanced this awareness. In his world-systems theory, Immanuel Wallerstein considered agriculture at length and he demonstrated that cash crops have been paramount in the rise of world capitalism. A cautious revaluation of agriculture is emerging in political economy as well. There is now a general awareness that the founders of this discipline formulated their ideas in an era before the Industrial Revolution. William Petty devised his brilliant theories based on his experiences as an agrarian settler in Ireland. Physiocrats such as François Quesnay and Turgot focused entirely on the agrarian sector. Even Adam Smith thought primarily in agrarian terms and argued: 'The capital [...] that is acquired to any country by commerce and manufactures, is all a very precarious and uncertain possession, till some part of it has been secured and realized in the cultivation and improvement of its lands'.[21]

In this volume we follow this train of thought. The preceding chapters demonstrate that the process of globalized production that has received so much attention lately also derives largely from agriculture. The idea that production sites that generate commodities for the global system may be transferred from one part of the world to another originated in agriculture – and gained ground in the processing industries only later on.[22]

Long-distance trade made temperate-climate traders and affluent consumers of luxury commodities – especially in East Asia and Europe – aware that in tropical and subtropical areas crops were grown that also appealed greatly to 'Northerners' as stimulants or food products, and for the garment industry. All the spices from Southern India, Ceylon and the Southeast-Asian archipelago were renowned in China and Europe as early as two millennia ago. When

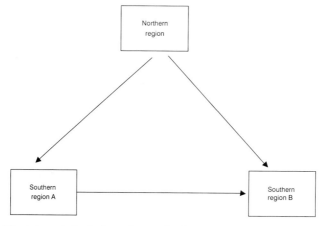

Figure 8.1 The 'triangulation' of agrarian production

150 *Marcel van der Linden*

capitalist influences increased, traders and settlers began to attempt to control the production of these profitable tropical and subtropical crops. Europeans began to transfer crops all over the world *within* the tropical and subtropical belt. They did so, for example, when they thought that expanding total production was certain to increase profits, or because in a certain region a crop was in danger of extinction from over-cropping. This led to a 'triangulation', in which the North organized the transfer (or expansion) of agrarian production systems within the South (Figure 8.1).

This triangle expresses the balance of power, in which states and companies from the North take decisions on work processes and ecological changes in the South. The preceding chapters explore these balances of power from several perspectives.

Global trajectories

Historical studies of cash crops and their transcontinental re-embedding have to cope with substantial source difficulties. In some countries there are hardly any early archives, either because these have been destroyed (as happened to the Thai archives when the city of Ayutthaya was burned down in 1767), or because the culture was illiterate for a long time. In other cases there are archives, but unarranged, or in a bad shape owing to air pollution or humidity. Most of the time, archives were produced by and for members of elites. Sometimes, however, archives can be read 'against the grain.' And for the more recent period, we often may be able to compensate the lack of documentary sources with oral sources, newspapers, etc.

The chapters collected in this volume reveal that despite all these limitations a wide variety of historical sources can be successfully applied to the study of plant transfers: diaries, reviews, scientific studies, surveys, petitions and reports. Naturally, all these different sources have their peculiarities, strengths and weaknesses, as Willem van Schendel has argued in the introductory chapter. But it is obvious that we frequently have more information at our disposal than we think.

The focus of the present volume is on the embedding of four agricultural commodities: indigo, coffee, cane sugar and tobacco. Their global trajectories have been very different – both in terms of space and time and in terms of political economy and labour exploitation.

Embedding indigo

Indigo is a blue dye that, paradoxically, is produced from the yellow, mauve, or pink flowers, and green leaves and stems of different plant species. In tropical areas, these plants are primarily of the *Indigofera* genus, in temperate-climate zones it is primarily woad (*Isatis tinctoria*). In Europe, there was a traditional indigo industry. Asian indigo, imported mainly via the Persian Gulf and Alexandria, had been known in Europe for some time and, thanks to its superior quality was sometimes added to the indigenous blue dye. After the Portuguese discovered a route to India by sea, larger quantities of the dye were sold in Europe, and this trade intensified considerably after it was taken over by the Dutch in the seventeenth century. Many European woad growers and traders were ruined by the rising import, forcing several sovereigns to take countermeasures. King Henri IV of France even made the usage of Asian indigo subject to the death penalty, and the substance came to be known as 'the devil's eye.'[23] Given the inferior quality of European indigo, however, the stakes were unequal and, despite all opposition, Asian indigo prevailed. In 1660, King Charles II of England had to recruit Belgian dyers to teach their English colleagues how to use indigo. It was only logical that the English East India Company would follow the example of the Dutch East India Company and began to import indigo from Asia, especially from Gujarat and Sind in India. Around 1750 the prohibition on Asian indigo had been lifted in most of Europe.[24]

Contemporary travellers have shared some information about the labour processes that producing indigo entailed in those days. In the late seventeenth century, the French traveller Jean-Baptiste Tavernier described the preparation process as follows:

> When they have cut the Herb, they throw it into Pits which they make with Lime, which becomes so hard, that you would judg it to be one intire piece of Marble. They are generally fourscore [eighty] of a hunder'd paces in circuit; and being half full of water, they fill them quite up with the Herb. Then they bruise and jumble it in the water till the leaf, for the stem is worth nothing, become like a kind of tick mud. This being done, they let it settle for some days; and when the settling is all at the bottom, and the water clear above, they let out all the water. When the water is all drain'd out, they fill several baskets with this slime, and in a plain Field you shall see several men at work, every one at his own basket, making up little pieces of *Indigo* flat at the bottom, at the top sharp like an egg. Though at *Amadabat* they make their pieces quite flat like a small cake.[25]

In later centuries, production methods were refined but they continued to be based on the preparation procedure described above.

Asian indigo came to dominate the global market as its production was stepped up considerably. This expansion was partly attributable to market changes: in Europe the production of military and other uniforms expanded massively and many of these uniforms were dyed blue.[26] This dominance of Asian indigo proved short-lived, for two reasons. The first was that the Asian indigo (mainly from Western India) was often adulterated:

> In some cases dirt became mixed with the balls when they were laid out to dry, but also certain clays of about the same consistency and of a similar color were regularly dug and sold to mix with indigo. In order to bring it nearer to buoyancy in water a little oil was added to the mixture. Customarily merchants burned a sample in order to ascertain what proportion was dirt.[27]

Indigo-bearing plants were soon found in the Americas, leading Spanish, Portuguese, French, and English settlers to grow indigo there as well. 'European skill and capital soon placed the enterprise on a footing which killed, or all but killed, the Indian trade'.[28] The Spaniards initiated indigo production in the viceroyalty of New Spain and the adjacent captaincy-general in Guatemala from the 1560s.[29] When opposition to non-woad-based indigo declined in Europe, the English and French began to grow indigo as well. The former started production in Jamaica after they had captured the island in 1655. The latter initiated indigo in the Guyanas and Martinique, among other places, and on Saint-Domingue (Haiti) from about 1670. In the 1720s indigo was grown in Louisiana as well.[30] Especially on Saint-Domingue indigo became economically significant. It was grown on large plantations and became the main source of income for the island's elite throughout the eighteenth century. On the eve of the revolution of 1791, an estimated 160 *indigoteries* existed in the colony.[31]

In British North America indigo cultivation was especially successful in South Carolina, where, from 1741, the industry was booming, only to enter a slump after a few decades, culminating in its demise in the mid-nineteenth century.[32] In Portuguese Brazil cultivation began somewhat later than in South Carolina, followed in the 1770s by a rapid rise in production, which was exported primarily to Portugal. After peaking around 1796, the industry collapsed, and little remained around 1820.[33]

Terry Sharrer has described agricultural practice in the Americas as follows:

> Planters began soil preparation some time in December, using slaves to clear the land of brush, trash, and trees. Planting started the following April, or as soon as the daily temperature stayed above 80° F [18°C]. Usually, the growing season ran until late August or early September. During this five-month period, planters could count on two cuttings of the plant, one in mid-July and another at the end of August. An uncommonly long growing season, however, allowed a third harvest in October. By comparison, West Indian and Guatemalan producers harvested six to eight times, at six-week intervals, because of the warmer and longer growing season.
>
> Slaves ploughed the fields in furrowed trenches. Then, walking along the furrows with a sack of tiny black seeds, they simply hoed the earth with a mattock, dropped in several seeds, and pressed the dirt over with their heels. Sowing at 18-inch intervals, a slave could plant a bushel of seed over 4 acres. Providing the weather remained warm, the first sprouts appeared above the ground in ten to fourteen days. The slaves then weeded, thinned the plants, and loosened the soil. As the indigo matured, planters had to guard against insects, especially caterpillars and grasshoppers. [...]
>
> About three months after the first sprouts appeared, the indigo reached full bloom and the planter readied for the harvest. Workers used reaping hooks to cut the plants. The cutting began, either early in the morning, when the

dew still lay heavy on the leaves, or in the evening, just before dark. At any other time in the day, the hot Carolina sun wilted the leaves as soon as the slaves cut the stems. In the cool of the early morning and late evening, one slave might harvest as much as 2 acres per day.[34]

Until somewhat more sophisticated techniques were introduced in India during the nineteenth century, the dye was manufactured by approximately the same techniques all over the world. The freshly-cut leaves, harvested from two to seven times a year, depending upon the locale, were placed in vats and allowed to ferment in warm water for several hours until a yellowish-orange pigment appeared. This slime was then drawn off to so-called beating vats, where it was agitated by bamboo sticks to induce oxidation, the resulting *indicum* gradually settling out as a blue precipitate which accumulated as sludge on the bottom of the vat. After the water had been drained off, the sludge was removed to another vat and immediately boiled to prevent further fermentation, which might injure the dye's quality. Then it was filtered and cut into cakes, which were stored to await transportation to market.[35]

The American hegemony was short-lived. Sugarcane often turned out to be even more profitable than indigo, so many planters switched to producing the sweetener in the course of the eighteenth century. The independence of the United States in 1776 rendered the British textile industry almost totally dependent on 'foreign' suppliers of blue dye. Deliveries from South Carolina could no longer be taken for granted, and the other major suppliers were colonies of other European powers. Moreover, the successful slave revolt on Saint-Domingue (1791–1804) brought the vast indigo production there to a standstill. Indigo production in Louisiana and Guatemala declined as well during the eighteenth century.[36]

In essence, the indigo supply from America diminished and became more tenuous. The directors of the English East India Company seized this opportunity and from 1780 systematically tried to revive Indian indigo production. They tempted European indigo planters from the West Indies to move to selected districts of Bengal.[37] From Delhi to Dhaka, indigo production thrived. 'There were 300 or 400 factories in Bengal, chiefly in Jessor, Krishnagar and Tirhoot, and in the Champaran District of Bihar. The best soils for growing indigo were those subject to inundation from the Ganges'.[38] The centre of gravity of international trade had now shifted back to South Asia. Willem van Schendel's chapter discusses this in depth and shows how ongoing conflicts between planters and peasants shaped the modalities of the crop transfer (Chapter 2).

At first, Indian indigo production was directly supervised by the East India Company:

> Prior to 1834, viz., before the renewal of the charter, private merchants usually took shelter under the shadow of some powerful covenanted servant of the Company and carried on indigo cultivation and manufacture as his partner or agent. The servant of the Company was also a powerful official, wielding almost despotic powers over the people residing within the limits

of his charge. Under this combination indigo culture flourished. The evils to which it led may be readily imagined.[39]

After 1833, however, when the Company lost its commercial character and henceforth had to limit its activities to managing the country, an enterprising group of planters arrived in Northern India that rented or purchased estates to grow indigo there. This system of direct cultivation soon proved insufficiently profitable. The resulting alternative was an elaborate system in which the planters issued advances to agricultural tenants (*raiyats*), 'on the condition that they cultivated a certain quantity of indigo on their holdings and sold the produce to the factory at fixed rates, the selling price to be adjusted against advances'.[40] This system rendered the tenants increasingly dependent on the planters. Lord Macaulay declared in a Memorandum that many *raiyats* had been 'reduced to a state not far removed from partial slavery'.[41] The attitude of the planters – British, French and 'Anglo-Indians' (of mixed race) – was harsh and cruel. They confined tenants in stocks and punished them with rattan. Many had worked as slave masters or slave overseers in the Caribbean and had brought their 'unfortunate ideas and practices' with them to South Asia.[42]

Mounting tensions ensued. In 1860, when indigo prices had been rising for several years while the *raiyats* continued to receive the same compensation that they had for the past 30 years, great riots broke out, the so-called *indigo disturbances*.[43] When the government, especially in Bengal, took measures to improve conditions for the *raiyats*, the result was an exodus of planters to other parts of the colony: Bihar, the North-Western Provinces (Upper India), and Madras.[44]

Around 1900, the great affluence of the indigo planters came to an end. In 1897 the Badische Anilin- und Soda-Fabrik (BASF) in Germany introduced large quantities of low-priced synthetic indigo on the market, and sales of natural indigo soon collapsed altogether.[45] Between 1894 and 1915 the land area used for growing indigo diminished by 90 per cent. During the First World War, there was a brief revival, but in the 1920s, the acreage once again became insignificant, this time permanently.[46]

Natural indigo has thus followed a circular pattern, but one that culminates in a fatal demise: starting as small-scale production in India, large-scale plantation production based on slave labour in the Americas took off and, subsequently, still on a large scale, returned to India, doomed there by competition from artificial substitution.

Embedding coffee

Coffee is made of berries from a shrub or tree that may grow to 15 metres in exceptional cases but usually reaches only 2 or 3 metres. The two main coffee varieties are *coffea arabica* and *coffea robusta*. The Robusta plant bears fruit throughout the year; the Arabica plant is less productive and provides a single annual harvest. Still, most coffee produced all over the world became and still is Arabica, thanks to its superior flavour.

The simplest way to grow coffee is to dig several small holes in the ground and place about 20 seeds in each hole – but seedlings of mature size may be planted as well. The young crop is protected by a practice dating back centuries: placing shade trees between the coffee plants. After some time, the plants are pruned, weeded and, possibly, mulched and manured. Once the berries are ripe and have turned red, they are stripped manually, 'swiftly but gently without injuring the tree'.[47]

The husk of each coffee berry ordinarily contains two seeds or beans. After they are harvested, the ripe berries need to be processed within 24 hours. There are two methods for doing this. The *dry method* entails drying the cherries immediately, usually by placing them in the sun; afterwards, they are threshed so that the dried pulp is separated from the beans. In the *wet method*, the beans are removed from the berries manually or mechanically and then fermented in water for 24 hours. Next, they are rinsed and dried. Both the wet and the dry method result in beans that are still surrounded by a seed coat. Removing this coating leaves green coffee beans that may be stored for several years. These green beans are transported to metropolitan distribution centres to be roasted. Neither the dry nor the wet method requires major investments, all the work may be done manually, using very simple tools – although over time machines have been devised to replace many of the manual operations. Coffee can thus be grown by small farmers and on large plantations alike.

Arabica coffee originated in Ethiopia and was initially used mainly for medicinal purposes, although it furthermore became acknowledged as a stimulant. Until the late seventeenth-century Yemen, with Mocha as the trading centre, was the main supplier.[48] Later on, the plant began a long trek across the world.[49] Around 1690, the Dutch brought the first coffee plants to Ceylon, but only around 1718 did regulated cultivation get under way. Coffee was planted in the coastal regions, where the VOC had the most power.[50]

Additionally, in the early eighteenth century, the VOC started to promote coffee growing in Java.[51] Several attempts at transfer failed, but in 1711, the first commercially cultivated coffee beans were shipped to the Netherlands. Everywhere the VOC resorted to indirect exploitation in coffee cultivation, reaching agreements with local rulers to give contingents and meet delivery quotas. The regents had to ensure that their subjects planted coffee, maintained the fields, and delivered the product in good condition. 'Company officials never interacted with the "little guy," so to speak. Only Batavia's Ommelanden [environs] were under direct Company control'.[52]

Coffee growing regularly met with resistance. Especially on Ceylon, the yield was disappointing, due to the renitent locals. Because at the same time the coffee supply from Java and the West Indies was increasing significantly, the Dutch abandoned production in Ceylon in 1739 – although the Sinhalese population seems to have continued planting on their own account: when the English later occupied part of the island, they still found many cultivated coffee plants.[53]

From Ceylon and Java, the coffee plant continued to spread, not only to other parts of Southeast Asia (Sumatra, Celebes, the Philippines), but also to the Americas. One coffee plant from Amsterdam's *hortus botanicus* figured most prominently in this trek. In 1714, the Amsterdam authorities presented some descendants of this plant to King Louis XIV of France. He had them transferred to the Jardin des Plantes in Paris, where they thrived. Next, cuttings were transferred to the Caribbean, first to Martinique (1723), somewhat later to Jamaica (1728), Cayenne, Cuba, Saint-Domingue and Bourbon. In 1719, some cuttings from Amsterdam ended up in Suriname so that the original plant from Amsterdam seems to have been the originator of all West-Indian coffee.[54]

In Brazil, the first coffee was planted in the state of Pará. Initially, the crop served domestic consumption; widespread production for export began only after the independence in 1822. Coffee was an ideal accessory to the rising capitalist society as it keeps one alert and accelerates physical and mental functions. Global coffee production met the equally rapid rise in consumer demand in North America and Europe.[55] 'Between 1853 and 1900 coffee consumption quadrupled in Germany and quintupled in France'.[56]

The Great Depression of the 1930s caused coffee prices to plummet. Brazil responded by destroying a considerable share of its harvest 'In the 14 years 1931–44 over 78 million bags of coffee went up in smoke – enough to supply world consumption requirements for at least three years'.[57] In many coffee-producing countries, larger growers took over the land of smaller growers, deepening the misery of the latter. In Central America resistance mounted among the

Figure 8.2 Picking coffee in Brazil in the early twentieth century

Table 8.2 World coffee production: geographical distribution, c. 1852–2010 (percentages)

	c. 1852	1909	1934	1945–50 average	1980	2010
Brazil	37.0	70.7	54.3	52.1	21.9	35.3
Central America	1.9	6.9	8.5		16.9	12.4
Caribbean	23.1	3.8	2.2	12.8	2.9	0.9
Venezuela	–	4.4	2.9	2.0	1.2	0.9
Colombia	–	3.3	11.9	16.1	15.0	6.2
Dutch East Indies/ Indonesia	27.3	2.4	5.2	1.1	6.1	8.3
Mexico	–	1.8	2.4	2.6	4.5	3.1
Africa	–	0.9	4.5	10.8	24.0	10.6
Vietnam	–	–	–	–	0.2	13.4
Rest of the world	10.7	5.8	8.1	2.5	7.3	5.1
Total	100.0	100.0	100.0	100.0	100.0	100.0
				(1,680,000 tonnes)	(4,839,224 tonnes)	(8,228,018 tonnes)

Sources: For c. 1852: John Crawford. 'History of Coffee', 53 (in lbs.), with the additional remark: 'the following has been considered probable, which is the utmost that can be said of this or any similar estimate'. On 1909: G. G. Huebner. 'The Coffee Market', Annals of the American Academy of Political and Social Science, 38:2 (1911), 294. On 1934: Henry C. Taylor and Anne Dewees Taylor. World Trade in Agricultural Products (New York: Macmillan, 1943), 80. On 1945–46/49–50: Wickizer, Coffee, Tea, and Cocoa), 68, 474. On 1980 and 2010: FAOSTAT.

poor farmers and farm workers, and states controlled by the coffee oligarchies responded with exceptionally repressive measures. In El Salvador, where at the time over 90 per cent of the export consisted of coffee, a military coup in 1931–2 resulted in a horrible bloodbath, named *La Matanza* (The Massacre); between 15,000 and 20,000 *campesinos* were murdered.[58]

Coffee production spread to other parts of the world. African countries (for example, Angola, Kenya, Mozambique and Natal) managed to conquer a part of world trade but, after peaking in the decade following the Second World War, decline set in. In the past quarter century, Vietnam has become a major producer. The French had previously introduced the coffee plant there in 1857, and the country already exported it abroad in the late nineteenth century. But production truly got under way only after the start of *Doi Moi*, privatization of the economy since 1986.

158   *Marcel van der Linden*

Coffee has traditionally been produced in two parallel productive systems, namely plantations and smallholdings, although production on smallholdings has dominated for quite a while.[59] Bhaswati Bhattacharya's chapter provides a good example of such smallholding production (Chapter 4). The corporate groups dominating coffee retail (Philip Morris, Nestlé, Sara Lee, etc.) never tried to gain widespread control of coffee farmers. Instead, they dominated the world market mainly through a chain of intermediaries.[60]

Embedding sugarcane

Sugarcane is a perennial grass. Nearly 40 species of the *saccharum* genus exist. They originate in South and Southeast Asia, and in the west of Oceania (the island of New Guinea). Processing sugarcane to make sugar is believed to have started in northern India in the fourth century BCE. From there, extraction technologies spread to China, to Arabia and Africa (via Oman) and to the Mediterranean (via Persia).[61] In North Africa, the Levant and southern Europe the sugar industry took off around 700 CE. Its heyday lasted several centuries and, remarkably but nonetheless indicative, around 1400 there were three sugarcane plantations on Cyprus, each with hundreds of slaves and other workers.[62]

Sugarcane ordinarily reproduces via cuttings rather than seeds. Capus and Bois described the cultivation method as follows:

> The cuttings are taken from the stems of the strongest and healthiest stalks and cut in lengths of 25 to 30 centimetres from the top half of the stem and comprising several nodes with buds. These cuttings are planted, either in holes made with a hoe or in ploughed furrows: *trouaison* or *sillonage*. Individual stems are usually planted 1.25 to 1.5 m apart in staggered rows with about 4,000 stalks per hectare. The terrain, from which the roots have been removed and the old cane rhizomes burned, is loosened through intersecting efforts [...], and the cuttings lie in the furrows or the holes or may be placed at oblique angles in less dry soil. They are then provided with suitable fertilizer and covered once again with earth. While the stalks are growing, the earth on the roots at the surface needs to be weeded, hoed, and lowered and to be cleared, i.e. by removing the rotten dry leaves from the stems that provide a breeding ground for parasitic diseases. The cane ripens after a year to eighteen months, depending on the varieties and the regional conditions. Under the most favourable conditions, harvesting follows eleven months after planting. The harvest is not postponed until after the plants blossom.[63]

Workers harvest the cane stalks by cutting them with machetes. The harvest is a major event on every sugar plantation: crucial for the owner and therefore also a strategic moment for workers to enforce their demands. As the technologist Noël Deerr has written, it is: 'an important item in the cost of production, and uses up a large proportion of the visible supply of labour, besides placing the owners at the mercy of an irresponsible population'.[64]

Over time, major changes occurred in subsequent processing methods. Until well into the nineteenth century large commercial plantations still used a method that is applied to this day by small farmers in India and elsewhere:

> [T]he cane was moved and compressed between vertical wooden or stone washers by people, buffaloes, or water. The syrup was boiled and evaporated in a measured quantity of slaked lime. While being boiled and reduced by evaporation, the boiling substance was regularly skimmed off. Once it was half boiled out, the resulting thickened syrup was poured in a settling tank to clear, and the cleared syrup was reduced by evaporation in a second set of pans to a filling compound. This was then poured into jars, closed at the bottom with a plug. After cooling and crystallizing, the plug was removed, allowing the syrup to drip out. Any remaining syrup was removed by pouring a mixture of water and clay on the sugar, to clay it. The sugar was then cast from the jars, dried in the sun, pulverized and packed into canisters.[65]

In the second half of the nineteenth century, countless modernizations were gradually introduced. These modernizations included steam engines and replacement of wooden and stone presses by iron ones with horizontal, ternary cylinders, the introduction of vacuum pans and centrifuges. Modern processing methods involve cutting the stems into pieces first or breaking them by using cutters, shredders or crushers. The pieces of the stems are then pre-crushed and post-crushed by cylinders rotating against each other. The syrup obtained is filtered and purified by adding lime. Heating and evaporation further concentrate the liquid, which is then boiled in a vacuum pan (a saucepan) at a temperature below 100 degrees, until sugar crystals become visible in the syrup that forms. After cooling sufficiently, the sugar crystals and syrup are separated by centrifuge.[66]

The system for producing cane sugar thus comprises distinct parts: first the agricultural part and then the industrial one. The second part meant that sugar production always required relatively large investments, including a separate building, with machines and skilled labour. The Mediterranean sugar industry may be seen as the laboratory in which the productive system was developed that was later widely used in tropical America and Asia.[67] This system, which Pierre Dockès has named the 'sugar paradigm',[68] roughly has the following characteristics:

- The crop is grown in areas naturally isolated from their surroundings: islands or places surrounded by mountains or large forests.
- Production takes place on vast plantations, with expansive 'gardens,' often divided into rectangles.
- Any indigenous population present is eliminated or driven out. The work is done by slaves living on the plantations and supervised by overseers.
- There would be one or more separate sugar mills on the plantation, factories where sugarcane was compressed and the resulting molasses purified.
- On the plantation was also a villa (*casa grande*) for the Master, the manager in charge.

The sugar paradigm is based in part on biology and in part on specific relations of labour exploitation. The sucrose content of sugarcane starts declining rapidly immediately after the harvest and it is gone within a few days. The cane must, therefore, be processed as quickly as possible, which is why the sugar mill is in close proximity to the fields.

From the Mediterranean, the Portuguese and Spanish brought sugar cultivation to the still uninhabited areas of Madeira, the Canaries en São Tomé.[69] By around 1506 there were some two thousand slaves who worked in São Tomé; by 1540, they numbered nearly six thousand. They came primarily from the Niger delta and Congo. Between 1530 and 1536 they revolted *en masse*. This rebellion appears to have been conducive to a racist ideology among the colonial rulers.[70]

In the 1530s the Portuguese introduced sugarcane in coastal Brazil; here they first exploited Indian slaves and later African ones. In 1630, the Dutch West India Company (WIC) conquered most of this area. With local assistance, the Dutch settlers soon began to master the art of producing sugar and, when they were chased out of Brazil in 1654, they brought the art of sugar cane cultivation along with them to the Caribbean, refining this art on several islands: in the British Caribbean (Jamaica, Barbados), on French islands such as Saint-Domingue, Martinique, and Guadeloupe, as well as in coastal areas on the mainland. This was where the so-called 'Sugar Revolution' began:

> The six central elements of the sugar revolution are commonly regarded as a swift shift from diversified agriculture to sugar monoculture, from production on small farms to large plantations, from free to slave labour, from sparse to dense settlement, from white to black populations, and from low to high value per caput output. More broadly, it is claimed that the sugar revolution had five effects: it generated a massive boost to the Atlantic slave trade, provided the engine for a variety of triangular trades, altered European nutrition and consumption, increased European interest in tropical colonies, and, more contentiously, contributed vitally to the industrial revolution.[71]

The clearest and earliest visible manifestation of the sugar revolution was on the small island of Barbados (1645–60). Elsewhere, the process was more gradual. One highly successful latecomer was Cuba, which became an immense producer in the second half of the eighteenth century, a trend that accelerated after the slave revolt on Saint-Domingue (renamed Haiti in 1802 and the first modern black state) had all but ended the plantation economy on that island. Following earlier attempts during the seventeenth and eighteenth centuries, sugarcane started to thrive in Asia and Oceania in the nineteenth century as well, in India, Java, Malaya, Taiwan, the Philippines, Queensland and Hawaii.[72]

In China, sugar had been produced since the fifteenth century, at first mainly in Guangdong and Fujian, later also in Taiwan and elsewhere. Unlike in the Atlantic region, however, here this industry was almost exclusively a smallholder economy. In the sixteenth and seventeenth centuries, it was the foundation for thriving intra-Asian foreign trade. After the rule of the Ming Dynasty ended (1644), rapid

Table 8.3 Sugarcane production, 1456–2010 (1,000 tonnes)

	Cyprus	Madeira	São Tomé	Brazil	Caribbean	Java/Indonesia	India	China	Rest of the world
1456	800	80							
1500	375	2,500							
1580		500	2,200	2,300					
1700				20,000	37,000				
1760				28,000	172,000				
1787				19,000	267,000				
1815				75,000	270,800				18,500
1859–60				50,000	504,000	134,000			
1895–96				225,000	595,800	605,025★	20,000★		1,491,752
1926–27				700	502,000	1,973			
1961				59,377	88,538	10,931	110,001	12,415	177,647
2010				717,462	19,761	24,450	292,300	111,454	570,110

★ Exports

Source: On 1456–1815: Angus Maddison. *The World Economy, vol. 1: A Millennial Perspective* (Paris: Development Centre of the OECD, 2007), 60. For 1895–96: John Franklin Crowell. 'The Sugar Situation in the Tropics,' *Political Science Quarterly,* 14:4 (1899), 610–1. On 1961 and 2010: FAOSTAT

commercial expansion followed under the aegis of Zheng Chenggong (known as Koxinga to the Dutch), involving at least ten mercantile groups, or *hang*. Their network extended from Persia to Japan. Around 1700, this empire made way for other Chinese networks while trade continued to grow and was economically important well into the nineteenth century. Chinese immigrants from Chaozhou even 'developed sugar plantations in Siam and began exporting to Singapore'.[73] See Table 8.3 for an overview of world sugarcane production.

During the nineteenth century, two major changes occurred. The abolition of slavery by England (1834), France (1848), and the Netherlands (1863) changed the sugar paradigm. Instead of slaves, the work was in many cases done by sharecroppers, indentured labourers and wage earners. In addition, following a slow start, competition from sugar beets increased – this was presumably the earliest example of an effort in the relatively advanced countries to use scientific agrarian methods to undermine tropical production.[74] Whereas in around 1850 almost 90 per cent of global sugar production was from cane, 50 years later this share was about half.[75] In the course of the twentieth century, however, sugarcane came back with a vengeance. In 2010, the ratio was: cane 88 per cent of world output, beets 12 per cent.

Embedding tobacco

Tobacco consists of dried leaves from an annual plant of the *nicotiana* genus. If properly cultivated, the plant may grow to three metres high and contain about 20 harvestable leaves. The crews on the ships of Columbus already acquired the Caribbean habit of smoking *toboca* or *tabaga* on their journeys to the New World, and tobacco production and consumption very rapidly spread all over the world, often rather spontaneously and sometimes even against the will of governments.[76] 'Tobacco was ideally suited to first generation settlers. It grew in varied soils under different climatic conditions, required little land and capital, and yielded a quick return. A crop could be grown in nine months'.[77] It was the first important cash crop to be brought from the Americas to Asia. The crop arrived in the Philippines in 1600 and reached Java only a year later.[78] Around 1620, the crop was present in both temperate and hot climates, in Northern and Southern Europe, in Russia, Turkey, South Asia, the East Indies, Japan, China, Korea, India and West Africa.[79] Hardly any reliable data are available from the seventeenth and eighteenth centuries about the geographic spread of tobacco production, in part because this production was under way in so many different places. Since the tobacco plant has very few requirements, it has been grown successfully from Argentina to Sweden. But it did deplete soil very rapidly and was, therefore, an extremely 'mobile' crop.[80] The quality of tobacco grown in so many different places, therefore, varies widely.

Tobacco may be sown directly or planted after cultivating seedlings in nurseries. The plants are then inspected periodically to catch any caterpillars, grasshoppers and other insects; they are also sprayed with water as needed. After a few months, buds and flowers appear and are systematically removed, as

Table 8.4 Tobacco production, unmanufactured in tonnes

	Average 1909–13	Average 1923–6	1961	2010
Caribbean	3.6% (49,800)	2.6% (53,700)	2.6% (92,322)	0.4% (30,777)
Brazil	3.2% (45,400)	3.0% (63,100)	4.7% (167,839)	11.4% (787,817)
United States	31.4% (451,800)	29.8% (619,900)	26.2% (935,000)	4.7% (325,766)
China	4.9% (70,000)	9.0% (187,500)	11.0% (395,854)	43.4% (3,005,928)
India★	15.7% (225,000)	16.4% (341,000)	8.6% (307,000)	10.8% (745,670)
Indonesia	5.6% (80,000)	3.8% (79,900)	2.4% (85,800)	2.0% (135,700)
Malawi	n.a.	n.a.	0.3% (12,202)	2.5% (172,922)
Zimbabwe	n.a.	n.a.	2.8% (99,890)	1.6% (109,737)
Rest of the world	35.6% (515,300)	35.4% (735,000)	41.4%	33.2%
World (100%) in tonnes	1,437,300	2,080,100	3,573,815	6,933,660

★India before 1947 is: British India.
Note on the years 1909–1926: 'Global tobacco production is difficult to determine. For some countries that are large producers, such as Russia and Persia, where valid statistics are difficult to obtain or entirely non-existent, the data are approximate and uncertain in the total, or the assessments are based on indirect data and mere estimation.' (Capus, Leulliot and Foëx. Tabac, 91)

Sources: For 1909–13 and 1923–6: Guillaume Capus, Fernand Leulliot and Etienne Foëx. Le Tabac (Paris: Société d'Editions géographiques, maritimes et coloniales, 1929–30), vol. 3, 94–5; for 1961 and 2010: FAOSTAT.

are bad leaves ('topping', 'suckering') so that all nutrients reach the promising leaves. The harvest that follows soon afterwards has been refined over time. An early twentieth-century study from the Netherlands Indies reads as follows:

> In the past the harvesting began only when the top leaves were ready to be harvested. People then harvested the trees and even had the bottom leaves fall from the tree prematurely, without harvesting them. Later the bottom leaves were harvested separately, before bringing in the others as tree harvest, i.e. including the stems. Nowadays the entire leaf is generally already taken to drying sheds as leaf harvest, first the bottom leaves, then the middle ones, next the top ones.[81]

After the leaves are picked, they are dried for three to four weeks by placing them in the sun or an oven, or hanging under a shelter. The leaves are then gathered and left to ferment for about ten weeks.

Production for the European market began in the seventeenth century. Virginia exported its first tobacco to England in 1612. Other regions gradually followed, first those in the Americas, later in Asia, and eventually in Africa as well. The Deli Company began important tobacco plantations on Sumatra from 1863 onward. In China tobacco cultivation began around 1914, was interrupted by the Civil War in the 1920s, and then cautiously resumed in the 1930s. After the People's Republic was proclaimed in 1949, tobacco cultivation was included in the planned economy. Yunnan has been the most important tobacco-growing area there since the 1970s.[82] In Africa tobacco began to be grown in Zimbabwe (Rhodesia), around 1890 (Table 8.4).

With the disclosure of scientific evidence that smoking is medically harmful, increasingly forceful campaigns against tobacco products have been launched in Europe and North America since the 1970s, culminating in official prohibitions on smoking in public spaces in a substantial number of countries.

Embedding crops: a sequence in time and space

These four narratives reveal how different the various historical cash-crop trajectories have been. Indigo was once in great demand but has been replaced almost entirely by artificial dyes for over a century. Coffee, on the other hand, has now become the strongest revenue-generating primary commodity worldwide, after crude oil. Some crops are labour-intensive, others require little work. Some crops tend to be grown on large plantations, others on small plots of land.

Many contingent factors helped to shape the global trajectories of cash crops: revolutions (such as the great slave rebellion of Saint-Domingue), wars and resultant power shifts, scientific discoveries, consumer preferences, and so on. Nevertheless, it is possible to discern a certain logic in developments – a logic that is not deterministic but reveals historical tendencies and opportunities. The process of long-distance plant transfer *always* consists of four necessary steps: 1) acquisition of seeds or seedlings; 2) transfer of these seeds and seedlings to new locations in the South; 3) growing and harvesting of the crops; 4) transport to and sale of these crops in the North.

Acquisition of seeds and seedlings

When relocating crops one first needs to acquire seeds or seedlings. Within the boundaries of colonial empires, this was often quite simple, provided that the would-be planters acted in accordance with the local authorities in the crop's area of origin. Things became more problematic if the authorities were opposed to a transfer, for example, because this could harm national export. Transfer then became an illegal act. There have been many of such illicit operations. A well-known example is that of the Englishman Henry A. Wickham, who, in defiance of a prohibition by the Brazilian authorities, gathered seeds from the rubber tree (*hevea brasiliensis*) along the Tapajoz River in 1876. Wickham managed to transport his delicate loot across many hundreds of kilometres to Belem and then to the Kew Botanical Gardens in England. A small share of the seeds survived the journey and these were cultivated. About two thousand seedlings were then transferred to botanical gardens in Ceylon, Malaya and Java.[83]

Transport was made easier by intermediate stops, so that the seeds and seedlings could recover from the hardships of travel, and could later continue their journey in a better condition. It was the botanical gardens that played the role of 'intermediate stops' – as in the case of Wickham's *hevea* seeds. Such gardens had a very long history, going back to antiquity, the early Islamic states and the Aztec empire. The first botanical gardens in Europe were probably established in Italy: in Pisa (1543), Padua (1545), Florence (1550) and Bologna (1568). These gardens were primarily meant to train students and not to facilitate the transfer of plants.

In the eighteenth century, botanical gardens gained economic significance. The less improvised cash-crop transfers became, the more important it became to have the practical know-how associated with these systematically organized and well-documented institutions. Botanical gardens thus developed into scientific nodes of plant transfers.[84] Therefore, it did not take long before colonial powers founded the first botanical gardens in tropical regions as bridgeheads for biological imperialism (Table 8.5).

Soon the botanical gardens formed a global network that exchanged data. An important resource was the so-called *Index semina* (sometimes called *Index seminum*), a list of seeds regularly published since the eighteenth century.[85]

Transfer of seeds and seedlings to new locations in the South

Seeds and seedlings had to be carried to new locations. For centuries, long-distance transfers of seeds and plants were particularly difficult: packaging

Table 8.5 Some botanical gardens that played a role in long-distance plant transfer, sixteenth–nineteenth centuries (founding years between brackets)

	British Empire	Dutch Empire	French Empire
Metropolitan	Royal Botanic Garden (Kew, 1759)	Hortus botanicus, Leiden (1590)	Jardin des plantes, Paris (1635)
Colonial	Kingstown, St. Vincent (1765) Howrah (near Calcutta), India (1787) Port of Spain, Trinidad (1818) Peradeniya, Ceylon (1821) Singapore (1822/1859)	Buitenzorgs (Bogor, Java) (1817)	Pamplemousses, Mauritius (1770)

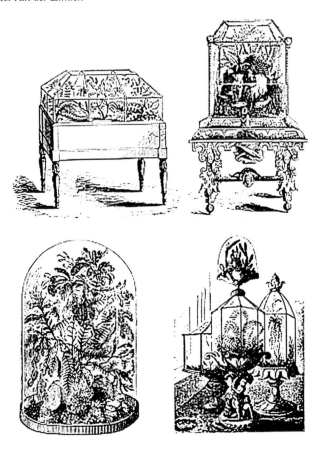

Figure 8.3 Wardian cases

methods were often imprecise and extended sea voyages very risky. Sarah Stetson described the problems as follows:

> Months might be spent in the painstaking gathering and careful preparation of specimens, which became a total loss in the course of the long sea voyage. The sailing ships which crossed the ocean were small affairs at best, dependent entirely upon wind and current for their speed; the length of the trip was a matter of weeks instead of days. Storms delayed the vessel until plants rotted and seeds lost their vitality; yet brisk winds and quiet sea might just as surely bring a ruined cargo to port, due to improper packing. It was an irregular traffic, with no tried and certain methods about it either in consignment or in transportation.[86]

Only after the 'Wardian case' was invented did the transfer of crops become less of an adventure. Around 1829, Dr Nathaniel Ward (1791–1868) built a kind of proto-herbarium that considerably facilitated safe transport of plants. It was first tested in 1833 when Ward successfully had two cases of ferns and grasses transported to Australia, a journey that lasted a few months.[87] Over the years, this case was used ever more frequently, thereby accelerating and increasing the number of transfers (Figure 8.3). Around the mid-nineteenth century, 'almost every domesticated plant had been transferred, at least experimentally, to every likely environment on earth'.[88]

Growing and harvesting of the crops

Once seeds and seedlings have been safely transferred to a new environment, their commercial exploitation is supposed to follow. In many cases, such relocations failed. Indigo did not do well in Senegal, cinchona was unsuccessful in Algeria, as was the Ford Company's attempt to develop a rubber plantation in Brazil. The factors influencing success are numerous and are often interconnected. On the one hand, we have elements affecting the prices received by the farmer for different products; they include market contingencies, transportation and handling costs. On the other hand, we have elements affecting the cost per unit of producing different products. Climate, soil and topography influence the yields, and hence the cost per unit, and labour relations and forms of workers' resistance also leads to different costs. These factors, which dictate both differences in prices and differences in cost, determine which products are most profitable.

Embedding – making crops an integral part of new surroundings – is an extremely complicated process. Agricultural 'globalizers' had to take into account a wide variety of aspects, including plant diseases, predators (insects, etc.), energy sources, water supply, labour recruitment, labour discipline, the relationship with financiers, transport facilities, the relationship with local authorities and market opportunities. Crop transfer was a difficult and risky enterprise, even though its history is often presented as a continuous success story. In reality, failures have probably far outnumbered successes. P. F. Knowles was justified in saying that: 'Often in early stages of a crop's development the best area of production is not known, mistakes may occur through ignorance, or unanticipated pests may appear. Usually the average yield is very low'.[89]

The following observation on the introduction of sugarcane in Hawaii is perhaps typical: 'Managers taught themselves how to organize a plantation and manufacture sugar (a delicate chemical process) by trial and error. Sugar mills broke down, burned down, and generally proved inadequate. [...] Often error led to business failure'.[90] Negative experiences with innovation may have contributed to conservatism among some cultivators, as Jonathan Curry-Machado shows in his chapter (Chapter 7).

An historian of technology, Nathan Rosenberg, articulated a commonplace when he wrote that 'there are many things that cannot be known in advance or deduced from some set of first principles'. This fundamental uncertainty 'has a very important implication: the [innovative] activity cannot be planned. No person, or group of persons, is clever enough to plan the outcome of the search process, in the sense of identifying a particular innovation target and moving in a predetermined way to its realization – as one might read a road map and plan the most efficient route to a historical monument'.[91] This is also the reason why pioneers are often 'punished'. As Karl Marx mentioned:

> [the] much greater costs that are always involved in an enterprise based on new inventions, compared with later establishments that rise up on its ruins, *ex suis ossibus*. The extent of this is so great that the pioneering entrepreneurs generally go bankrupt, and it is only their successors who flourish, thanks to their possession of cheaper buildings, machinery, etc. Thus, it is generally the most worthless and wretched kind of money-capitalists that draw the greatest profit from all new developments of the universal labour of the human spirit and their social application by combined labour.[92]

As the knowledge of agricultural 'globalizers' increased over time, their mutual competition became more sophisticated. During the eighteenth century, former soldiers and other 'meritorious' Europeans were rewarded with a piece of land so that they could have a farm or plantation there. But this became almost impossible at a later stage, owing to the enormous know-how that had meanwhile been accumulated. For example, in his 1956 manual on *Modern Coffee Production*, A. E. Haarer cautioned:

> The time has long since passed when ex-soldier land settlement schemes are of any value. Nor is it wise for a banker, a stockbroker, or a lawyer to throw up his profession and start planting coffee. [...] Nowadays a farm requires a technically trained farmer, and an orchard needs a man who is trained in horticulture though agriculture and horticulture are complementary. Money has been wasted and land misused far too often in the past by men who knew little about either of these trades.[93]

Let me highlight three essential conditions for a successful agricultural enterprise in the tropics or subtropics: ecology, business organization and labour.

Ecology

Ecology is of great importance since plants do not grow everywhere but require specific surroundings. For example, coffee can be cultivated between 24° northern and 24° southern latitude, at an elevation of no more than 800 meters, and at temperatures between 17 and 23 °C; rainy and dry seasons should alternate while both extended droughts and long-lasting precipitation are harmful; and the soil should be highly porous, with a stable structure and moisture permeability.[94] This already sounds quite constraining, but many more aspects come into play, such as acidity of the soil, the need of plants for shade or the need *not* to be in the shade. The spectrum of growth-promoting factors for individual plants is very broad. Nowadays, based on such parameters, we can more or less determine the *potential growing areas* for every cash crop – the regions where a given crop would theoretically prosper. Such potential growing areas tend to be considerably larger than the actual growing areas, partly because many other factors may be relevant, such as wind, running water, and partly because of competition from other crops and land use.[95]

The parameters may be very specific. When clove trees were transferred from the Moluccas to the East-African coast, the effort was only barely successful. After all, rainfall is far heavier in the Moluccas than in Africa. On Amboina annual precipitation is about 1,360mm, whereas in Zanzibar it is approximately 600mm, and in Pemba 800mm. In their new surroundings, clove trees had to subsist on an absolute minimum of moisture, which probably explains why the crop did better in Pemba than on Zanzibar.[96] Throughout history, out of ignorance European agriculturalists have made countless unsuccessful attempts to grow plant crops outside their potential growth areas. Over the course of time, 'globalizers' have learned through trial and error where the best locations for certain crops can be found.

Business organization

Business organization is a second major factor. In principle, it is possible to cultivate every crop with every type of business organization. But clearly there are elective affinities. Sugarcane, for instance, is preferably grown in large-scale plantations, while tobacco is often produced by small farmers. At least two factors create such affinities.

First, there is the crop's *gestation period*. Some crops bear fruit within a few months, others take many years. The classical plantation crops are so-called perennials, that is crops which, after planting, need several years before they can be first harvested (palm oil, rubber, cacao). So-called annuals, on the other hand, yield a harvest after one year (cotton, jute, tobacco, or groundnuts). The economic implications of this contrast are several. The production of annuals can be adjusted easily to changes in demand. Perennials, however, are less flexible. They will, therefore, be grown 'either as a secondary crop on a food farm or by a large corporation which can afford to wait out the period between planting and production'. And in addition, 'the decisions to make extra plantings are taken five to ten years before the crops begin to bear, thus accounting for the violent fluctuations in supply'.[97]

Second, *processing* is a major factor. After harvesting, some crops, such as sugarcane and indigo, have to be processed quickly. Green coffee beans, however, can be kept for months and, therefore, do not need immediate roasting. In the case of sugarcane, this can either lead to large plantations with their own central mills, or to a co-operative sugar mill shared by a large number of smallholders. In both cases,

> the mill's profitability largely depended on the minimization of the average fixed costs of producing sugar. This, in turn, depended on the mill working continuously at full capacity during the harvesting season. Thus, the

provision of adequate supplies of cane and the coordination of the pace of harvesting, transport, and milling was of prime concern.[98]

The co-operative approach frequently led to higher transaction costs because harvesting and milling had to be coordinated between numerous smallholders, and this increased the risks borne by the mill. 'It was in these ways that the capital requirements of crushing mills hindered the growth of the smallholding system in sugar cane farming'.[99]

The *combination* of these two influences goes some way towards explaining how agricultural enterprise was organized in separate places. Perennials and costly processing favoured large-scale businesses while annuals and low processing costs favoured small-scale production. Small-scale production could be indirect or direct. In the first case, Northern entrepreneurs did no more than make (often coercive) deals with local Southern elites who then were supposed to periodically deliver a certain amount of crops by exploiting 'their' peasantry. In the second case, smallholder production was stimulated by economic incentives, money taxes or taxes in kind – as under the Cultivation System (1830–1870) in the Netherlands Indies, analysed in Ulbe Bosma's chapter (Chapter 3). The large-scale option would be for 'globalizers' to start their own farms and plantations. Frequently, this choice was the least popular.[100]

Labour

The labour requirements for crops diverge widely. Some crops, such as cotton or tobacco, need substantial labour for short periods while other crops have labour requirements that can be spread more evenly over the year.[101] And some plants do not need much labour at all. The coconut was sometimes referred to as the 'lazy man's crop', for 'once the tree is well started, the owner may, figuratively, recline under it the rest of his life with coconuts falling in his lap. The coconut palm has a very long productive life, with a maximum not clearly determined but appearing to approach one hundred years'.[102] Labour demand for most crops fluctuates seasonally. Harvest time is a busy period, and requires lots of workers while fewer people are necessary during other parts of the year. Agriculturalists generally have two options to resolve this problem. One option is to employ a small group of workers permanently and, in addition, hire large numbers of temporary workers for shorter periods. This is how it is done on the *fincas* or *cafetales* in the coffee region of La Guaca in Colombia:

> Because coffee beans must be picked at just the right time, before they become over-ripened, a relatively large and dependable labor force must be available. Coffee harvesting takes place twice a year in this highland temperate zone. The collection of coffee beans is tedious and exhausting work. [...] Coffee harvesting is task labor and the pickers are paid according to the quantity collected each day. [...] Because of the large numbers of people (whole families participate) involved in the harvest and the rapidity

with which the bushes are cleared, there are only a few days when the picking is financially rewarding for the workers. Between the harvest seasons work is extremely scarce for the majority of the population, and there are about three months during the year (June-August) when there is no work on the coffee farms for most of the *campesinos*. Many Guaqueños supplement their low and sporadic wages with subsistence gardening or petty commodity production. They also hire themselves out as common day-laborers whenever the occasion may arise.[103]

The other option is to have *all* the work done by permanent workers, even if these workers would then be idle for a part of the year. This option is only attractive for agriculturalists if they can keep the cost of these workers extremely low. Slaves on sugar plantations in the English West Indies were a case in point. They had only three tools: an ax, a hoe and a bill:

> Men did the work of animals. Such tasks as planting and cultivating, performed on English and North American farms by horse-driven plows and harrows, were carried out in the Indies entirely by hand. Caribbean farm implements were few and simple. [... The reason for all this inefficiency was] to keep the slaves busy year-round. Cane cultivation, like most farming is seasonal. The planter needs a large labor force at crop time, but not during the slow six months of the year from July through December. Yet the seventeenth-century slave-owning planter had to keep his laborers fully occupied in the slow months, as well as in crop time, to forestall mischief and rebellion. So he put them to work in the fields with hoes instead of horse-drawn plows. The slave's appointed tasks were exceedingly monotonous and degrading, and he executed them unwillingly, unskilfully, and inefficiently.[104]

Transport to and sale in the North

If the crop yielded a good harvest, the product had to be transferred to distribution centres in the North. By no means all crops were suited to this purpose. Whether long-distance transfers were commercially viable depended on which means of transport were available; if such means of transport had limited carrying capacity, or if transport took a long time and entailed serious risks, then only crops that could be easily preserved and had a high value-weight density, such as spices, were eligible to be transferred. As transport became faster, cheaper, and less risky, bulkier vegetable products entered the picture as well. And when, moreover, at the end of the nineteenth century good refrigeration techniques became available, perishable goods, such as bananas and other fruits, could be transported across long distances as well.[105]

It was a multi-faceted transport revolution that radically changed the world market for cash crops from the late nineteenth century onward. In the shipping industry, the wooden ships that were still dominant around 1870 rapidly gave way to larger, faster and more reliable ships powered by steam engines.[106] Furthermore, the opening of the Suez Canal in 1871 and the Panama Canal in 1914 enormously shortened sea routes from Asia and the Americas to Europe. Construction of railways enabled huge advances in the tropics, where in many regions colonial authorities, assisted by willing investors or multinationals, such as the United Fruit Company, established connections between plantations and harbours along the coast.[107]

In addition to benefiting from the invention of refrigeration systems, transport of perishable items also benefited greatly from the introduction of canning techniques – originally invented by Nicolas Appert in 1809 to supply Napoleon's troops across long distances and perfected in the decades that followed for increasingly broad application.[108] The success of this new method is illustrated by the development on Hawaii, where the number of canned pineapple cases increased from 1,893 in 1903 to 8,728,580 in 1925. In the 1920s, the archipelago was home to the largest fruit cannery in the world:

> It employs 2,000 persons and is filled with special machinery for economical, sanitary operation. Much of the machinery has been invented in Hawaii and is of special manufacture. The fruit is not touched by human hands during the process of canning. Tin cans are manufactured in a plant next door to the cannery and are brought on an endless belt for immediate use. Some 200,000,000 cans a year are made.[109]

Considering all these interconnected influences, it is obvious that plant transfer has been an extremely complicated process, which we still understand only partly.

Conclusion

Towards the end of the nineteenth century, the possibilities for commercially attractive crop transfers became increasingly exhausted. Most possible plant relocations had been tested in practice. The focus shifted from transfers of plants to refinement and genetic manipulation of seeds.[110] It was no longer *one* science (botany) that studied all plants, but many sciences together focused on single plants:

> Instead of transferring plants from one area to another, scientists now manipulate familiar plants, adjusting their characteristics to human requirements and to specific environments. Geneticists have replaced the traditional domesticated plants with new and far more productive varieties, while soil scientists, agricultural chemists, plant pathologists, and entomologists have learned to improve the environment in which the plants can grow.[111]

The first symptom of this new trend was the founding of agricultural research stations. Building on the work of the pioneer of agricultural chemistry,

Justus von Liebig (1803–1873), Germany introduced such stations from 1861 and shortly thereafter began to export the practice to other countries.[112] In Brazil, in 1885, for example, the German agronomist Franz Wilhelm Dafert founded an agricultural research station in the coffee region of Campinas.[113] The colonial empires followed suit. In British West Africa eight stations were established between 1890 and 1909. In French Africa similar stations were almost simultaneously initiated while in the Netherlands Indies so-called *proefstations* (testing stations) were founded for sugarcane (1893), tobacco (1894), cacao (1901) and other crops.[114] Kathinka Sinha-Kerkhoff provides us with a vivid description of one such research station, in Pusa (India) (Chapter 6). The work of the research stations led to remarkable results, such as the introduction of nobilized sugarcane and hybrid maize in the 1920s.[115]

Production per hectare of most crops rose, at first gradually and then explosively after the Second World War. With three of the four plants examined here, productivity was greatly increased (Table 8.6). The exception is indigo, which after all is hardly grown anymore.

One important driver of this growth is known as the Green Revolution, which changed much of agriculture in the Global South from the 1960s by introducing new crop varieties, irrigation, pesticides and fertilizers. This campaign, supported primarily by US institutions, served explicitly to avert a 'Red Revolution.'[116]

Increasingly globalized production and distribution of cash crops not only changed our consumption habits but it also drastically modified labour relations, landscapes and ecologies. Agricultural output has increased tremendously and our daily menu has become much more variegated. But mankind had to pay a high price. Millions of slaves were worked to death on farms and plantations. And with the coming of modern colonialism, peasants and farm labourers became, as Mike Davis has argued convincingly, 'dramatically more pregnable to natural disaster after 1850 as their local economies were violently incorporated into the world market'. Not only was traditional food security undermined by 'the forcible incorporation of smallholder production into commodity and financial circuits controlled from overseas', but it was also true that 'the integration of millions of tropical cultivators into the world market during the late nineteenth century was accompanied by a dramatic deterioration in their terms of trade'.[117]

Table 8.6 Development of productivity on a world scale

Crop	1961			2011		
	Area harvested (ha)	Production quanity (tonnes)	Tonnes/ha	Area harvested (ha)	Production quantity (tonnes)	Tonnes/ha
Tobacco	3,398,158	3,573,815	1.05	4,251,760	7,568,208	1.78
Sugarcane	8,911,877	447,977,518	50.27	25,436,924	1,794,359,190	70.54
Coffee	9,757,455	4,527,872	0.46	10,476,355	8,284,135	0.79

Often, this led to acts of resistance, as in the case of the tobacco-shed burnings described in Ratna Saptari's chapter (Chapter 5).

But it was not just the social consequences that were enormous. The ecological consequences of agricultural globalization have been equally massive. The expansion of coffee cultivation has often 'coincided with territorial expansion, the movement of settlers into frontier zones where tropical forests were destroyed, "new forests" of coffee and shade planted, towns established, roads and railroads built, regional identities forged'.[118] And what is more,

> In periods of rising prices, cultivated acreage has frequently expanded in regions whose arid and erratic climate or steep slope make them unfit for permanent cultivation. Soil depletion has often occurred during and after a period of prosperity for certain cash crops (for example, wheat, cotton, tobacco, sugar cane, rubber) which expanded as monocultures or near-monocultures in areas suitable for permanent cultivation only under a diversified system of farming.[119]

The Green Revolution seems to have amplified these problems. For example, many coffee-producing farms underwent dramatic changes in the last quarter of the previous century. Coffee plants were long grown in the shade of fruit trees and other trees, which were a natural habitat for insects and animals. Therefore, coffee farms were forest-like agro-ecosystems,

> 'providing protection from soil erosion, favorable local temperature and humidity regimes, constant replenishment of the soil organic matter via leaf litter production, and home to an array of beneficial insects that can act to control potential economic pests without the use of toxic chemicals.'

Moreover, the combination of trees and coffee plants enabled farmers to diversify production and thus to derive additional income from selling fruit, timber and the like. During the Green Revolution international agencies and national governments propagated what was known as 'technification' – nowadays also called 'modernization' – which consisted of replacing traditional varieties of coffee (*típica*, *bourbón*) with varieties capable of growing without shade, enabling the density of coffee plants to be increased from 1,100–1,500 plants per hectare to 4,000–7,000 plants per hectare. The new-style coffee farms look 'industrial', with long rows of coffee plants in the sun, regularly sprayed with fertilizers and chemical pesticides.[120] While coffee output has clearly increased, farmers have become more dependent than in the past on a single source of income, the eco-system has deteriorated, and bio-diversity has been reduced.[121] The globalization of agriculture has been a profoundly ambivalent process of world-historical importance.

Notes

1 Arthur Young. *Political Essays Concerning the Present State of the British Empire* (London: W. Strahan and T. Cadell, 1772), 274.
2 David Grigg. *The Agricultural Systems of the World: An Evolutionary Approach* (Cambridge: Cambridge University Press, 1992), Ch. 3; Jonathan D. Sauer. *Historical Geography of Crop Plants* (Boston, MA: CRC Press, 1993), 37ff.
3 Donald D. Brand. 'The Origin and Early Distribution of New World Cultivated Plants,' *Agricultural History*, 13:2 (1939), 112–3; Herbert G. Baker. 'The Evolution of the Cultivated Kapok Tree: A Probable West African Product.' In David Brokensha (ed.) *Ecology and Economic Development in Tropical Africa* (Berkeley, CA: Institute of International Studies, University of California, 1965), 185–216.
4 Wouter van der Weijden, Rob Leeuwis and Pieter Bol. *Biological Globalisation: Bioinvasions and Their Impacts on Nature, the Economy and Public Health* (Utrecht: KNNV Publishing, 2007), 22.
5 Judith A. Carney and Richard Nicholas Rosomoff, *In the Shadow of Slavery: Africa's Botanical Legacy in the Atlantic World* (Berkeley and Los Angeles: University of California Press, 2009).
6 Arthur W. Hill. 'The History and Functions of Botanic Gardens,' *Annals of the Missouri Botanical Garden*, 2:1/2 (1915), 185–6.
7 Arend de Roever. *De jacht op sandelhout. De VOC en de tweedeling van Timor in de zeventiende eeuw* (Zutphen: Walburg Pers, 2002), 44; R.A. Donkin. *Between East and West: The Moluccas and the Traffic in Spices up to the Arrival of Europeans* (Philadelphia: American Philosophical Society, 2003), 16.
8 Reinhardt Wendt. 'Globalisierung von Pflanzen und neue Nahrungsgewohnheiten: zur Funktion botanischer Gärten bei der Erschließung natürlicher Ressourcen der Überseeischen Welt.' In Thomas Beck, Horst Gründer, Horst Pietschmann and Roderich Ptak (eds.) *Überseegeschichte: Beiträge der jüngeren Forschung. Festschrift anläßlich der Gründung der Forschungsstiftung für vergleichende europäische Überseegeschichte 1999 in Bamberg* (Stuttgart: Franz Steiner Verlag, 1999), 208n.
9 Herbert Pruns. *Europäische Zuckerwirtschaft, vol. I: Europa auf der Suche nach Zucker in einheimischen Kulturpflanzen* (Berlin: Albert Bartens, 2004), 50–56.
10 Andrew M. Watson. *Agricultural Innovation in the Early Islamic World* (Cambridge: Cambridge University Press, 1983), esp. 9–73.
11 The biologist Wes Jackson has noted: 'We seldom appreciate how narrow our food requirements really are. But of the 350,000 plant species worldwide, only two dozen are of particular importance to us for food. Of the top 18 sources, 14 come from but two flowering plant families, the grasses and legumes.' Wes Jackson. 'Toward a Unifying Concept for an Ecological Agriculture.' In Richard Lowrance, Benjamin R. Stinner and Garfield J. House (eds.) *Agricultural Ecosystems: Unifying Concepts* (New York [etc.]: John Wiley & Sons, 1984), 212.
12 Yung-ho Ts'ao. 'Pepper Trade in East Asia,' *T'oung Pao*, 68:4/5 (1982), 242.
13 Els M. Jacobs. *Merchant in Asia: The Trade of the Dutch East India Company during the Eighteenth Century* (Leiden: CNWS Publications, 2006), 60.
14 On the Columbian Exchange, see Alfred Crosby. *The Columbian Exchange: Biological and Cultural Consequences of 1492* (Westport, CT: Greenwood Press, 1973); Alfred Crosby. *Ecological Imperialism: The Biological Expansion of Europe, 900–1900* (Cambridge: Cambridge University Press, 1986); and Alfred Crosby. *Germs, Seeds, and Animals: Studies in Ecological History* (Armonk, NY: M.E. Sharpe, 1994). See also John F. Richards. *The Unending Frontier: An Environmental History of the Early Modern World* (Berkeley: University of California Press, 2003). On the Magellan Exchange, see James Gerber and Lei Guang (eds.) *Agriculture and Rural Connections in the Pacific, 1500–1900* (Aldershot: Ashgate, 2006).
15 Jacques Gernet. *Le Monde chinois*. Third revised edition (Paris: Armand Colin, 1990), 420.

16 R.N. Kapil and A.K. Bhatnagar. 'Portuguese Contributions to Indian Botany,' *Isis*, 67:3 (1976), 452; José Honório Rodrigues. 'The Influence of Africa on Brazil and of Brazil on Africa,' *Journal of African History*, 3:1 (1962), 63.
17 Clifford A. Wright. 'The Medieval Spice Trade and the Diffusion of the Chile,' *Gastronomica*, 7:2 (2007), 42.
18 Robert O. Collins and James M. Burns. *A History of Sub-Saharan Africa* (Cambridge: Cambridge University Press, 2007), 198–9.
19 Gernet, *Le Monde chinois*, 420–1.
20 Friedrich Schiller. 'Was heißt und zu welchem Ende studiert man Universalgeschichte?' *Der Teutsche Merkur*, 4 (1789), 118.
21 Adam Smith. *An Inquiry into the Nature and Causes of the Wealth of Nations* (London: Methuen & Co., 1776), Book III, Ch. 4, 24.
22 Porcelain is probably the most significant exception to this rule. In the early eighteenth century the Chinese production process was 'reinvented' in Saxony and was subsequently disseminated across Europe, and later to other parts of the world.
23 David H. Rembert Jr. 'The Indigo of Commerce in Colonial North America.' *Economic Botany*, 33:2 (1979), 128.
24 George Watt, George, Edgar Thurston and T.N. Mukerji. 'Indigofera.' In George Watt et al. *Dictionary of the Economic Products of India, Vol IV* (Calcutta: Government Printing, 1890), 392–3.
25 Jean-Baptiste Tavernier. *The Six Travels of John Baptista Tavernier, Baron of Aubonne, Through Turky and Persia to the Indies [...]. Part II: Describing India and the Isles Adjacent.* Trans. J. Phillips (London: no publisher, 1678), 128.
26 Alexander Engel. *Farben der Globalisierung: Die Entstehung moderner Märkte für Farbstoffe 1500–1900* (Frankfurt am Main: Campus, 2009), 220–5.
27 Daniel H. Buchanan *The Development of Capitalist Enterprise in India* (New York: Macmillan, 1934), 36.
28 Watt et al. 'Indigofera,' 393.
29 Robert S. Smith. 'Indigo Production and Trade in Colonial Guatemala,' *Hispanic American Historical Review*, 39:2 (1959), 181–211.
30 Dauril Alden. 'The Growth and Decline of Indigo Production in Colonial Brazil: A Study in Comparative Economic History,' *Journal of Economic History*, 25:1 (1965), 42; Jack Holmes. 'Indigo in Colonial Louisiana and the Floridas,' *Louisiana History*, 8:4 (1967), 329–49.
31 Gabriel Debien. 'Une indigoterie à Saint-Domingue à la fin du XVIIIe siècle,' *Revue d'histoire des colonies*, 33 (1940–1946), 1–49; Alden. 'Growth and Decline,' 42.
32 G. Terry Sharrer. 'Indigo in Carolina 1671–1796,' *South Carolina Historical Magazine*, 72:2 (1971), 94–103; G. Terry Sharrer. 'The Indigo Bonanza in South Carolina, 1740–90,' *Technology and Culture*, 12:3 (1971), 447–55; David L. Coon. 'Eliza Lucas Pinckney and the Reintroduction of Indigo Culture in South Carolina,' *Journal of Southern History*, 42:1 (1976), 61–76.
33 Alden, "Growth and Decline".
34 Sharrer. 'Indigo Bonanza, 449–50.
35 Alden. 'Growth and Decline,' 36; detailed descriptions appear in Kenneth H. Beeson. 'Indigo Production in the Eighteenth Century,' *Hispanic American Historical Review*, 44:2 (1964), 214–8; and in Sharrer. 'Indigo Bonanza,' 451–3.
36 Alden. 'Growth and Decline,' 59–60; Holmes. 'Indigo in Colonial Louisiana,' 102.
37 Watt et al. 'Indigofera,' 393; Buchanan, *Development of Capitalist Enterprise*, 36.
38 M.S. Randhawa, *A History of Agriculture in India*, vol. III: 1757–1947 (New Delhi: Indian Council of Agricultural Research, 1983), 154.
39 Asiaticus. 'The Rise and Fall of the Indigo Industry in India.' *Economic Journal*, 86 (1912), 240.
40 Buchanan. *Development of Capitalist Enterprise*, 38.
41 Asiaticus. 'Rise and Fall,' 241.

42 Buchanan. *Development of Capitalist Enterprise*, 37–8; Randhawa. *History of Agriculture in India*, vol. 3, 155.
43 Colin M. Fisher. 'Planters and Peasants: The Ecological Context of Agrarian Unrest on the Plantations of North Bihar 1820–1920.' In Clive Dewey and Anthony G. Hopkins (eds.) *The Imperial Impact: Studies in the Economic History of Africa and India* (London: Athlone Press, 1978), 114–31.
44 Asiaticus. 'Rise and Fall,' 244–5.
45 Evelin Wiedenmann. *Die Konstruktion der richtigen Formel: Strukturaufklärung und Synthese des Indigblau, dargestellt an Hand des Briefwechsels Baeyer-Caro* (Munich: Beck, 1978), 2 vols.; Ernst Homburg. 'The Emergence of Research Laboratories in the Dyestuff Industry, 1870–1900,' *British Journal for the History of Science*, 25 (1992), 91–111; Carsten Reinhardt. *Forschung in der chemischen Industrie: Die Entwicklung synthetischer Farbstoffe bei BASF und Hoechst, 1863 bis 1914* (Freiberg: TU Bergakademie, 1997); Carsten Reinhardt and Anthony S. Travis. *Heinrich Caro and the Creation of Modern Chemical Industry* (Dordrecht: Kluwer Academic, 2000); Engel. *Farben der Globalisierung*, 105–9.
46 Buchanan. *Development of Capitalist Enterprise*, 52. A quantitative account of the development between 1896 and 1956 appears in Padmini Tolat Balaram. 'Indian Indigo.' In Andrea Feeser, Maureen Daly Goggin and Beth FowkesTobin (eds.) *The Materiality of Colour: The Production, Circulation, and Application of Dyes and Pigments, 1400–1800* (Farnham: Ashgate, 2012), 150.
47 A.E. Haarer. *Modern Coffee Production* (London: Leonard Hill, 1956), 239.
48 C. van Arendonk. 'Kahwa.' In *Encyclopaedia of Islam. New Edition, vol. IV* (Leiden: Brill, 1978), 449–53. On coffee export from Ethiopia in the early modern period, see Merid W. Aregay. 'The Early History of Ethiopia's Coffee Trade and the Rise of Shawa,' *Journal of African History*, 29 (1988), 19–25.
49 A map depicting coffee migrations appears in Mark Pendergrast. *Uncommon Grounds: The History of Coffee and How It Transformed Our World* (New York: Basic Books, 1999), xx–xxi.
50 G. Mundt. *Ceylon en Java: Aanteekeningen van een theeplanter* (Batavia: Ogilvie, 1886), 12. Mundt bases his work on N.P. van den Berg. 'Historisch-statistische aanteekeningen over de voortbrenging en het verbruik van koffie,' *Tijdschrift van Nijverheid en Landbouw in Nederlandsch Indië*, 24 (1879), 427. See also P. W. A. van Spall. *Verslag over de koffij- en kaneel-kultuur op het eiland Ceylon in het jaar 1861* (Batavia: W. Ogilvie, 1863), 41–2.
51 NN. 'Invoering der koffijkultuur op Java, 1700–1750,' *Bijdragen tot de Taal-, Land- en Volkenkunde*, 6 (1859), 53–71.
52 K. W. van Gorkom. *De Oost-Indische Cultures in betrekking tot handel en nijverheid* (Amsterdam: J.H. de Bussy, 1881), vol. I, 216–7.
53 Van Spall. *Verslag over de koffij- en kaneel-kultuur*, 42, 44.
54 Van Gorkom. *Oost-Indische Cultures*, vol. I, 218; John Crawford. 'History of Coffee,' *Journal of the Statistical Society of London*, 15:1 (1852), 52–3.
55 Boris Fausto. *A Concise History of Brazil* (Cambridge: Cambridge University Press, 1999), 106.
56 Catherine M. Tucker. *Coffee Culture: Local Experiences, Global Connections* (New York: Routledge, 2011), 44.
57 V.D. Wickizer. *Coffee, Tea, and Cocoa: An Economic and Political Analysis* (Stanford, CA: Stanford University Press, 1951), 27–8.
58 Alastair White. *El Salvador* (New York: Praeger, 1973).
59 A typical example is Kenya, where in 1966 estates and small farms each still accounted for half the coffee produced. Robert W. Maxon. 'Small-Scale and Large-Scale Agriculture since Independence.' In William R. Ochieng and Robert W. Maxon (eds.) *An Economic History of Kenya* (Nairobi: East African Educational Publishers, 1992), 287.

178 *Marcel van der Linden*

60 Laura Waridel. *Coffee with Pleasure: Just Java and World Trade* (Montréal: Black Rose, 2002).
61 J. H. Galloway. *The Sugar Cane Industry: An Historical Geography from Its Origins to 1914* (Cambridge: Cambridge University Press, 1989), 19–27.
62 Marie-Louise von Wartburg. 'Entwurf und Technologie einer mittelalterlichen Rohrzuckerfabrik: Eine industriearchäologische Fallstudie in Cypern.' In Hans Berger, Christoph H. Brunner and Otto Sigg (eds.) *Mundo Multa Miracula: Festschrift für Hans Conrad Peyer* (Zürich: Verlag Neue Zürcher Zeitung, 1992), 207–20, 251–4.
63 G. Capus and D. Bois. *Les produits coloniaux: Origine, production, commerce* (Paris, Armand Colin, 1912), 320.
64 Noël Deerr, *Cane Sugar: A Textbook on the Agriculture of the Sugar Cane, the Manufacture of Cane Sugar, and the Analysis of Sugar House Products*, 2nd edition (London: Norman Rodger, 1921), 175.
65 C. J. van Lookeren Campagne. 'Suiker.' In Joh. F. Snelleman (ed.) *Encyclopaedie van Nederlandsch-Indië, Vol. IV* (The Hague: Martinus Nijhoff, and Leiden: E.J. Brill, n.d. [1905 or 1906]), 165–6. For a description of contemporary sugar production in Gorakhpur (India), see Shahid Amin, *Sugarcane and Sugar in Gorakhpur: An Inquiry into Peasant Production for Capitalist Enterprise in Colonial India* (New Delhi: Oxford University Press, 1984), 53–61.
66 Van Lookeren Campagne. 'Suiker,' 167–8. A very detailed description of the new production process appears in Deerr. *Cane Sugar*, Chapters 11–21.
67 Galloway. *Sugar Cane Industry*, 32.
68 Pierre Dockès. 'Le paradigme sucrier (XIe–XIXe siècle).' In Fred Célimène and André Legris (eds.) *L'économie de l'esclavage colonial: Enquête et bilan du XVIIe au XIXe siècle* (Paris: CNRS Editions, 2002), 111–3; Pierre Dockès. *Le sucre et les larmes: Bref essai d'histoire et de mondialisation* (Paris: Descartes & Cie, 2009), 23–4.
69 Virginia Rau. 'The Settlement of Madeira and the Sugar Cane Plantations,' *A.A.G. Bijdragen*, 9 (1964), 3–12; Sidney Greenfield. 'Madeira and the Beginnings of New World Sugar Cane Cultivation and Plantation Slavery: A Study in Institution Building.' In Vera Rubin and Arthur Tuden (eds.) *Comparative Perspectives on Slavery in New World Plantation Societies* (New York, 1977), 536–52; Galloway. *Sugar Cane Industry*, 48ff.
70 Marian Małowist. 'Les débuts du système de plantations dans la période des grandes découvertes,' *Africana – Bulletin of the Centre of African Studies at the University of Warsaw*, 10 (1969), 9–30.
71 B. W. Higman. 'The Sugar Revolution,' *Economic History Review*, New Series, 53:2 (2000), 213.
72 For an interesting comparison of sugarcane's embedding in India and Indonesia, see Ulbe Bosma, *The Sugar Plantation in India and Indonesia: Industrial Production, 1770–2010* (Cambridge: Cambridge University Press, 2013).
73 Chinese sugar production is analysed in detail in Sucheta Mazumdar. *Sugar and Society in China: Peasants, Technology, and the World Market* (Cambridge, MA: Harvard-Yenching Institute Monograph Series, 1998). The passage quoted appears on page 112.
74 Vladimir P. Timoshenko and Boris C. Swerling. *The World's Sugar: Progress and Policy* (Stanford: Stanford University Press, 1957), 235.
75 H. C. Prinsen Geerligs. *The World's Cane Sugar Industry: Past and Present* (Manchester: N. Rodger, 1912), 21.
76 G. B. Masefield. 'Crops and Livestock.' In E. E. Rich and C. H. Wilson (eds.) *The Cambridge Economic History of Europe, vol. IV: The Economy of Expanding Europe in the Sixteenth and Seventeenth Centuries* (Cambridge: At the University Press, 1967), 283.
77 James Pritchard. *In Search of Empire: The French in the Americas, 1670–1730* (Cambridge: Cambridge University Press, 2004), 130–1.
78 Grigg. *Agricultural Systems*, 34.

Globalization's agricultural roots   179

79 Henry Hobhouse. *Seeds of Wealth: Four Plants That Made Men Rich* (Washington, DC: Shoemaker & Hoard, 2003), 189.
80 Pritchard. *In Search of Empire*, 130–1.
81 C. J. van Lookeren Campagne. 'Tabak.' In Joh. F. Snelleman (ed.) *Encyclopaedie van Nederlandsch-Indië, Vol. IV* (The Hague: Martinus Nijhoff and Leiden: E.J. Brill, n.d. [1905 or 1906]), 235.
82 Irene Eng. 'Agglomeration and the Local State: The Tobacco Economy of Yunnan, China,' *Transactions of the Institute of British Geographers*, New Series, 24:3 (1999), 315–29.
83 Ernest P. Imle. 'Hevea Rubber – Past and Future,' *Economic Botany*, 32:3 (1978), 265. See also the description in Warren Dean. *Brazil and the Struggle for Rubber: A Study in Environmental History* (Cambridge [etc.]: Cambridge University Press, 1987), 11–22.
84 Norbert Ortmayr. "Kulturpflanzen: Transfers und Ausbreitungsprozesse im 18. Jahrhundert.' In Margarete Grandner and Andrea Komlosy (eds.) *Vom Weltgeist beseelt. Globalgeschichte 1700–1815* (Vienna: Promedia, 2004), 74.
85 Sometimes scientific curiosity could hinder economic utility, as became clear in Calcutta's botanical garden during the early nineteenth century: 'The Court of Directors were disturbed by the growing emphasis on science. Since the foundation of the Calcutta Garden they had never ceased to view it as a horticultural establishment, above all else designed to foster economic botany on the periphery. Its scientific function was limited to the domestication of profitable plants and the collection of samples which could be studied by scientists *in Europe*.' Marika Vicziany. 'Imperialism, Botany and Statistics in Early Nineteenth-Century India: The Surveys of Francis Buchanan (1762–1829),' *Modern Asian Studies*, 20:4 (1986), 641–2.
86 Sarah P. Stetson. 'The Traffic in Seeds and Plants from England's Colonies in North America,' *Agricultural History*, 23:1 (1949), 47. Precisely because transfers entailed so many risks, their success was often attributable to coincidence and luck. Alexander von Humboldt reported about a black slave in New Spain, who, while preparing rice, 'had found three or four grains of wheat among the rice intended to feed the Spanish army: these grains appeared to have been planted before 1530. [...] Historical records mention a Spanish lady, Marie d'Escobar, wife of Diego de Chaves, who was the first to bring some grains of wheat to the city of Lima, then known as Rimac. The product of harvests from which she obtained these grains was distributed for three years among the new settlers, so that each farmer received twenty or thirty grains.' Alexander von Humboldt. *Essai politique sur la Royaume de la Nouvelle-Espagne* (Paris: F. Schoell, 1811), vol. 3, 67–8. This was how wheat spread across South America. See also James A. Robertson. 'Some Notes on the Transfer by Spain of Plants and Animals to Its Colonies Overseas,' *The James Sprunt Historical Studies*, 19:1 (1927), 14.
87 David Hershey, "Doctor Ward's Accidental Terrarium", *American Biology Teacher*, 58 (1996), pp. 276–281.
88 Daniel R. Headrick, "Technological Change", in: B.L. Turner et al. (eds), *The Earth as Transformed by Human Action. Global and Regional Changes in the Biosphere over the Past 300 Years* (Cambridge: Cambridge University Press, 1990), pp. 55–67, at 61.
89 P. F. Knowles. 'New Crop Establishment,' *Economic Botany*, 14:4 (1960), 267.
90 Carol A. MacLennan. 'Foundations of Sugar's Power: Early Maui Plantations, 1840–1860,' *Hawaiian Journal of History*, 29 (1995), 43, 53.
91 Nathan Rosenberg. 'Economic Experiments,' *Industrial and Corporate Change*, 1:1 (1992), 186–7.
92 Karl Marx, *Capital*. Trans. David Fernbach (Harmondsworth: Penguin, 1981), vol. 3, 199.
93 Haarer. *Modern Coffee Production*, 138.
94 Gunther Franke. *Nutzpflanzen der Tropen und Subtropen, vol. I* (Leipzig: S. Hirzel Verlag, 1980).

180 Marcel van der Linden

95 Olof Jonasson. 'The Potential Areas of Coffee-Growing and Their Relation to the Settlement of the White Man,' *Geografiska Annaler*, 40:2 (1958), 94. The Swedish geographer Jonasson was probably the first to examine this subject matter. See his study *Kaffet och kaffeländer* [Coffee and the Coffee Lands] (Stockholm: Kooperativa Förbundets Press, 1932). He was driven by colonial and racist motivations and intended to indicate 'the regions within the tropics where possible future cultivation [...] might extend the settlement and successful permanent occupancy by the white race of certain favorable equatorial regions.; Olof Jonasson. 'Natural Conditions for Coffee Culture,' *Economic Geography*, 9:4 (1933), 356. For a considerable refinement of Jonasson's approach, see Jen-Hu Chang. 'Potential Photosynthesis and Crop Productivity,' *Annals of the Association of American Geographers*, 59 (1969), 92–101; Jen-Hu Chang. 'Global Distribution of Net Radiation According to a New Formula,' *Annals of the Association of American Geographers*, 60 (1970), 340–351; Jen-Hu Chang. 'Tropical Agriculture: Crop Diversity and Crop Yields,' *Economic Geography*, 53:3 (1977), 241–54; Philip W. Porter. 'A Note on Cotton and Climate: A Colonial Conundrum.' In Allen Isaacman and Richard Roberts (eds.) *Cotton, Colonialism, and Social History in Sub-Saharan Africa* (London: James Currey, 1995), 43–9.
96 G. E. Tidbury, *The Clove Tree* (London: Crosby Lockwood & Son, 1949), 23–4.
97 Grigg, *Agricultural Systems*, 211.
98 Ralph Shlomowitz. 'Plantations and Smallholdings: Comparative Perspectives from the World Cotton and Sugar Cane Economies, 1865–1939,' *Agricultural History*, 58:1 (1984), 7.
99 Shlomowitz. 'Plantations and Smallholdings,' 9.
100 'Plantations covered only 1.01 per cent of the cultivated area of British India in 1895.' Irfan Habib. *Indian Economy 1858–1914* (New Delhi: Tulika, 2006), 78. One consideration may have been, that 'family labour does not require as much supervision as hired labour. This is partly because family members can be expected to share an emotional bond, and so to a great extent can trust one another not to shirk.' Partha Dasgupta. *An Inquiry into Well-Being and Destitution* (Oxford: Clarendon Press, 1993), 222.
101 Grigg. *Agricultural Systems*, 211–3.
102 J. E. Spencer and Ronald J. Horvath. 'How Does an Agricultural Region Originate?' *Annals of the Association of American Geographers*, 53:1 (1963), 82.
103 William R. James. 'Subsistence, Survival and Capitalist Agriculture: Aspects of the Mode of Production among a Colombian Proletariat,' *Latin American Perspectives*, 2:3 (1975), 88–9.
104 Richard S. Dunn. *Sugar and Slaves: The Rise of the Planter Class in the English West Indies, 1624–1713* (Chapel Hill: University of North Carolina Press, 1972), 198, 200.
105 Hans-Jürgen Teuteberg. 'Zur Geschichte der Kühlkost und des Tiefgefrierens,' *Zeitschrift für Unternehmensgeschichte*, 36:3 (1991), 139–155. Not only did natural disasters, robbers, and pirates, or flawed navigation techniques endanger the transport, but so did economic vicissitudes. In the sixteenth century the supply and price levels of long-distance crops were uncertain. In addition to the constant occurrence of exogenous shocks, such as clashes between principalities, which impeded deliveries, there was what Peter Musgrave has called a 'doubly-opaque market system': long distances and minimal communication opportunities across these distances meant that essential economic information (about current prices, supply, etc.) were lacking – and this allowed rumours to spread, while the long-term absence of a single warehouse caused the supply to be distributed among myriad trading hubs. Peter Musgrave. 'The Economics of Uncertainty: The Structural Revolution in the Spice Trade, 1480–1640.' In P. L. Cottrell and D. H. Aldcroft (eds.) *Shipping, Trade and Commerce: Essays in Memory of Ralph Davis* (Leicester: Leicester

University Press, 1981), 15. All these factors affected both intra-Asian trade (e.g. by the Chinese) and trade between Europe and Asia. Because earnings could vary considerably from year to year, and the danger of bankruptcy was always very real, traders ordinarily sought to maximize their short-term returns. Only a high profit in a 'good' year might offset the serious risk.

106 For a quantitative overview of the changes between 1850 and 1950. see W. S. Woytinski and E. S. Woytinsky. *World Commerce and Governments. Trends and Outlook* (New York: The Twentieth Century Fund, 1955), 433 (Table 154).

107 W. Arthur Lewis. 'The Export Stimulus.' In W. Arthur Lewis (ed.) *Tropical Development, 1880–1913: Studies in Economic Progress* (London: George Allen & Unwin, 1970), 14; Virginia Scott Jenkins. *Bananas: An American History* (Washington and London: Smithsonian Institution Press, 2000), 18.

108 On Appert (1749–1841), see Rosemonde Pujol. *Nicolas Appert: l'inventeur de la conserve* (Paris: Denoël, 1985) and Jean-Paul Barbier. *Nicolas Appert: inventeur et humaniste* (Paris: Royer, 1994). The course of events is described in Marin Bruegel. '"Un sacrifice de plus à demander au soldat": l'armée et l'introduction de la boîte de conserve dans l'alimentation française, 1872–1920,' *Revue historique*, 294:2 (1995), 259–84; Marin Bruegel. 'Du temps annuel au temps quotidien: la conserve appertisée à la conquête du marché, 1810–1920,' *Revue d'histoire moderne et contemporaine*, 44:1 (1997), 40–67; J. C. Graham. 'The French Connection in the Early History of Canning,' *Journal of the Royal Society of Medicine*, 74 (1981), 374–81.

109 Otis W. Freeman. 'Economic Geography of the Hawaiian Islands,' *Economic Geography*, 5:3 (1929), 268.

110 Dwight H. Perkins. *Agricultural Development in China 1368–1968* (Edinburgh: University Press, 1969), 51.

111 Headrick. 'Technological Change,' 62.

112 Wolfgang Krohn and Wolf Schäfer. 'Ursprung und Struktur der Agrikulturchemie.' In Gernot Böhme et al., *Starnberger Studien 1: Die gesellschaftliche Orientierung des wissenschaftlichen Fortschritts* (Frankfurt am Main: Suhrkamp, 1978), 23–68; Mark R. Finlay. 'The German Agricultural Experiment Stations and the Beginnings of American Agricultural Research,' *Agricultural History*, 62:2 (1988), 41–50; Nathalie Jas. *Au carrefour de la chimie et de l'agriculture. Les sciences agronomiques en France et en Allemagne, 1840–1914* (Paris: Ed. des Archives contemporaines, 2001); Frank Uekötter. *Die Wahrheit ist auf dem Feld: Eine Wissensgeschichte der deutschen Landwirtschaft* (Göttingen: Vandenhoeck und Ruprecht, 2010). On the worldwide spread of agricultural research see Lawrence Busch and Carolyn Sachs. 'The Agricultural Sciences and the Modern World System.' In Lawrence Busch (ed.) *Science and Agricultural Development* (Totowa, NJ: Allanheld, Osmun, 1981), 131–56.

113 Warren Dean. 'The Green Wave of Coffee: Beginnings of Tropical Agricultural Research in Brazil (1885–1900),' *Hispanic American Historical Review*, 69:1 (1989), 91–115.

114 Montague Yudelman. 'The Transfer of Agricultural Techniques.' In Peter Duignan and L. H. Gann (eds.) *Colonialism in Africa, 1870–1960, vol. 4: The Economics of Colonialism* (Cambridge: Cambridge University Press, 1969), 329–59; 'Stations (proef-).' In D. G. Stibbe (ed.) *Encyclopaedie van Nederlandsch-Indië*. Second printing (The Hague: Martinus Nijhoff, and Leiden: Brill, 1921), vol. 4, 94–103.

115 Headrick, 'Technological Change,' 62.

116 William Gaud, director of the United States Agency for International Development, coined the term 'Green Revolution.' In 1968 he called the changes in agriculture 'a new revolution. It is not a violent Red Revolution like that of the Soviets, nor is it a White Revolution like that of the Shah of Iran. I call it the Green Revolution.' William S. Gaud. 'The Green Revolution: Accomplishments and Apprehensions' (March 8, 1968), reprinted in *AgBioWorldArchives*, <www.agbioworld.org/biotech-info/topics/borlaug/borlaug-green.html>.

117 Mike Davis. *Late Victorian Holocausts: El Niño Famines and the Making of the Third World* (London and New York: Verso, 2001), 288–90.
118 William Roseberry. 'Introduction.' In William Roseberry, Lowell Gudmundson and Mario Samper Kutschbach (eds.) *Coffee, Society, and Power in Latin America* (Baltimore and London: the Johns Hopkins University Press, 1995), 3.
119 S. von Ciriacy-Wantrup. 'Resource Conservation and Economic Stability,' *Quarterly Journal of Economics*, 60:3 (1946), 417.
120 <www.nrdc.org/health/farming/ccc/chap3.asp>. Consulted on 15 April 2015.
121 In general, one can say that, as a consequence of the Green Revolution, significant productivity gains were realized. However, the middle peasantries were the main beneficiaries, while the position of poor farmers worsened. There were also harmful environmental effects, such as greater water use, soil erosion, and chemical runoff. See, for example, R. E. Evenson and D. Gollin. 'Assessing the Impact of the Green Revolution, 1960 to 2000,' *Science* (2 May 2003), 758–62; Prabhu L. Pingali. 'Green Revolution: Impacts, Limits, and the Path Ahead,' *Proceedings of the National Academy of Sciences of the United States of America (PNAS)*, 109:31 (2012), 12302–8. Vandana Shiva therefore regards the Green Revolution mainly as a failure: 'It has led to reduced genetic diversity, increased vulnerability to pests, soil erosion, water shortages, reduced soil fertility, micronutrient deficiencies, soil contamination, reduced availability of nutritious food crops for the local population, the displacement of vast numbers of small farmers from their land, rural impoverishment and increased tensions and conflicts. The beneficiaries have been the agrochemical industry, large petrochemical companies, manufacturers of agricultural machinery, dam builders and large landowners. The 'miracle' seeds of the Green Revolution have become mechanisms for breeding new pests and creating new diseases.' Vandana Shiva. 'The Green Revolution in the Punjab,' *The Ecologist*, 21:2 (March-April 1991). http://livingheritage.org/green-revolution.htm (Accessed 14 April 2015).

References

Alden, Dauril. 'The Growth and Decline of Indigo Production in Colonial Brazil: A Study in Comparative Economic History,' *Journal of Economic History*, 25:1 (1965), 35–60.

Alpern, Stanley B. 'The European Introduction of Crops into West Africa in Precolonial Times,' *History in Africa*, 19 (1992), 13–43.

Amin, Shahid. *Sugarcane and Sugar in Gorakhpur: An Inquiry into Peasant Production for Capitalist Enterprise in Colonial India* (New Delhi: Oxford University Press, 1984).

Aregay, Merid W. 'The Early History of Ethiopia's Coffee Trade and the Rise of Shawa,' *Journal of African History*, 29 (1988), 19–25.

Asiaticus. 'The Rise and Fall of the Indigo Industry in India,' *Economic Journal*, 86 (1912), 237–47.

Baker, Herbert G. 'The Evolution of the Cultivated Kapok Tree: A Probable West African Product.' In David Brokensha (ed.) *Ecology and Economic Development in Tropical Africa* (Berkeley, CA: Institute of International Studies, University of California, 1965), 185–216.

Balaram, Padmini Tolat. 'Indian Indigo.' In Andrea Feeser, Maureen Daly Goggin and Beth Fowkes Tobin (eds.) *The Materiality of Color: The Production, Circulation, and Application of Dyes and Pigments, 1400–1800* (Farnham: Ashgate, 2012), 139–54.

Barbier, Jean-Paul. *Nicolas Appert: inventeur et humaniste* (Paris: Royer, 1994).

Beeson, Kenneth H. 'Indigo Production in the Eighteenth Century,' *Hispanic American Historical Review*, 44:2 (1964), 214–18.

Brand, Donald D. 'The Origin and Early Distribution of New World Cultivated Plants,' *Agricultural History*, 13:2 (1939), 109–17.

Bruegel, Marin. '"Un sacrifice de plus à demander au soldat": l'armée et l'introduction de la boîte de conserve dans l'alimentation française, 1872–1920,' *Revue historique*, 294:2 (1995), 259–84.

Bruegel, Marin. 'Du temps annuel au temps quotidien: la conserve appertisée à la conquête du marché, 1810–1920,' *Revue d'histoire moderne et contemporaine*, 44:1 (1997), 40–67.

Buchanan, Daniel H. *The Development of Capitalist Enterprise in India* (New York: Macmillan, 1934).

Busch, Lawrence, and Carolyn Sachs. 'The Agricultural Sciences and the Modern World System.' In Lawrence Busch (ed.) *Science and Agricultural Development* (Totowa, NJ: Allanheld, Osmun, 1981), 131–56.

Capus, G., and D. Bois. *Les produits coloniaux: Origine, Production, Commerce* (Paris, Armand Colin, 1912).

Capus, Guillaume, Fernand Leulliot and Etienne Foëx. *Le Tabac* (Paris: Société d'Editions géographiques, maritimes et coloniales, 1929–30), 3 vols.

Carney, Judith A., and Richard Nicholas Rosomoff. *In the Shadow of Slavery: Africa's Botanical Legacy in the Atlantic World* (Berkeley, CA: University of California Press, 2009).

Chang, Jen-Hu. 'Potential Photosynthesis and Crop Productivity,' *Annals of the Association of American Geographers*, 59 (1969), 92–101.

Chang, Jen-Hu. 'Global Distribution of Net Radiation According to a New Formula,' *Annals of the Association of American Geographers*, 60 (1970), 340–51.

Chang, Jen-Hu, 'Tropical Agriculture: Crop Diversity and Crop Yields,' *Economic Geography*, 53:3 (1977), 241–54.

Collins, Robert O., and James M. Burns. *A History of Sub-Saharan Africa* (Cambridge: Cambridge University Press, 2007).

Coon, David L. 'Eliza Lucas Pinckney and the Reintroduction of Indigo Culture in South Carolina,' *Journal of Southern History*, 42:1 (1976), 61–76.

Cosby, Alfred. *The Columbian Exchange: Biological and Cultural Consequences of 1492* (Westport, CT: Greenwood Press, 1973).

Cosby, Alfred, *Ecological Imperialism: The Biological Expansion of Europe, 900–1900* (Cambridge: Cambridge University Press, 1986).

Cosby, Alfred, *Germs, Seeds, and Animals: Studies in Ecological History* (Armonk, NY: M.E. Sharpe, 1994).

Crawford, John. 'History of Coffee,' *Journal of the Statistical Society of London*, 15:1 (1852), 50–8.

Crowell, John Franklin. 'The Sugar Situation in the Tropics,' *Political Science Quarterly*, 14:4 (1899), 610–1.

Dasgupta, Partha. *An Inquiry into Well-Being and Destitution* (Oxford: Clarendon Press, 1993).

Davis, Mike. *Late Victorian Holocausts: El Niño Famines and the Making of the Third World* (London and New York: Verso, 2001).

Dean, Warren. *Brazil and the Struggle for Rubber: A Study in Environmental History* (Cambridge: Cambridge University Press, 1987).

Dean, Warren. 'The Green Wave of Coffee: Beginnings of Tropical Agricultural Research in Brazil (1885–1900),' *Hispanic American Historical Review*, 69:1 (1989), 91–115.

Debien, Gabriel. 'Une indigoterie à Saint-Domingue à la fin du XVIIIe siècle,' *Revue d'histoire des colonies*, 33 (1940–1946), 1–49.

Deerr, Noël. *Cane Sugar: A Textbook on the Agriculture of the Sugar Cane, the Manufacture of Cane Sugar, and the Analysis of Sugar House Products*, 2nd edition (London: Norman Rodger, 1921).

De Roever, Arend. *De jacht op sandelhout. De VOC en de tweedeling van Timor in de zeventiende eeuw* (Zutphen: Walburg Pers, 2002).

Dockès, Pierre. 'Le paradigme sucrier (XIe–XIXe siècle).' In Fred Célimène and André Legris (eds.) *L'économie de l'esclavage colonial: Enquête et bilan du XVIIe au XIXe siècle* (Paris: CNRS Editions, 2002), 109–26.

Dockès, Pierre. *Le sucre et les larmes: Bref essai d'histoire et de mondialisation* (Paris: Descartes & Cie, 2009).

Donkin, R. A. *Between East and West: The Moluccas and the Traffic in Spices up to the Arrival of Europeans* (Philadelphia, PA: American Philosophical Society, 2003).

Dunn, Richard S. *Sugar and Slaves: The Rise of the Planter Class in the English West Indies, 1624–1713* (Chapel Hill, NC: University of North Carolina Press, 1972).

Eng, Irene. 'Agglomeration and the Local State: The Tobacco Economy of Yunnan, China,' *Transactions of the Institute of British Geographers*, New Series, 24:3 (1999), 315–29.

Engel, Alexander. *Farben der Globalisierung. Die Entstehung moderner Märkte für Farbstoffe 1500–1900* (Frankfurt am Main: Campus, 2009).

Evenson, R. E., and D. Gollin. 'Assessing the Impact of the Green Revolution, 1960 to 2000,' *Science* (2 May 2003), 758–62.

Fausto, Boris. *A Concise History of Brazil* (Cambridge: Cambridge University Press, 1999).

Finlay, Mark R. 'The German Agricultural Experiment Stations and the Beginnings of American Agricultural Research,' *Agricultural History*, 62:2 (1988), 41–50.

Fisher, Colin M. 'Planters and Peasants: The Ecological Context of Agrarian Unrest on the Plantations of North Bihar 1820–1920.' In Clive Dewey and Anthony G. Hopkins (eds.) *The Imperial Impact: Studies in the Economic History of Africa and India* (London: Athlone Press, 1978), 114–31.

Franke, Gunther. *Nutzpflanzen der Tropen und Subtropen*, vol. I (Leipzig: S. Hirzel Verlag, 1980).

Freeman, Otis W. 'Economic Geography of the Hawaiian Islands,' *Economic Geography*, 5:3 (1929), 260–76.

Galloway, J. H. *The Sugar Cane Industry: An Historical Geography from Its Origins to 1914* (Cambridge: Cambridge University Press, 1989).

Gaud, William S. 'The Green Revolution: Accomplishments and Apprehensions' (March 8, 1968), reprinted in *AgBioWorldArchives*, www.agbioworld.org/biotech-info/topics/borlaug/borlaug-green.html.

Gerber, James, and Lei Guang (eds.) *Agriculture and Rural Connections in the Pacific, 1500–1900* (Aldershot: Ashgate, 2006).

Gernet, Jacques. *Le Monde chinois*. Third revised edition (Paris: Armand Colin, 1990).

Graham, J. C. 'The French Connection in the Early History of Canning,' *Journal of the Royal Society of Medicine*, 74 (1981), 374–81.

Greenfield, Sidney. 'Madeira and the Beginnings of New World Sugar Cane Cultivation and Plantation Slavery: A Study in Institution Building.' In Vera Rubin and Arthur Tuden (eds.) *Comparative Perspectives on Slavery in New World Plantation Societies* (New York: New York Academy of Sciences, 1977).

Grigg, David. *The Agricultural Systems of the World: An Evolutionary Approach* (Cambridge: Cambridge University Press, 1992).

Haarer, A. E. *Modern Coffee Production* (London: Leonard Hill, 1956).

Habib, Irfan. *Indian Economy 1858–1914* (New Delhi: Tulika, 2006).

Headrick, Daniel R. 'Technological Change.' In B. L. Turner et al. (eds.) *The Earth as Transformed by Human Action: Global and Regional Changes in the Biosphere over the Past 300 Years* (Cambridge: Cambridge University Press, 1990), 55–67.

Hershey, David. 'Doctor Ward's Accidental Terrarium,' *American Biology Teacher*, 58 (1996), 276–81.

Higman, B. W. 'The Sugar Revolution,' *Economic History Review*, New Series, 53:2 (2000), 213–36.

Hill, Arthur W. 'The History and Functions of Botanic Gardens,' *Annals of the Missouri Botanical Garden*, 2:1/2 (1915), 185–240.

Hobhouse, Henry. *Seeds of Wealth: Four Plants That Made Men Rich* (Washington, DC: Shoemaker & Hoard, 2003).

Holmes, Jack. 'Indigo in Colonial Louisiana and the Floridas,' *Louisiana History*, 8:4 (1967), 329–49.

Homburg, Ernst. 'The Emergence of Research Laboratories in the Dyestuff Industry, 1870–1900,' *British Journal for the History of Science*, 25 (1992), 91–111.

Huebner, G. G. 'The Coffee Market,' *Annals of the American Academy of Political and Social Science*, 38:2 (1911), 292–302.

Imle, Ernest P. 'Hevea Rubber – Past and Future,' *Economic Botany*, 32:3 (1978), 264–77.

Jackson, Wes. 'Toward a Unifying Concept for an Ecological Agriculture.' In Richard Lowrance, Benjamin R. Stinner and Garfield J. House (eds.) *Agricultural Ecosystems: Unifying Concepts* (New York: John Wiley & Sons, 1984), 209–21.

Jacobs, Els M. *Merchant in Asia: The Trade of the Dutch East India Company during the Eighteenth Century* (Leiden: CNWS Publications, 2006).

James, William R. 'Subsistence, Survival and Capitalist Agriculture: Aspects of the Mode of Production among a Colombian Proletariat,' *Latin American Perspectives*, 2:3 (1975), 84–95.

Jas, Nathalie. *Au carrefour de la chimie et de l'agriculture: Les sciences agronomiques en France et en Allemagne, 1840–1914* (Paris: Ed. des Archives contemporaines, 2001).

Jenkins, Virginia Scott. *Bananas: An American History* (Washington and London: Smithsonian Institution Press, 2000).

Jonasson, Olof. *Kaffet och kaffeländer* [Coffee and the Coffee Lands] (Stockholm: Kooperativa Förbundets Press, 1932).

Jonasson, Olof. 'Natural Conditions for Coffee Culture,' *Economic Geography*, 9:4 (October 1933), 356–67.

Jonasson, Olof. 'The Potential Areas of Coffee-Growing and Their Relation to the Settlement of the White Man,' *Geografiska Annaler*, 40:2 (1958), 89–100.

Kapil, R. N., and A. K. Bhatnagar. 'Portuguese Contributions to Indian Botany,' *Isis*, 67:3 (1976), 449–52.

Knowles, P. F. 'New Crop Establishment,' *Economic Botany*, 14:4 (1960), 263–75.

Krohn, Wolfgang, and Wolf Schäfer. 'Ursprung und Struktur der Agrikulturchemie.' In Gernot Böhme et al. *Starnberger Studien 1: Die gesellschaftliche Orientierung des wissenschaftlichen Fortschritts* (Frankfurt am Main: Suhrkamp, 1978), 23–68.

Lewis, W. Arthur. 'The Export Stimulus.' In W. Arthur Lewis (ed.) *Tropical Development, 1880–1913: Studies in Economic Progress* (London: George Allen & Unwin, 1970), 13–45.

MacLennan, Carol A. 'Foundations of Sugar's Power: Early Maui Plantations, 1840–1860,' *Hawaiian Journal of History*, 29 (1995), 33–56.

Maddison, Angus. *The World Economy, vol. I: A Millennial Perspective* (Paris: Development Centre of the OECD, 2007)

Małowist, Marian, 'Les débuts du système de plantations dans la période des grandes découvertes,' *Africana – Bulletin of the Centre of African Studies at the University of Warsaw*, 10 (1969), 9–30.

Marx, Karl, *Capital. vol. 3*. Trans. David Fernbach (Harmondsworth: Penguin, 1981).

Masefield, G. B. 'Crops and Livestock.' In E. E. Rich and C. H. Wilson (eds.) *The Cambridge Economic History of Europe, vol. IV: The Economy of Expanding Europe in the Sixteenth and Seventeenth Centuries* (Cambridge: Cambridge University Press, 1967), 276–301.

Maxon, Robert W. 'Small-Scale and Large-Scale Agriculture since Independence.' In William R. Ochieng and Robert W. Maxon (eds.) *An Economic History of Kenya* (Nairobi: East African Educational Publishers, 1992), 273–96.

Mazumdar, Sucheta. *Sugar and Society in China: Peasants, Technology, and the World Market* (Cambridge, MA: Harvard-Yenching Institute Monograph Series, 1998).

Mundt, G. *Ceylon en Java: Aanteekeningen van een theeplanter* (Batavia: Ogilvie, 1886).

Musgrave, Peter. 'The Economics of Uncertainty: The Structural Revolution in the Spice Trade, 1480–1640.' In P. L. Cottrell and D. H. Aldcroft (eds.) *Shipping, Trade and Commerce: Essays in Memory of Ralph Davis* (Leicester: Leicester University Press, 1981), 9–21.

NN. 'Invoering der koffijkultuur op Java, 1700–1750,' *Bijdragen tot de Taal-, Land- en Volkenkunde*, 6 (1859), 53–71.

Ortmayr, Norbert. 'Kulturpflanzen: Transfers und Ausbreitungsprozesse im 18. Jahrhundert.' In Margarete Grandner and Andrea Komlosy (eds.) *Vom Weltgeist beseelt: Globalgeschichte 1700–1815* (Vienna: Promedia, 2004) 73–99.

Pendergrast, Mark, *Uncommon Grounds: The History of Coffee and How It Transformed Our World* (New York: Basic Books, 1999).

Perkins, Dwight H. *Agricultural Development in China 1368–1968* (Edinburgh: Edinburgh University Press, 1969).

Pingali, Prabhu L. 'Green Revolution: Impacts, Limits, and the Path Ahead,' *Proceedings of the National Academy of Sciences of the United States of America (PNAS)*, 109:31 (2012), 12302–8.

Porter, Philip W. 'A Note on Cotton and Climate: A Colonial Conundrum.' In Allen Isaacman and Richard Roberts (eds.) *Cotton, Colonialism, and Social History in Sub-Saharan Africa* (London: James Currey, 1995), 43–9.

Prinsen Geerligs, H. C. *The World's Cane Sugar Industry: Past and Present* (Manchester: N. Rodger, 1912).

Pritchard, James. *In Search of Empire: The French in the Americas, 1670–1730* (Cambridge: Cambridge University Press, 2004).

Pruns, Herbert. *Europäische Zuckerwirtschaft, vol. I: Europa auf der Suche nach Zucker in einheimischen Kulturpflanzen* (Berlin: Albert Bartens, 2004).

Pujol, Rosemonde. *Nicolas Appert: l'inventeur de la conserve* (Paris: Denoël, 1985).

Randhawa, M. S. *A History of Agriculture in India, vol. III: 1757–1947* (New Delhi: Indian Council of Agricultural Research, 1983).

Rau, Virginia. 'The Settlement of Madeira and the Sugar Cane Plantations,' *A.A.G. Bijdragen*, 9 (1964), 3–12.

Reinhardt, Carsten. *Forschung in der chemischen Industrie. Die Entwicklung synthetischer Farbstoffe bei BASF und Hoechst, 1863 bis 1914* (Freiberg: TU Bergakademie, 1997).

Reinhardt, Carsten, and Anthony S. Travis. *Heinrich Caro and the Creation of Modern Chemical Industry* (Dordrecht: Kluwer Academic, 2000).

Rembert Jr., David H. 'The Indigo of Commerce in Colonial North America,' *Economic Botany*, 33:2 (1979), 128–34.

Richards, John F. *The Unending Frontier: An Environmental History of the Early Modern World* (Berkeley, CA: University of California Press, 2003).

Robertson, James A. 'Some Notes on the Transfer by Spain of Plants and Animals to Its Colonies Overseas,' *The James Sprunt Historical Studies*, 19:1 (1927), 7–21.

Rodrigues, José Honório. 'The Influence of Africa on Brazil and of Brazil on Africa,' *Journal of African History*, 3:1 (1962), 49–67.

Roseberry, William. 'Introduction.' In William Roseberry, Lowell Gudmundson, and Mario Samper Kutschbach (eds.) *Coffee, Society, and Power in Latin America* (Baltimore and London: The Johns Hopkins University Press, 1995), 1–37.

Rosenberg, Nathan. 'Economic Experiments,' *Industrial and Corporate Change*, 1:1 (1992), 181–203.

Sauer, Jonathan D. *Historical Geography of Crop Plants* (Boston, MA: CRC Press, 1993).

Schiller, Friedrich. 'Was heißt und zu welchem Ende studiert man Universalgeschichte?' *Der Teutsche Merkur*, 4 (1789), 105–35.

Sharrer, G. 'Indigo in Carolina 1671–1796,' *South Carolina Historical Magazine*, 72:2 (1971), 94–103.

Sharrer, G., 'The Indigo Bonanza in South Carolina, 1740–90,' *Technology and Culture*, 12:3 (1971), 447–55.

Shiva, Vandana. 'The Green Revolution in the Punjab,' *The Ecologist*, 21:2 (1991), http://livingheritage.org/green-revolution.htm (Accessed 14 April 2015).

Shlomowitz, Ralph. 'Plantations and Smallholdings: Comparative Perspectives from the World Cotton and Sugar Cane Economies, 1865–1939,' *Agricultural History*, 58:1 (1984), 1–16.

Smith, Adam. *An Inquiry into the Nature and Causes of the Wealth of Nations* (London: Methuen & Co., 1776).

Smith, Robert S. 'Indigo Production and Trade in Colonial Guatemala,' *Hispanic American Historical Review*, 39:2 (1959), 181–211.

Spencer, J. E., and Ronald J. Horvath, 'How Does an Agricultural Region Originate?' *Annals of the Association of American Geographers*, 53:1 (1963), 74–92.

'Stations (proef-).' In D. G. Stibbe (ed.) *Encyclopaedie van Nederlandsch-Indië*. Second printing (The Hague: Martinus Nijhoff/Leiden: Brill, 1921), vol.4, 94–103.

Stetson, Sarah P. 'The Traffic in Seeds and Plants from England's Colonies in North America,' *Agricultural History*, 23:1 (1949), 45–56.

Tavernier, Jean-Baptiste. *The Six Travels of John Baptista Tavernier, Baron of Aubonne, Through Turky and Persia to the Indies [...]. Part II: Describing India and the Isles Adjacent*. Trans. J. Phillips (London: no publisher, 1678).

Taylor, Henry C., and Anne Dewees Taylor. *World Trade in Agricultural Products* (New York: Macmillan, 1943).

Teuteberg, Hans-Jürgen. 'Zur Geschichte der Kühlkost und des Tiefgefrierens,' *Zeitschrift für Unternehmensgeschichte*, 36:3 (1991), 139–55.

Tidbury, G. E. *The Clove Tree* (London: Crosby Lockwood & Son, 1949).

Timoshenko, Vladimir P., and Boris C. Swerling. *The World's Sugar: Progress and Policy* (Stanford, CA: Stanford University Press, 1957).

Ts'ao, Yung-ho. 'Pepper Trade in East Asia,' *T'oung Pao*, 68:4/5 (1982), 221–47.

Tucker, Catherine M. *Coffee Culture: Local Experiences, Global Connections* (New York: Routledge, 2011).

Uekötter, Frank. *Die Wahrheit ist auf dem Feld: Eine Wissensgeschichte der deutschen Landwirtschaft* (Göttingen: Vandenhoeck und Ruprecht, 2010).

Van Arendonk, C. 'Kahwa.' In *Encyclopaedia of Islam. New Edition*, vol. IV (Leiden: Brill, 1978), 449–53.

Van den Berg, N. P. 'Historisch-statistische aanteekeningen over de voortbrenging en het verbruik van koffie,' *Tijdschrift van Nijverheid en Landbouw in Nederlandsch Indië*, 24 (1879), 427.

Van der Weijden, Wouter, Rob Leeuwis and Pieter Bol. *Biological Globalisation: Bio-invasions and Their Impacts on Nature, the Economy and Public Health* (Utrecht: KNNV Publishing, 2007).

Van Gorkom, K. W. *De Oost-Indische Cultures in betrekking tot handel en nijverheid* (Amsterdam: J.H. de Bussy, 1881).

Van Lookeren Campagne, C. J. 'Suiker.' In Joh. F. Snelleman (ed.) *Encyclopaedie van Nederlandsch-Indië, Vol. IV* (The Hague: Martinus Nijhoff and Leiden: E.J. Brill, n.d. [1905 or 1906]), 145–75.

Van Lookeren Campagne, C. J. 'Tabak.' In Joh. F. Snelleman (ed.) *Encyclopaedie van Nederlandsch-Indië, Vol. IV* (The Hague: Martinus Nijhoff and Leiden: E.J. Brill, n.d. [1905 or 1906]), 220–54.

Van Spall, P. W. A. *Verslag over de koffij- en kaneel-kultuur op het eiland Ceylon in het jaar 1861* (Batavia: W. Ogilvie, 1863).

Vicziany, Marika. 'Imperialism, Botany and Statistics in Early Nineteenth-Century India: The Surveys of Francis Buchanan (1762–1829),' *Modern Asian Studies*, 20:4 (1986), 625–60.

Von Ciriacy-Wantrup, S. 'Resource Conservation and Economic Stability,' *Quarterly Journal of Economics*, 60:3 (1946), 412–52.

Von Humboldt, Alexander. *Essai politique sur la Royaume de la Nouvelle-Espagne* (Paris: F. Schoell, 1811).

Von Wartburg, Marie-Louise. 'Entwurf und Technologie einer mittelalterlichen Rohrzuckerfabrik: Eine industriearchäologische Fallstudie in Cypern.' In Hans Berger, Christoph H. Brunner and Otto Sigg (eds.) *Mundo Multa Miracula: Festschrift für Hans Conrad Peyer* (Zürich: Verlag Neue Zürcher Zeitung, 1992), 207-20, 251–54.

Waridel, Laura. *Coffee with Pleasure: Just Java and World Trade* (Montréal: Black Rose, 2002).

Watson, Andrew M. *Agricultural Innovation in the Early Islamic World* (Cambridge: Cambridge University Press, 1983).

Watt, George, Edgar Thurston and T.N. Mukerji. 'Indigofera.' In George Watt et al. *Dictionary of the Economic Products of India*, Vol. 4 (Calcutta: Government Printing, 1890), 383–469.

Wendt, Reinhardt. 'Globalisierung von Pflanzen und neue Nahrungsgewohnheiten: zur Funktion botanischer Gärten bei der Erschließung natürlicher Ressourcen der Überseeischen Welt.' In Thomas Beck, Horst Gründer, Horst Pietschmann and Roderich Ptak (eds.) *Überseegeschichte: Beiträge der jüngeren Forschung. Festschrift anläßlich der Gründung der Forschungsstiftung für vergleichende europäische Überseegeschichte 1999 in Bamberg* (Stuttgart: Franz Steiner Verlag, 1999), 206–20.

White, Alastair. *El Salvador* (New York: Praeger, 1973).

Wickizer, V. D. *Coffee, Tea, and Cocoa: An Economic and Political Analysis* (Stanford, CA: Stanford University Press, 1951).

Wiedenmann, Evelin. *Die Konstruktion der richtigen Formel: Strukturaufklärung und Synthese des Indigblau, dargestellt an Hand des Briefwechsels Baeyer-Caro* (Munich: Beck, 1978), 2 vols.

Woytinski, W. S., and E. S. Woytinsky. *World Commerce and Governments: Trends and Outlook* (New York: The Twentieth Century Fund, 1955).
Wright, Clifford A. 'The Medieval Spice Trade and the Diffusion of the Chilli,' *Gastronomica*, 7:2 (2007), 35–43.
Young, Arthur. *Political Essays Concerning the Present State of the British Empire* (London: W. Strahan and T. Cadell, 1772).
Yudelman, Montague. 'The Transfer of Agricultural Techniques.' In Peter Duignan and L. H. Gann (eds.) *Colonialism in Africa, 1870–1960, vol. 4: The Economics of Colonialism* (Cambridge: Cambridge University Press, 1969), 329–59.

Index

Abdussalam, K. 87
Africa 58–60, 132, 146–8, 157–8, 160, 162, 184, 169, 173
Agete, F. 119–41
agricultural commodity 1–8, 23, 36, 58, 70, 80, 85, 93, 102, 104, 121–2, 146–74
Allison, F.V. 136
America 12–3, 59, 64, 99, 102–3, 111, 127, 131, 140, 146–8, 152–7, 159, 162, 164, 171–2
Appert, N. 172
Arabia 7, 11, 51, 59, 158
Arabica 58, 154–5
areca nut *see* betel nut
Argentina 127, 162
arson *see* tobacco–shed burning
Asia 7, 12, 41, 56, 58–9, 66, 69, 100, 102, 130, 146–7, 149–51, 153–5, 158–60, 162, 164, 172
Atkins, E. 131
Australia 11, 167
Ayutthaya 150

Baba Budan *see* Dada Hayat
Baba Budan Hills 61–2
Bandarage, A. 66
Bangladesh 1–2, 7, 16
Bantam 43
Barbados 106, 130, 132, 160
BASF 154
Batavia 37, 40, 45, 78, 126, 155
Beattie, R. 133
Bengal 5–7, 11–29, 80, 100–1, 103–4, 153–4
Bennett, H.H. 136
Berkholst, J.G. 86
Besoeki 78–93
betel nut 59, 63, 67
Bhattacharya, B. 6, 23, 79, 102, 158

Bihar 6–7, 79, 99–118, 153–4
Birnie, G. 85–7, 90
Bois, D. 158
book review 1–2, 30–54, 150
Bosma, U. 5, 23, 62, 170
Bosman, J. 88
botanical garden 60, 109, 112, 131, 147, 155–6, 165
Bowring, L. 57
Brazil 67, 147, 152, 156–7, 160–1, 163, 165, 167, 173,
Britain 2, 11–15, 21, 55–6, 101, 104, 108, 113, 151, 162, 164–5
British India *see* India, Bangladesh
Broekveldt, F.L. 84, 92
Broersma, R. 85–7, 89–90

Calcutta 13, 15, 21–2, 24, 28–9, 60, 165
Cannon, Mr. 62
Capus, G. 158
cardamom 59
Caribbean 7, 13, 59, 99, 119–45, 152, 154, 156–7, 160–3, 171
Carpentier Alting, Mr. 87–9, 93
cash crop *see* agricultural commodity
cashew nut 147–8
cassava 146–8
Ceylon *see* Sri Lanka
Chikmagalur 59–60, 66
Chile 11
chilli pepper 147–8
China 13, 100, 147, 149, 158, 160–4
Chinese 37, 146–7, 162
citrus 146, 148
Clarence–Smith, W.G. 70
Cleghorn, H.F.C. 62
clove 169
coconut 146, 148, 170

Index

coffee 1–2, 5–7, 11, 23, 31, 33, 35–7, 42, 45, 55–77, 101–2, 121, 124, 148, 150, 154–8, 164, 168–71, 173–4
coir 59
Coke, E. 56
colonial rule 2, 4–7, 13–14, 22–3, 30–48, 56, 58–9, 62, 69, 78–9, 85–6, 91, 93, 100, 103, 105, 160, 164–5, 172–3
Columbian Exchange 147–8
Columbus 148, 162
commodity chain 1, 3–5, 8
Coorg 58, 60–1, 66–8, 70
cotton 21, 33, 101, 146, 169–70, 174
Coventry, B. 104
Cox, H. 114
Cuba 1–2, 6–7, 23, 69, 119–45, 156, 160
Cubbon, M. 62
Cultivation System 5, 7, 23, 30–54, 61, 84–5, 170
Curry–Machado, J. 6, 23, 69–70, 99, 167
Curzon, Lord 102, 104

Dada Hayat 59
Dafert, F.W. 173
Davis, M. 173
Davis, N.Z. 55
Deerr, N. 158
Delhi 56, 105, 153
Dhaka 153
diary 1–2, 11–29, 150
disembedding 4–7, 23, 141 disembed
Dockès, P. 159
Dominican Republic 122
Doup, C.H. 86
Douwes Dekker, E. *see* Multatuli

El Salvador 157
Elliot, H.M. 57
Elliot, R.H. 65, 67–8
Elson, R.E. 7
embedding 1–8, 13–14, 16, 23, 30–1, 33, 36–7, 44, 47–8, 58, 61, 69–70, 80, 99–105, 109, 113–14, 119, 121–3, 125, 140–1, 150, 154, 158, 162, 164–72
England *see* Britain
Ethiopia 58, 155
Europe 2, 4, 6–7, 12–14, 17, 23, 31, 37, 39, 41, 45–8, 55–6, 58–69, 71, 78, 80, 84–7, 89, 91–2, 101–2, 104–5, 107–9, 146–53, 156, 158, 160, 162, 164–5, 168–9, 172
Evans, B. 66

Fasseur, C. 36, 45

fertilizer 4, 64, 110, 122–3, 126, 128, 136–7, 139, 158, 173–4
flax 21, 146
France 12, 55, 59, 64, 151, 156, 162
Fransen van de Putte, I.D. 35–6, 42, 45, 47, 86

Gama, V. da 148
Germany 13, 59, 154, 156, 173
ginger 63
global triangle 148–50
Global South 4, 173
globalization 1, 7, 146–89
Goodman, J. 100
Granovetter, M. 3
Great Britain *see* Britain
Green Revolution 173–4
groundnut 106, 147–8, 169
Guatemala 12, 152–3

Haarer, A.E. 168
Hafid, J. 86–7
Haiti 12, 121, 152, 160, 164
Havana 126, 131, 139
Hawaii 124, 160, 167, 172
hemp 21
historian's craft 3
historical source 1–3, 11–12
Hong Kong 11
Howard, A. 101, 106–14
Howard, G.L.C. (Matthaei) 101, 106–14
Howard, L. 106–9
Hunter, W.W. 103

imperialism 32–3, 48–9, 101, 165
India 1–2, 5–7, 11–29, 33, 55–77, 99–118, 128, 146–7, 149, 151, 154, 158–63, 165, 173
indigo 1–2, 5, 7, 11–29, 31, 36–7, 42, 63, 69, 80, 101, 103–4, 106, 150–4, 164, 167, 169, 173
Indonesia 1, 7, 13, 23, 30–54, 58–9, 78–99, 146, 157, 161, 163
Industrial Revolution 149, 160
intercropping 64, 66, 69

Jamaica 60, 152, 156, 160
Japan 100, 147, 162
Java 5–7, 23, 30–54, 59, 61, 64, 68, 78–98, 123–4, 126–32, 137, 139, 141, 155, 160–2, 165
jute 101, 169

kapok 146

Index

Knowles, P.F. 167
Kolkata *see* Calcutta
Kooiman, D. 66
Korea 147, 162

labour 5, 12–14, 17, 20–1, 31, 33, 36–8, 40, 42, 44–8, 50–2, 59, 63, 66, 68, 70, 72–4, 76–9, 81, 83–5, 88–91, 122–4, 126, 131, 150–1, 154, 158–60, 162, 164, 167–8, 170, 173
land 13–16, 18, 20–1, 31, 36–8, 44–8
Lebak 39–41, 43–5, 50
Liebig, J. von 173
Lieftinck, Mr. 92
Lonsdale, W. 56–8, 61–3, 66–7, 69
Louis XIV 156
Ludden, D. 7

Macaulay, Lord 154
Machell, T. 11–29
Mackenzie, D.P. 57, 63, 66–7
Madurese 78, 86–8
Magellan Exchange 147–8
mailrapport *see* 'mail report'
'mail report' 1–2, 78
maize 146–8, 173
Marquesas Islands 11
Marx, K. 148, 168
Mataram 37
Matthaei, E.C.H. 107
Mauritius 126, 165
Max Havelaar 30–55
Mediterranean 147, 158–60
Mexico 12, 157
migration 59, 86–9, 92, 133, 142, 162
'mobile production' 7, 162
Mocha 59, 155
monetization 37–8
monoculture 64, 66, 124, 126, 160, 174
Moore, J.D. 65
Multatuli 30–55,
Mysore 7, 55–77

Napoleon 46, 59, 172
Netherlands 2, 30–55, 59–60, 155, 162
Netherlands East Indies *see* Indonesia
New Spain 152
Ngawi 41

oil palm 146, 169
opium 13
Opium War 11
Ortiz, F. 7
Ottley, C. 56

Pacific islands 126
Panama Canal 172
Pasuruan 43, 128
Pelzer, K.J. 7
pepper 147–8
petition 1–2, 21, 55–77, 150
Petty, W. 149
Philippines 13, 152, 160, 162
pineapple 147–8, 172
plant *see* agricultural commodity
plant transfers 7, 59, 106, 125–6, 128, 130, 146–7, 149–50, 153, 155–6, 164–9, 171–2
plantain 63
Polanyi, K. 3
Port of Spain 165
Porter, J.F. 57, 67–8
potato 64, 146–8
Puerto Rico 122, 127, 130
Pusa 102–13, 173

Quesnay, F. 149

Raman, B. 56
'reluctant embedding' 6, 119, 121, 123, 125, 130, 140
Rembang 47
Reynoso, A. 122–5, 131, 136–41
rice 33, 37, 69, 89, 146, 148
Robusta 58, 154
Roque, J. de la 59
Rosenberg, N. 167
Roxburgh, W. 60
rubber 68, 146, 148, 165, 167, 169, 174

sago 33
Saint–Domingue *see* Haiti
sandalwood 59, 146
San Salvador 12
Santiago de las Vegas 128–9, 132, 139
Saptari, R. 6, 23, 62, 99, 174
Schagen van Soelen, B. 84
Schiller, F. 148
school 21–2
scientific report 1–2, 99–115
Shanghai 147
silk 13, 21
Sinha–Kerkhoff, K. 6, 23, 62, 79, 93, 173
Shen Nung 146
slavery 12, 39, 122, 124, 146–7, 152–4, 158–60, 162, 164, 171, 173
Smith, A. 149
South Africa 132
South Carolina 152–3

South–South trade 4
Spanish 2, 7, 12, 119, 121, 123, 147, 152, 160
Sri Lanka 58–60, 65–8, 149, 155, 165
Stubbs, J. 93
Suez Canal 172
sugar 1–2, 5–7, 13, 15, 23, 36, 38, 42, 45, 47–8, 64, 69, 99, 105–6, 119–45, 147–8, 150, 153, 158–62, 167, 169–71, 173–4
sugar paradigm 159–60
Sumatra 31, 48, 64, 78, 85, 147, 155, 164
survey 1–2, 47, 80, 107, 119–45, 150
sweet potato 146–8

taro 147
Tavernier, J.B. 151
taxation 13–14, 37, 56–7, 66–9, 71, 86, 170
tea 58, 63, 68, 101
Thiselton–Dyer, W.T. 105
tobacco 1, 6–7, 21, 23, 42, 47, 49, 69, 78–118, 121, 124, 148, 150, 162–4, 169–70, 173–4
tobacco–shed burning 78–93
Toer, P. A. 34
tomato 146, 148
triangulation 149–50, 160
Turgot, A.R.J. 149
turmeric 63

Uhlenbeck, D.J. 86

Uncle Tom's Cabin 33, 39
United States 12, 59, 99–100, 102, 120, 124, 131, 133, 135, 140, 153, 163, 171

Van den Bergh van Heinenoord, Mr. 78–84, 88, 90, 92
Van den Bosch, J. 37–8, 43
Van der Linden, M. 7
Van Hasselt, W.J.C. 43
Van Lennep, J. 35, 43
Van Schendel, W. 5, 80, 93, 101, 104, 150, 153
Veth, P.J. 30–55

Wallerstein, I. 149
Wallich, N. 60
Ward, N. 166–7
Wardian case 166–7
West Indies *see* Caribbean
White, B. 93
Wickham, H.A. 164–5
woad 12, 150–2

yam 63, 147
Yemen 59, 155
Yorkshire 11
Yunnan 147, 164

zamindar 14–16, 18–19
Zheng Chenggong 162

Taylor & Francis eBooks

Helping you to choose the right eBooks for your Library

Add Routledge titles to your library's digital collection today. Taylor and Francis ebooks contains over 50,000 titles in the Humanities, Social Sciences, Behavioural Sciences, Built Environment and Law.

Choose from a range of subject packages or create your own!

Benefits for you
- Free MARC records
- COUNTER-compliant usage statistics
- Flexible purchase and pricing options
- All titles DRM-free.

Benefits for your user
- Off-site, anytime access via Athens or referring URL
- Print or copy pages or chapters
- Full content search
- Bookmark, highlight and annotate text
- Access to thousands of pages of quality research at the click of a button.

REQUEST YOUR FREE INSTITUTIONAL TRIAL TODAY

Free Trials Available
We offer free trials to qualifying academic, corporate and government customers.

eCollections – Choose from over 30 subject eCollections, including:

Archaeology	Language Learning
Architecture	Law
Asian Studies	Literature
Business & Management	Media & Communication
Classical Studies	Middle East Studies
Construction	Music
Creative & Media Arts	Philosophy
Criminology & Criminal Justice	Planning
Economics	Politics
Education	Psychology & Mental Health
Energy	Religion
Engineering	Security
English Language & Linguistics	Social Work
Environment & Sustainability	Sociology
Geography	Sport
Health Studies	Theatre & Performance
History	Tourism, Hospitality & Events

For more information, pricing enquiries or to order a free trial, please contact your local sales team:
www.tandfebooks.com/page/sales

 The home of Routledge books

www.tandfebooks.com